THE BONHOEFFER LEGACY

THE
BONHOEFFER
LEGACY

Post-Holocaust Perspectives

STEPHEN R. HAYNES

Fortress Press
Minneapolis

THE BONHOEFFER LEGACY
Post-Holocaust Perspectives

Unless otherwise noted, scripture quotations are from the New Revised Standard Version Bible, copyright © 1989 by the Division of Christian Education of the National Council of the Churches of Christ in the USA and used by permission.

Cover design: Brad Norr Design
Book design: Ann Delgehausen
Author photo: Kevin Barre

Library of Congress Cataloging-in-Publication Data

Haynes, Stephen R.
  The Bonhoeffer legacy: post-Holocaust perspectives /
  Stephen R. Haynes. p. cm.
  Includes bibliographical references and index.
  ISBN 0-8006-3815-8 (alk. paper)
  1. Bonhoeffer, Dietrich, 1906–1945. I. Title.
BX4827.B57H37 2006
230'.044092—dc22
                                                                2005037896

The paper used in this publication meets the minimum requirements of American National Standard for Information Sciences—Permanence of Paper for Printed Library Materials, ANSI Z329.48-1984.

Manufactured in the U.S.A.

10   09   08   07   06   1   2   3   4   5   6   7   8   9   10

For John J. Carey,

Teacher, Scholar, Mentor, Friend

CONTENTS

PREFACE

Bonhoeffer in Light of the Holocaust

In 2004 I wrote *The Bonhoeffer Phenomenon: Portraits of a Protestant Saint*, which may be read as a sort of preface to the present volume. Unlike that book, which was essentially a meta-analysis of Bonhoeffer's reception over time, the present study focuses on one aspect of the Bonhoeffer legacy—its relevance for Christian understandings of Jews, Judaism, and Christian-Jewish relations. The premise of this book is that while the Bonhoeffer legacy contains real significance for post-Holocaust Christianity, this has been neither fully explored nor accurately described. Among the reasons for this are superficial reading, hopeful interpretation, and overactive speculation.

Another element is that Bonhoeffer scholars have invoked the expression "post-Holocaust" without carefully defining it. In this book, the phrase "post-Holocaust Christianity" will be used to describe a state of awareness rather than an epoch, to denote thinking and acting that are informed by the ways in which Christians and Christianity prepared the way for the Holocaust through viewing Jews as objects of contempt, victimizing them, and making them vulnerable to other victimizers. Post-Holocaust theology strives to revise Christianity in light of what the Holocaust teaches us about the effects of Christian thought, scriptural interpretation, preaching, worship, and catechesis, and seeks to detect the presence of traditions that are implicated in anti-Judaism. The term "post-Holocaust," then, ought to imply an unflinching critique of Christian faith in light of its consequences for Jewish life.

This book seeks to improve our grasp of Bonhoeffer's post-Holocaust legacy by reviewing and critiquing popular and scholarly perceptions of "Bonhoeffer and the Jews" and by offering perspectives designed to provoke further reflection. It engages in a critical examination of Bonhoeffer's function as an exemplar of Jewish-Christian rapprochement, concluding that his chief role in the conflicted space between Jews and Christians is not, as is often argued, as a guide for the reconstruction of Christian theology in light of the Holocaust, but as an aid to interpreting the varieties of (flawed) human response to Nazi anti-Semitism. Only in light of such an examination, I think, can Bonhoeffer become the pioneering figure for post-Holocaust theology that Eberhard Bethge and others have claimed him to be.

Actions Louder than Words

Some may sincerely wonder whether it is reasonable to criticize Bonhoeffer's thoughts and actions with regard to "the Jews." He was, after all, a more incisive and committed advocate of Jewish rights than virtually any other Christian leader in Nazi Germany. Who are we to find fault with a man who sacrificed himself in the struggle against tyranny and hate, and who undertook a variety of courageous deeds on behalf of the Jewish victims of Nazism? Among these well-documented actions are the following:

- treasonous discussions with Paul Lehmann in 1933 concerning the transfer of information about conditions in Germany to American rabbi Stephen Wise[1]
- refusal to seek a church post in Berlin in 1933 for fear of "betraying [his] solidarity with the Jewish Christian pastors"[2]
- energetic attempts to inform delegates to the World Alliance meeting in Sofia, Bulgaria, in September 1933 of the Jewish Question (*die Judenfrage*) in Germany, culminating in a resolution deploring "state measures against the Jews in Germany"[3]
- an unsuccessful campaign at the National Synod in Wittenberg the same month to place the Jewish Question on the church's agenda
- repeated admonitions to "open thy mouth for the dumb" (Prov. 31:8, KJV)[4]

- condemnation of the Confessing Church after the 1935 Steglitz Synod for its failure to transcend a limited concern for Jewish Christians[5]
- aid to Jewish-Christian refugees in London between 1933 and 1935[6]
- shelter (at Finkenwalde) for Willy Sussbach, a young pastor of Jewish origin who had been attacked by the SA (Storm Troops)[7]
- help for his sister Sabine and her Jewish husband, Gerhard Leibholz, to emigrate to Switzerland in 1938[8]
- participation in "Operation-7," a plot to spirit German Jews to Switzerland as Abwehr agents[9]
- work on a report detailing Nazi deportation of Jews from Berlin in 1941[10]
- a deeply negative reaction to a fellow prisoner's anti-Semitic remark[11]

Awe before this litany of brave deeds gives rise to an understandable reluctance to pass judgment. In 1979 Pinchas E. Lapide warned those tempted to do so that

> whoever would analyze Bonhoeffer's statements toward Jews and Judaism must above all avoid the hubris of retrospect. Without a full realization of the eclipse of God in those satanic years, in which a man's life often hung on a single word and compassion was a political offense, without considering all this as the ubiquitous background to Bonhoeffer's drama, no one may draw a smug conclusion, nor pass posthumous sentence in academic safety.[12]

It has rarely been necessary to repeat this warning. The saintly portrait conveyed by these actions implies that Bonhoeffer's reflection and praxis were of a piece, that, as Gregory the Great wrote of St. Benedict, "the holy man cannot have taught otherwise than as he lived."[13] Indeed, many who are impressed by his sacrificial acts on behalf of Jews presume that Bonhoeffer must have thought in ways that were radically pro-Jewish as well. Catalyzed by his unusual integrity, the conviction that Jewish suffering was "the decisive stimulus to [Bonhoeffer's] repudiation of the regime from the beginning"[14] contributes to the image of a man whose actions were an outgrowth of his theology.

Yet nowhere has it been more difficult than on the issue of "the Jews"[15] to determine the standing of Bonhoeffer's theology, nor more tempting to suppose that Bonhoeffer's behavior sprung from the soil of theological reflection. Among laypeople the tendency is simply to align Bonhoeffer's thought with his praxis and assume that his martyrdom by the Nazis makes him a reliable model for post-Holocaust Christianity. Scholars, of course, do not treat the matter so glibly; yet the wish to identify harmony between Bonhoeffer's thought and behavior is evident in insistent claims that by the time of his martyrdom Bonhoeffer's "theology of Israel"[16] had been purified—or was in the process of being purified—of traditional anti-Jewish elements. In the words of Stephen Plant, such claims reflect "the mistaken view that the compelling story of [Bonhoeffer's] anti-Nazi resistance, ending on the gallows, serves to justify the quality of his theology." "Many who have died bravely have thought unclearly," Plant observes, concluding that "if Bonhoeffer is to speak to this new century as to the last then his theology must be capable of standing on its own feet."[17]

Faced with evidence of a bifurcation between thought and deed, some scholars have conceded that, with regard to "the Jews" at least, Bonhoeffer's actions were superior to his theology. This view has been advanced by both Ruth Zerner and Franklin H. Littell, who writes:

> The sad truth is that Bonhoeffer was much better than his theology. The man who fought Hitler as a citizen but not as a churchman was better than his theological tradition. . . . The man whose humanity and decency led him to run risks for Jews and to oppose practical Antisemitism was better than the bad theology which laid the foundations for Christian Antisemitism.[18]

If for some Bonhoeffer's deeds reflect the demands of discipleship more than conceptual clarity, others consider Bonhoeffer's actions on behalf of Jews as compensation for a flawed theology. William J. Peck writes that because deeds must proceed from words, Bonhoeffer "took back his sentence about the curse laid on the name of the Jews, in the only way in which he could take it back, by entering into solidarity with the victims of the Holocaust through his death."[19] Craig Slane opines that, as in the case of Jesus, "Bonhoeffer's death as a martyr accomplished something his theology alone could not," namely, an "answer to the anti-Semitic knot he was never able fully to disentangle intellectually."

His death in solidarity with Jews, Slane contends, is tantamount to a theological position.[20]

Still other scholars perceive a paradoxical relationship between Bonhoeffer's problematic theology and his anti-Nazi resistance. "As objectionable as many today find his problematic readings of his theological inheritance," Richard L. Rubenstein points out, "without them he would have had no Archimedean point with which to transcend his culture and oppose Hitler and National Socialism."[21] Andreas Pangritz concurs, noting that "without a theological conception of the close relationship between the church and Israel, without the so-called 'witness people myth,' Bonhoeffer probably would not have been able to develop such a paradoxical form of 'patriotism.'"[22]

As I will argue in chapter 7, thought and behavior may be considered together in Bonhoeffer's relationship to "the Jews" if we focus on the *roles* vis-à-vis Nazi anti-Semitism he occupied at various points in his career. But whatever we conclude about the relationship between Bonhoeffer's deeds and his theology of Israel, it is paramount that we keep in view the distinction between Bonhoeffer the anti-Nazi hero and Bonhoeffer the putative post-Holocaust theologian. To insist on this distinction is to acknowledge the inevitable gap between praxis and reflection in situations of crisis. As we shall see, illuminating this gap through careful assessment of the deep theological structures revealed in Bonhoeffer's initial response to the Jewish Question and the lingering ambivalence toward Jews and Judaism in his later writings will allow us to clarify his post-Holocaust significance.

Despite the good faith of Bonhoeffer scholars, this process of clarification has been delayed by the need for heroes whose moral brilliance can help dispel the darkness of the Nazi era, as well as by Christians' eagerness to move beyond the Holocaust without fully coming to terms with what it has to teach us. Rabbi A. James Rudin has written that we do not need "a mythological Bonhoeffer who is larger than life, a Bonhoeffer without ambivalences, ambiguities, and complexities." This is especially true, he stresses, with regard to Christian-Jewish relations and Bonhoeffer's perceptions of Jews and Judaism.[23] The truth, however, is that we *desperately* need such a Bonhoeffer, which is why it has been so difficult to accurately gauge the implications of his theology for Christian-Jewish relations, a problem this book begins to address.

ACKNOWLEDGMENTS

I have been working on the material in this book, off and on, for ten years. How does one acknowledge all the debts one incurs during such a long swath of professional life? Since one must try, I wish to thank my beautiful and supportive wife, Alyce, my students and colleagues at Rhodes College, the Lilly Endowment Inc., librarian Kenan Padgett, and students Becca Eza and Stephen Ogden. I am particularly appreciative of members of the International Bonhoeffer Society who have welcomed my contributions to Bonhoeffer research and taken them seriously enough to critique them. Clifford Green, Martin Rumscheidt, Michael Lukens, and Ruth Zerner are members of the IBS who deserve special thanks. For permission to use material originally published in "Who Needs Enemies? Jews and Judaism in Anti-Nazi Religious Discourse," *Church History* 71: 2 (June, 2002), 341–67, I express thanks to the editors of that journal.

This book is dedicated to someone who is not a Bonhoeffer scholar but who is responsible for introducing me to the critical study of modern theology. John J. Carey was my teacher for a course titled "Modern Western Religious Thought" over twenty years ago, and I am still reaping the benefits of having been his student. John is not only the most inspiring teacher I ever had, but the one who is most influential in my own quest to be an inspiring teacher. Beyond that, John is the sort of professional mentor every junior faculty member needs but few are fortunate enough to have. In recent years he has been like a father to me, the sort of father I want to be to my children, Christiana, Matthew, and Braden. It is not possible to repay such a debt; only to acknowledge it. Thank you, John.

BONHOEFFER AND THE JEWS IN POPULAR MEMORY

"The Jews" and Bonhoeffer's Reception

It should not be surprising that, particularly in America, the trajectory of interest in Bonhoeffer's relationship to "the Jews" reflects growth in popular concern with the Holocaust. As Peter Novick demonstrates in *The Holocaust in American Life*, the "Holocaust" as we have come to know it is a post-1960s cultural phenomenon. Just so, the image of Bonhoeffer as pro-Jewish advocate (as opposed to anti-Nazi crusader or progenitor of radical theology) has come into focus very gradually since then. Novick maintains that the Holocaust as a distinct species of Nazi crime did not reach public awareness in America until the mid-1960s. Similarly, "the Jews" were barely discernible in studies of Bonhoeffer before this time, while most studies published since have devoted at least superficial attention to the subject.[1]

Along with the Holocaust's gradual emergence into public consciousness, other factors have been responsible for generating interest in Bonhoeffer's relationship to the Jewish people. One of these was the initiation in the 1960s of genuine efforts to grapple with the Christian beliefs and attitudes that made the Holocaust possible, a process that received momentum in Germany from the Adolf Eichmann trial and the establishment of the "Jews and Christians" committee of the German Evangelical Church Convention. In America, the Vietnam War and the civil rights movement seem to have influenced perceptions of Bonhoeffer as well. A. James Rudin has argued, in fact, that "it was only after the often violent struggle for black civil rights in the 1960s, . . . the wrenching and divisive war in Southeast Asia, and the Watergate scandal that resulted in a U.S. President's resignation from office" that American religious leaders were prepared "to look closely at . . . Dietrich Bonhoeffer."[2]

It was during this same period that historiography of the German Church Struggle, hitherto characterized by a "tendency to hagiography," underwent a revisionist shift and began to acknowledge and explore the less heroic aspects of the church's career under Nazism.[3] In addition, the 1960s brought to light new data related to Bonhoeffer and "the Jews." Of particular importance was the English publication of No Rusty Swords in 1965 and its inclusion of "The Church and the Jewish Question" in a section titled "The Aryan Clauses." The German publication of Eberhard Bethge's definitive biography of Bonhoeffer in 1967 also gave impetus to considerations of this topic. In a now-famous letter to Bethge, Karl Barth credited the biography with bringing to light the fact that "in 1933 and the years following, Bonhoeffer was the first and almost the only one to face and tackle the Jewish question so centrally and energetically."[4]

Bonhoeffer's relevance for understanding Christian responses to the Jewish Question during the Third Reich did not immediately displace interest in his role as resister or constructive theologian. For instance, the proceedings of the inaugural Scholars' Conference on the German Church Struggle and the Holocaust in 1970 included dozens of references to Bonhoeffer, but no mention of his relationship with Jews or his theology's post-Holocaust import.[5] And Larry Rasmussen's classic 1972 study of Bonhoeffer's resistance activities barely mentioned Jews. Among the first signs that "the Jews" were emerging as a legitimate theme in Bonhoeffer studies came in 1973, when William Jay Peck made the previously unintelligible claim that Bonhoeffer's "relation to the Jews" had "a decisive place in his theology, his political decisions, and his concept of religion."[6] Over the next several years, Bonhoeffer scholars devoted so much attention to evaluating and expanding this claim that in 1990 an article in the Encyclopedia of the Holocaust could declare that Bonhoeffer's "theological influence has been significantly instrumental in the post-Holocaust rethinking of Christian relationships with the Jewish people."[7] Unsurprisingly, this reassessment of Bonhoeffer's theology has also affected portrayals of his life. In 2004 a brief pictorial biography of Bonhoeffer contained a section titled "Contacts with Jews."[8]

This chapter explores some of the forces that continue to shape interpretation of Bonhoeffer's relationship with "the Jews."

The Bethge Effect

It is difficult to overstate the role of Eberhard Bethge in fashioning Bonhoeffer's reception in the postwar world. The recent biography of Bethge by John W. de Gruchy offers considerable insight into the way he influenced understandings of Bonhoeffer's legacy from the 1950s until his death in 2000. "There is no doubt," de Gruchy writes, "that, after 1945, Bethge's interpretation of his friend's life and thought took Bonhoeffer's theology in the direction he thought it would have gone — admittedly, a speculative enterprise."[9] De Gruchy honestly considers the extent to which "the Bonhoeffer we know today is the creation of Bethge"; he concludes that while Bethge did not manufacture the Bonhoeffer legacy, in interpreting it "he inevitably left his own distinct impression upon it."[10]

Despite the influence of his 1967 biography in clarifying Bonhoeffer's leadership in the church's response to the Jewish Question, Bethge later acknowledged this work was plagued by a "blindness . . . regarding the topic of the Jews."[11] The nature of this blindness, how Bethge came to acknowledge it, and what he did to correct it are questions explored in de Gruchy's biographical study. During the 1970s, according to de Gruchy, several factors affected Bethge's evolving understanding of the meaning Jews and Judaism had for Bonhoeffer.[12] One was his participation in the Annual Scholars' Conference on the Holocaust and the Church Struggle, where he interacted with Christian and Jewish scholars engaged in post-Holocaust reflection. Bethge's contribution to the first Scholars' Conference in 1970 dealt with the "half-hearted" German Church Struggle. This paper, which Bethge later said cost him friendships in Germany, is emblematic of his early quest to understand the implications of the Church Struggle for post-Holocaust Christian-Jewish relations.[13]

Another influence on Bethge's interpretation of Bonhoeffer during the 1970s was South African apartheid, about which he had remained informed while serving as a pastor in London between 1953 and 1961. De Gruchy indicates that during the '70s the struggle against apartheid became the prism through which Bethge interpreted Bonhoeffer's own struggle on behalf of Jews. When Eberhard and Renate Bethge visited South Africa in 1973, they found that "the plight of black South Africans was a powerful reminder of the plight of the Jews in the Third Reich."[14] By 1974 Bethge was leading a seminar on Black Theology in Germany, and "his encounter with black theology and the Church Struggle in South Africa made him more aware of the ongoing relevance of Bonhoeffer's legacy within his own German context and elsewhere."[15]

In a public discussion of confession and resistance in the Third Reich and South Africa in 1983, Bethge related the need for solidarity with Jews under National Socialism with the call for solidarity with the victims of apartheid. Through the 1980s, in fact, Bethge continued to reflect on the relationship between confession and resistance, between the Barmen Declaration of 1934 and the churches' attempts at authentic confession in South Africa. By the middle of the decade,

> history had turned a complete circle. When Bethge came to South Africa the question was what could South Africans learn from the German *Kirchenkampf* and from the legacy of Bonhoeffer. But over the years the question had become what could and should Germans learn from the church struggle in South Africa, from the testimony of black theologians, the Belhar Confession, and now finally from the *Kairos Document*.[16]

One thing Bethge learned was that the German churches had work to do in the area of Jewish-Christian relations. Indeed, another factor affecting Bethge's interpretation of Bonhoeffer after 1970 was his increasing involvement in German discussions of the Holocaust and Christian-Jewish relations. De Gruchy observes that as Bethge reflected on the Nazi era, "he increasingly came to recognize the enormity of the Holocaust or *Shoa* and its challenge to the church." Rightly remembering and connecting those murdered for resisting tyranny and the victims of the Holocaust "became his special passion during the last two decades of his life."[17] In preparation for the 1980 synod of his Rhineland church, Bethge led a commission that produced the most progressive statement on Christian-Jewish relations to emerge from postwar

Germany—"Towards a Renewal of the Relationship of Christians and Jews." With this statement, Bethge wrote,

> finally, guilt consisted primarily no longer in sins of weakness, but in sins of strength practiced for centuries. This was the result of long phases of a dialog finally begun, which Jews had granted us for many years. Of course there were sins of fear, but now also sins of not seeing what Americans have called the "theology of contempt" toward Jews. This insight, with its immense consequences for almost all of church life—for preaching, instruction, liturgy, hymnbooks, and creed—arrived only after decades.[18]

Significantly, Bethge credited Bonhoeffer with being the guide for post-Holocaust Christian-Jewish dialogue who "pointed out to us the beginning of a new path."[19]

In light of his personal history, Bethge's leadership in post-Holocaust Jewish-Christian dialogue in Germany represented a profound development. In his more autobiographical moments, Bethge admitted that a religiously homogeneous rural background combined with the effects of an inner-looking German Protestantism had produced in him an attitude of "indifferent innocence" toward the Jewish Question. In later life, as he explored the depths of his own anti-Jewish instincts, Bethge became increasingly sensitive to this concern in Bonhoeffer's career. "Nothing challenged him more than this issue," de Gruchy writes, "in retrieving Bonhoeffer's legacy, in developing his own theology."[20] In other words, compensation for his own "blindness" on this issue seems to have influenced Bethge's changing understanding of the meaning of Jews and Judaism for Bonhoeffer. Thus, when assessing Bethge's assertion that Dietrich was seeking "a new kind of teaching about the relation of Christians and Jews,"[21] it is fair to ask whether this statement refers more to Bonhoeffer or to himself. In any case, by the end of the '80s, Bethge was widely honored for "continuing Bonhoeffer's struggle after his death and . . . developing the basis for a radically new Christian theology on Jews and Judaism."[22]

Influences on Bethge that are not explored in de Gruchy's biography include personal encounters with Jews in New York during the 1950s[23] and early responses to Bonhoeffer among Jewish scholars of the Holocaust. An essay Bethge wrote in 1991 contains an enticing clue to the way Jewish attitudes shaped his understanding of Bonhoeffer's relationship to the Holocaust. In 1978 Eberhard and Renate attended a conference on the Holocaust in San Jose, California. Half of the conference participants were American Jews, some of them world-famous scholars. When the Bethges described "the tormenting logic of conspiratorial resistance," which required members of the resistance group around Admiral Wilhelm Canaris to collaborate even with SS officers, they found "no understanding whatever." In fact, they met with "conscious indifference on the part of those eminent Jews" who said that the July 20th plot to assassinate Hitler meant nothing to them. "They did not even grant," Bethge remembers, "that some members of the resistance, as we had mentioned, had taken risks for their—the Jews'—sake."[24] It is no coincidence that shortly after this experience Bethge began to emphasize that for Bonhoeffer and his family "the Jews were the main reason for sharing in the conspiracy."[25]

Another dimension of the Jewish response to Bonhoeffer, one that also seems to have influenced Bethge, was the ringing endorsement by Pinchas E. Lapide. In a study titled "Bonhoeffer und das Judentum" published in 1979, Lapide described Bonhoeffer's theology with considerably generosity.[26] In fact, when Bethge took up the topic "Bonhoeffer and the Jews" in earnest around 1980, he highlighted Lapide's reading of Bonhoeffer as a counterpoint to less charitable Jewish interpretations. As Bethge happily noted, Lapide's point of departure was "the prisoner in Tegel whose capacity for interpretation and sense of solidarity were fostered by martyrdom."[27] The contested status of Bonhoeffer's relationship to the Jews made Lapide's embrace of Bonhoeffer both a boon to Bethge and a watershed in interpretation. While it is not possible to demonstrate that Lapide's influence on Bonhoeffer scholars was mediated by Bethge, it is suggestive that the sentence from "Bonhoeffer und das Judentum" one reads again and again is the one quoted by Bethge: "From a Jewish perspective, Bonhoeffer is a pioneer and forerunner of the slow, step-by-step re-Hebraisation of the churches in our days."[28]

With encouragement from Lapide, over the last two decades of his life Bethge was able to forge a tripartite consensus that concern for Jews was the engine that drove Bonhoeffer's sacrificial resistance to the Nazis, that in 1938 and after Bonhoeffer atoned for his mistakes of 1933, and that Bonhoeffer's theological writings represented a promising foundation for Christian-Jewish rapprochement. This consensus has held sway in part because Bethge knew Bonhoeffer and Bonhoeffer's theology better than any living person, and in part because he himself effectively utilized Bonhoeffer's legacy as a foundation for post-Holocaust reconciliation between Christians and Jews.

In his biography, de Gruchy stresses that in evaluating Bonhoeffer's relationship to the Jewish Question, Bethge demonstrated more care than other scholars. While most early interpreters assumed that Bonhoeffer's "clear and undisputed record of resistance against the Nazi state was based upon his solidarity with the Jewish victims of Nazism, Bethge was far more cautious about drawing conclusions about Bonhoeffer's thinking in this area."[29] De Gruchy adds that Bethge was painfully honest in pointing to the presence of anti-Jewish sentiments in the German resistance. In a letter to a German critic, Bethge acknowledged that "even extraordinary resistance fighters were at the same time still sunken in the kind of language and attitudes whose anti-Jewish content could only be made clear decades after 1945."[30]

However, what is important for comprehending the status of "Bonhoeffer and the Jews" in popular memory is not the accuracy of Bethge's interpretation but the fact that he authoritatively established "the Jews" as a legitimate topic in Bonhoeffer studies, encouraged others to pursue the theme, and personally embodied the link between Bonhoeffer's legacy and concern for post-Holocaust Christian-Jewish relations. Indeed, the Bethge effect is discernible in every study of Bonhoeffer and the Jews after 1980, by Jews and non-Jews alike. If the past three decades have witnessed the emergence of a consensus regarding Bonhoeffer's significance for post-Holocaust Christianity, this has no doubt been made *necessary* by the growing realization that Christians failed miserably during the Nazi years to "open their mouths for the dumb" (Prov. 31:8, KJV, slightly modified). But in a real sense the consensus has been made *possible* through the influence of Bethge, who became a leading post-Holocaust theologian and in the process turned Bonhoeffer into one as well.

Harlem and Berlin

Complementing the Bethge effect in shaping perceptions of Bonhoeffer's salience for a post-Holocaust world is the compelling image of the committed anti-racist. Many familiar with Bonhoeffer's biography have concluded that his activism on behalf of European Jews was the culmination of a developing solidarity with "the oppressed." Earlier stages in this development are seen in his encounter with the proletariat in Barcelona and his ministry with working-class youth in Berlin. But it was Bonhoeffer's Harlem sojourn, the thinking goes, that taught him to identify with the victims of racial oppression.

Taken by Bonhoeffer's concern for ethnic minorities on two continents, contemporary memory has made him the epitome of Christian passion for racial rapprochement.[31] Winfried Maechler, one of Bonhoeffer's students, recalls that Bonhoeffer "saw parallels" between the oppression of blacks and the oppression of Jews, which is "why he so quickly stepped in for the Jews, because he had had this experience in America."[32] Similarly, an overview of Bonhoeffer's intellectual progress declares that "the encounter with racism in America paved the way for his opposition to the racist anti-Semitism of National Socialism."[33] But this way of interpreting Bonhoeffer's experience overlooks the fact that it was class alienation and not racial oppression that occupied him in the years prior to the Nazi takeover.

Viewing Bonhoeffer's involvement in the Church Struggle through the lens of his immersion in Harlem also risks overstating the parallels between anti-black and anti-Jewish ideologies. Without question there are similarities, as both are quasibiblical belief systems that eventually became embedded in pseudoscientific racial hierarchies. But anti-black racism nearly always perceives people of African heritage as less than human, lacking qualities found in "higher" human types (e.g., honor, self-control, intelligence, maturity, culture, governability). While racist anti-Semitic rhetoric also traffics in images of subhumanity, its distinctive element is the contention that Jews are *more* than human. Jews may appear harmless, the anti-Semite warns, but are in fact extremely dangerous because they participate in subtle and not-so-subtle plots to control society, undermine traditional values, and destroy civilization.

One implication of this difference is that anti-black racism typically dictates that "white" society can be maintained only if blacks are controlled (sexually, politically, or physically), while the racial anti-Semite claims that the survival of non-Jews mandates Jews' "removal." An effect of this distinction is that the black and Jewish "threats" are apprehended differently in the racial imagination. Whites develop mythologies of black criminality, hypersexuality, and lack of intellectual capacity; but the presence of blacks in society does not provoke cosmic conspiracies in which they do the devil's work.

For these reasons, an assumption of continuity between American racism and German anti-Semitism can give rise to the misconception that Bonhoeffer reacted to the Jewish Question apart from theological concerns, as simply another example of violated human rights. As we shall see, this is far from the case.

Fictional Bonhoeffers

Given the drama inherent in his life it was perhaps inevitable that Bonhoeffer's story would be adapted for popular media. And since fictionalized accounts of Bonhoeffer's story now exist by the dozens, it is not surprising that they reflect perceptions of his relationship to Jews. One recurring image is Bonhoeffer the innate and consistent philosemite. This image emerges in shorthand descriptions of Bonhoeffer's passion that refer to him as "a Christian theologian who gave his life to save Jewish people"[34] as well as in narrative accounts of Bonhoeffer's life, where the philosemitic Bonhoeffer is imagined with considerable ingenuity.

Michael Phillips, an author of "Christian fiction" who has sold over five million books, features Bonhoeffer in *The Eleventh Hour*, the first volume in his series The Secret of the Rose.[35] Although *The Eleventh Hour* is not a recounting of Bonhoeffer's life, the theologian does play an increasingly prominent supporting role as the story unfolds. When Bonhoeffer enters the novel, it is 1937. Baron Heinrich von Dortmann has just returned to his Pomeranian country estate from a visit to Finkenwalde, where he has been auditing Bonhoeffer's lectures on the Sermon on the Mount. In a conversation with his wife, von Dortmann expresses both admiration and concern for Bonhoeffer, who seems unafraid of death: "He has been flying in the Nazis' face for years, making enemies with his bold pro-Jewish sentiments and his pronouncements to the church to awaken from its complacency."[36] After Gestapo agents close the seminary, Bonhoeffer asks for refuge at *Lebenshaus*, the von Dortmann country estate.

When Bonhoeffer next appears in the novel, it is February 1938. While supervising "collective pastorates" in the region, Bonhoeffer visits *Lebenshaus* and confides to the baron that he has made contact with the German resistance. "I have prayed and prayed for years about what should be our response as Christians to the Nazi evil. . . . My conscience tells me that the Nazi evil against the Jews is of such magnitude that bringing force against it may be necessary," Bonhoeffer says. Despite differing views of their faith's political implications, the two men agree on the necessity of taking personal risks to aid persecuted Jews.

A portrait of Bonhoeffer the pro-Jewish crusader is elaborated in great detail in Denise Giardina's critically acclaimed biographical novel *Saints and Villains*. If the Bonhoeffer fashioned by Michael Phillips in *The Eleventh Hour* is the quintessential evangelical, Giardina's Bonhoeffer is the consummate liberal. He smokes cigarettes, engages in premarital sex, is a committed pacifist, and is influenced by ecumenical contacts in other countries and denominations. The two novels are united, however, in the certainty that Bonhoeffer's contemporary relevance cannot be divorced from his awareness of the intimate connection between Christians and Jews. Both books celebrate a camaraderie with and empathy for threatened Jews, and both make clear that Bonhoeffer's distress at Jewish suffering launched him on the path toward political resistance.

Saints and Villains is the story of Bonhoeffer's public opposition to the Nazis, and its plot is fueled by his private aversion to anti-Semitism. The novel's opening chapter implies that this aversion was virtually innate. While hiking through the Thüringer Wald, Dietrich and his twin sister, Sabine, are caught in a snowstorm. A woman who shelters the teenagers remarks off-handedly that their hometown of Berlin contains "too many Jews." "Why do you say that? Do you know any Jews?" Dietrich testily responds.[37] This incident dramatizes Bonhoeffer's natural inclination to champion Germany's Jews and foreshadows his inevitable collision with Nazism. Dietrich's affinity for things Jewish is underscored when he falls in love with a Jewess named Elisabeth

Hildebrandt. As the narrator points out, Bonhoeffer commits his first act of treason when he makes love to Elisabeth in violation of the Nazi Nuremberg laws.

In subsequent passages, Bonhoeffer's sympathy for Jews as Jews is repeatedly confirmed. His parishioners describe him as "obsessed with the Jewish Question"; he wanders through Berlin's Jewish district in search of Elisabeth, whom he later helps escape from Germany; he pleads with his co-conspirators to do something for the Jews, though his brother-in-law must remind him that "the saving of Jews is not your assignment"; he daydreams of pulling a trainload of Jews to freedom; he walks the streets of the German capital while "thousands of people wearing yellow stars flowed past him—some carrying suitcases and boxes, others wandering confused and empty-handed—beneath the watchful eyes of armed SS guards"; Schindler-like, he bribes an SS official in an effort to save Elisabeth's husband from deportation.[38] Then, in the book's final scene, while in transit to his own execution site, Bonhoeffer passes

> a caravan of Jews being driven on foot from Auschwitz and Treblinka to the Reich. Dietrich watches through a crack between the slats of the truck's wooden sides as the scarecrow men, women, and children make their painful way, driven by armed guards like draft horses ready to die in the traces. The passing truck forces them from the road, and they do not look at it but stand with heads bowed taking what rest they can as they wait to be forced on.
>
> "The absent ones," Dietrich says.
>
> And thinks he is better off on the road with them.[39]

Artificial though it may be, in highlighting Dietrich's longing to identify and suffer with Jewish victims of the Third Reich, this scene is faithful to the Bonhoeffer Giardina has portrayed in the previous 450 pages.

Mary Glazener's *The Cup of Wrath* is another work of historical fiction that accentuates Bonhoeffer's response to anti-Jewish persecution.[40] It does so through references to documented history (such as Bonhoeffer's opposition to his church's adoption of the Aryan clause, his reaction to *Kristallnacht*, and his role in "Operation-7"), accounts of his influence on other characters, and fabricated episodes in which Bonhoeffer comes to the aid of vulnerable Jewish men. In one such scene, Dietrich and his cousin are walking the streets of Berlin when two members of the SA forcibly remove a Jew from an "Aryan only" bench. As the brown shirts prepare to give the offending "non-Aryan" a thrashing, Bonhoeffer moves into action:

> With three quick steps Dietrich passed the storm troopers, addressing the hapless victim as he went, "Ah, Johannes, have I kept you waiting? I'm terribly sorry. I was held up at the university." He winked at the startled Jew, put his hand on his shoulder, and steered him to the path, where Hugo waited in obvious amazement. In a voice loud enough to be heard by the storm troopers, Dietrich said, "I'd like you to meet my cousin, Herr Councilor von der Lutz, of the Justice Department." He tried to reassure the frightened man with a look, then turned to Hugo. "My friend, Herr Johannes Ertzberger." Without a backward glance, Dietrich nudged them forward. Hugo, three inches taller than Dietrich, towered above the man walking between them.
>
> "We'd better hurry or we'll be late for the matinee," said Dietrich, and continued in the same vein until they were out of earshot of the SA men . . . .[The Jew] said, with tears in his eyes, "Thank you. Thank you very much. Those men—there's no telling—."[41]

Another fictional scene depicting Bonhoeffer's putative philosemitism appears in Michael van Dyke's *Bonhoeffer: Opponent of the Nazi Regime*. Shocked to realize that his Tübingen fraternity does not accept Jews, the young Bonhoeffer reflects on the situation:

> Could it be true that the Hedgehogs are truly haters of Jews, he asked himself. Then he remembered the songs he sang in Hedgehog meetings about "Germany, pure and strong," "the blood of Christian men," and so forth. . . . Suddenly it seemed like his entire world had come crashing down. He closed his philosophy book, laid his head down upon it, and began to weep softly.[42]

Such products of the imagination are the results of backward extrapolation from Bonhoeffer's mature opposition to Nazism. They assure us that, at least with regard to the issue of anti-Semitism, Bonhoeffer's heart and mind were in the right place from the beginning. These novelistic creations may faithfully reflect Bonhoeffer's character; yet they leave readers with the mistaken impression that Bonhoeffer publicly and consistently intervened on behalf of Jews he did not know. For this reason, narrative portraits of Bonhoeffer as an instinctive opponent of Nazi anti-Semitism make difficult a fair appraisal of his relationship to the Jewish Question and his legacy for Christian-Jewish relations.

The Confessing Church in Myth and History

Popular conceptions of the Confessing Church and its opposition to Nazism represent another influence on perceptions of Bonhoeffer's relationship to "the Jews." As a resister associated with the *Bekennende Kirche*, Bonhoeffer's image has long been part of the church's "iconography of self-justification, evidence that the Christian Church could—did—speak of justice and brought forth martyrs in every dark age."[43] But as our understanding of the German Church Struggle has been revised by historiography that deromanticizes the Confessing Church and places it against the background of the church's overall failure vis-à-vis Nazism, the image of Bonhoeffer has undergone revision as well. Franklin H. Littell was among the first to complicate romantic images of the confessors. "The cheap and easy view of the Church Struggle," he wrote in 1975, "is that it was like the persecutions of old in which martyrs and confessors stood to the death against heathenism." In fact, however, "the record of most theologians and churchmen . . . was confused and weak where not outright wicked. The conduct of the masses of baptized Christians covered the scale from enthusiastic apostasy to accommodation."[44]

Alice Eckardt concurs. If we consider the total picture of the churches' role during the years of the Nazi regime, she argues, the term "Church Struggle" becomes "almost farcical, certainly misleading":

> Essentially it was a struggle by the institutional churches to preserve for themselves an area that was separate from the state and national life, an area in the sacraments, and care for those in need of solace. . . . The churches and their hierarchies did not raise objections . . . to the government's repudiation of democracy, persecution of Communists

and Socialists, the concentration camps, the multitude of anti-Jewish decrees and violent actions, the wars of aggression, oppressive occupation policies, use of foreign slave labor, or the "Final Solution" itself.[45]

Eckardt's sobering conclusion is that the German Church Struggle teaches us what to *avoid* in any similar situation. Eberhard Bethge has been similarly unsparing in his criticisms of the Confessing Church, whose concern to confess Christ alone meant that "the problems of anti-Semitism and peace remained marginal for a long time."[46] As measures of the Confessing Church's failure, Bethge points to its silence in the wake of *Kristallnacht* and its ministers' record of volunteering for military service at the outbreak of World War II.[47] Geffrey Kelly, who refers to the Barmen Declaration of 1934 as "something Hitler could live with," is among the many scholars who have criticized this emblem of Confessing Church resistance for its insensitivity to the plight of Jews.[48]

Nonetheless, despite a chorus of scholarly voices eager to correct misleading images of the church's response to Nazism, among laypeople popular conceptions of the Church Struggle remain largely undisturbed. American evangelical publications routinely recall the courageous stand of the Confessing Church and the heroic actions of Barth, Bonhoeffer, and Martin Niemöller.[49] And mainline Protestants wishing to harness the moral authority of the *Bekennende Kirche* have launched the "confessing church movement," in part to oppose the ordination of openly homosexual persons. In contemporary America, the loudest claimant to the mantle of the *Bekennende Kirche* is the confessing church movement within the Presbyterian Church (USA), which emerged in western Pennsylvania in the spring of 2001.[50]

As in the case of the radical pro-life movement, use of the name "Confessing Church" is part of a strategy of establishing symbolic connections between Nazi Germany and contemporary America.[51] The analogy lends a patina of heroism and victimhood to those who are committed to resisting a departure from tradition that would allow gay and lesbian pastors and elders. Leaders of the Presbyterian Church (USA) "confessing churches" allege that, just as in Nazi Germany, mainline Protestants have been unfaithful to basic tenets of the faith and overly accommodating to contemporary culture.[52]

The first impulse of many who are familiar with the *Bekennende Kirche*'s struggle against Nazi-sympathizing German Christians has been to point out the incongruity—indeed, the obscenity—of American claims to wear the mantle of the Confessing Church. Critics of the movement have observed how poorly Protestant sexuality debates conform to the Church Struggle in Nazi Germany, and more liberal Presbyterians have called the choice of the name "confessing church movement" amusing, inappropriate, and highly offensive. Some have even argued that the claim of sexual purists to stand in the shadow of the German "confessors" is profoundly ironic since, as William Stacy Johnson succinctly notes, "the term 'confessing church' has stood for people risking their lives for the conviction that the gospel of grace extends to everyone."[53]

Indeed, contemporary confessing church movements thrive on a naive conception of the German Church Struggle built from superficial perceptions of saints and martyrs who stood for Christ and for Jews in the face of Nazi terror. As long as such views of the church under Nazism flourish in the popular mind, it will be difficult to view the confessors' responses to the Jewish Question with anything like objectivity.

A Conflicted Legacy

Another influence on perceptions of "Bonhoeffer and the Jews" has been the unsuccessful campaign to have the German theologian recognized as one of the "righteous among the nations" by Yad Vashem: The Holocaust Martyrs' and Heroes' Remembrance Authority in Jerusalem. Inasmuch as he is a beacon of hope for those concerned with righting the ship of post-Holocaust Christian-Jewish relations, Bonhoeffer seems the very model of the Righteous Gentile. For many Christians, he represents the promise that Christianity can remain faithful to its Jewish founder by demonstrating special concern for its sibling faith; for many Jews, Bonhoeffer's sacrificial actions instill hope that some Gentiles may be as committed to Jewish survival as they are. Yet despite the widespread view that he "struggled passionately on behalf of rescuing Jews,"[54] since the mid-1980s Bonhoeffer has been turned down by Yad Vashem on several occasions.

A new campaign to have Bonhoeffer counted among the 20,000 "Righteous Gentiles" acknowledged by Yad Vashem was launched in 1998. In an article in the *Christian Century* titled "Why Isn't Bonhoeffer Honored at Yad Vashem?" Stephen A. Wise noted that among the persons honored as "righteous among the nations" are men such as Armen Wegner who did not actually rescue Jews. Bonhoeffer did so, according to Wise, in a number of activities that aided Jewish victims of the Nazi regime. Wise provides the details of "Operation-7," a scheme devised by Bonhoeffer's brother-in-law Hans von Dohnanyi and the Abwehr's Admiral Wilhelm Canaris to supply fourteen German Jews with false papers and spirit them across the border to neutral Switzerland during August and September of 1942.[55] Bonhoeffer aided the operation by calling on his ecumenical contacts to arrange visas and sponsors for the rescuees.[56]

Responding to the objection that most of these rescuees were converts to Christianity, Wise reminds us that "according to Nazi law, a person with a single Jewish grandparent or great-grandparent was considered Jewish, even if he or she had been baptized."[57] Not only was Bonhoeffer directly involved in rescuing Jews, Wise maintains, but he opposed Hitler by speaking out repeatedly against mistreatment of Jews by the Nazis and violated the High Treason Law by sending descriptions of deportation procedures to Wise's grandfather, who had ties to President Roosevelt.[58] Wise recounts these and other features of Bonhoeffer's opposition to Nazi Jewish policy in an attempt to demonstrate that he risked "life, freedom, and safety" to protect Jews (a direct appeal to Yad Vashem's requirements).

Despite his seemingly unassailable argument, Wise's twenty-six-page petition (which included an affidavit from an "Operation-7" rescuee and a newly found copy of the indictment charging Bonhoeffer with trying to help an imprisoned Jewish professor) was rejected. In an October 1998 letter to Wise, Mordecai Paldiel, director of Yad Vashem's Department for the Righteous Among the Nations, informed him that in Bonhoeffer's case three important pieces of data were lacking: evidence of personal involvement in assisting Jews at considerable risk to himself, open defiance and condemnation of Nazi anti-Jewish policies, and "direct linkage between the man's arrest and his stance on the Jewish issue."[59]

Yad Vashem's position was further delineated in a *Jerusalem Post* article in which Paldiel acknowledged that although Bonhoeffer was surely a martyr in the struggle against Nazism, he was not among those "non-Jews who specifically addressed themselves to the Jewish issue, and risked their lives in the attempt to aid Jews." In Paldiel's view, Bonhoeffer opposed Hitler on church-state issues and his imprisonment and execution stemmed from "involvement in the anti-Hitler plot of July 1944, and not, to the best of our knowledge and the known record, to any personal aid rendered to Jews." As for "Operation-7," Paldiel opined that since the action had "the full backing of the highest authority in the *Abwehr*," honoring those involved would make a "laughing matter" of the Righteous program. The same article quoted Peter Hoffman, a scholar of the German resistance, who surmised that Bonhoeffer's close ties to government insiders in the resistance were a chief obstacle to his recognition by Yad Vashem.[60]

In the summer of 2000, Yad Vashem again refused to honor Bonhoeffer with the designation "righteous among the nations." In the process, Paldiel revealed what many had long suspected—that Bonhoeffer's candidacy was troubled by his words as well as his putative actions. "On the Jewish issue," Paldiel wrote, "the record of Bonhoeffer is to publicly condone certain measures by the Nazi state against the Jews (save only baptized Jews), and to uphold the traditional Christian delegitimization of Judaism, coupled with a religious justification of the persecution of Jews." Paldiel went on to assert that while Bonhoeffer's condemnations of Nazi anti-Jewish measures were uttered "in private and among trusted colleagues; his denunciations of Judaism and justification of the initial anti-Jewish measures were voiced in writing."[61]

The matter received rigorous scholarly attention later that year at the 2000 annual meeting of the American Academy of Religion, where the AAR's Bonhoeffer Group sponsored a session titled "Bonhoeffer, the Jews, and Judaism." The session featured a presentation by Richard L. Rubenstein titled "Was Dietrich Bonhoeffer a 'Righteous Gentile'?" as well as responses from leading Bonhoeffer scholars. Rubenstein concluded that it is quite possible to regard Bonhoeffer as a "righteous gentile," with or without Yad Vashem's imprimatur.[62]

Despite the negative attention that has resulted from its refusal to honor Bonhoeffer as a Righteous Gentile, Yad Vashem has not budged. Meanwhile, Bonhoeffer's repeated failure to earn this accolade has provoked strong reactions among his supporters.[63] Their pique was intensified in October 2003 when Hans von Dohnanyi, Bonhoeffer's brother-in-law and comrade in the conspiracy, was honored as one of the "righteous among the nations" in an official ceremony in Berlin. The same year, the Center for Jewish Pluralism of the Reform Movement, represented by Stephen Wise, sued Yad Vashem before the Supreme Court of Israel for access to protocols from discussion of Bonhoeffer's case. Yad Vashem, whose privacy was upheld by the court, reiterated in a press release that its decision in the Bonhoeffer case (which, it revealed, had been unanimous) was based on its view that

> his assistance towards the Jews was limited to speaking up for Jewish converts who belonged to the Christian church that were being persecuted by the Nazis because of their Jewish roots. This was not a case of saving them, but of protecting their rights as Christians. Moreover, Bonhoeffer did not oppose the Nazis per se, but a faction within the church that sought to negate the rights of converts. There is no proof that he was involved in saving Jews.[64]

Whether the official position of Yad Vashem reflects a cautious approach to history or the murky politics of the Jewish community, Yad Vashem's characterization of Bonhoeffer as "someone whose actions did not include any efforts to try to save Jews or to speak out against Jewish persecution" has cast a shadow of suspicion over his relationship to the Jewish people. While the Yad Vashem controversy is just one of the forces affecting Bonhoeffer's place in popular memory, this particular post-Holocaust perspective indicates the conflicted nature of Bonhoeffer's legacy.

BONHOEFFER AND THE JEWS IN SCHOLARSHIP

In the charged space between the Bethge effect and the Yad Vashem controversy, between the portrayals in historical fiction and the romantic associations of the Church Struggle, scholars have been laboring for decades to clarify Bonhoeffer's relationship to the Jewish people. The survey of scholarship in this chapter will illumine the ways Bonhoeffer's post-Holocaust legacy has been assessed. While not exhaustive, it is illustrative of the questions that have occupied scholars and the various conclusions they have proposed.

Jewish Perspectives

The importance of "the Jews" as a topic in Bonhoeffer studies can be credited in part to the contributions of leading Jewish scholars and rabbis including Stephen S. Schwarzschild, Eugene B. Borowitz, Emil L. Fackenheim, Stanley R. Rosenbaum, James A. Rudin, Richard L. Rubenstein, Pinchas E. Lapide, Albert H. Friedlander, and Irving Greenberg.

The 1960s

The first Jewish scholars to take notice of Bonhoeffer were primarily concerned not with how he understood Jews, but with how Jews ought to understand him. Among the earliest to address this question was Steven S. Schwarzschild, whose 1960 survey of liberal Protestant theological literature in the journal *Judaism* dedicated considerable space to Bonhoeffer. Schwarzschild observed that "Jews owe it to Dietrich Bonhoeffer to become acquainted with his theology"—not only because he was a martyr to Nazism, but because his teachings "exhibit many marks of kinship with basic Jewish orientation," a fact not surprising given that he "increasingly went back to what to him was the 'Old Testament' and thus drank from the same well from which Judaism is nourished."[1] In a similar review of current theological literature in *Judaism* five years later, Eugene B. Borowitz expressed an equally favorable impression of Bonhoeffer's significance for Jews. "For a post-Hitler Jew," Borowitz wrote, Bonhoeffer's "human credentials . . . are impeccable. He was not only an avid supporter of the Barmen Declaration, but also a major figure in the Confessing Church which stood up to the Nazi regime." Despite recent questioning of the motives of the various German resistance efforts, Borowitz concluded, Bonhoeffer's standing as "one of the 'saints'" remains unblemished.[2]

The same year, however, following the publication *No Rusty Swords*, Schwarzschild illumined a different facet of Bonhoeffer's image. According to Schwarzschild, the matter of Bonhoeffer's resistance to Nazism required "some elucidation from a Jewish point of view," from which perspective it appeared "quite dubious—to put it mildly." Schwarzschild drew upon a letter Bonhoeffer wrote in 1934 as well as the essay of April 1933 titled "The Church and the Jewish Question" (both of which appeared in *No Rusty Swords*) in order to "make clear the ambiguity of the best of Protestant Christians in a decisive hour, to set the historical record right, to stimulate whatever questions sensitive people may wish to deduce from these circumstances, and to warn against any facile, simplistic interpretation of the phenomenon of Dietrich Bonhoeffer."[3]

In 1967 prominent Jewish philosopher Emil L. Fackenheim assessed Bonhoeffer's life and theology in a journal article that represented the first attempt by a Jewish scholar to engage the prison letters. Fackenheim conveyed appreciation for Bonhoeffer's encounter with the "modern-secular world," his emphasis on "the Biblical God['s]" concern with this-worldly life, and the "radical Biblical authenticity" that sweeps aside all "apologetic nineteenth-century half-heartedness."[4] He perceived "Hebraic inspiration" in Bonhoeffer's Christian affirmations from prison and judged that Jews were bound to be moved by them; yet he regarded "profoundly problematical" Bonhoeffer's musings on "'man come of age,' happy in his secularity and free of guilt." Fackenheim called it a tragic irony that Bonhoeffer should have cleared this man of guilt at the precise time when he became implicated, all around him, in a guilt without historical precedent: not only when his "work" was to drive gas-chamber trucks or to fight Hitler's war, but also when it was merely to clean the streets—and hold his peace.[5]

Accusing Bonhoeffer of "a nearly incredible lack of realism," Fackenheim penned a critique of the German theologian's apparent obliviousness to the Final Solution that would reverberate through subsequent assessments of Bonhoeffer's relationship to Jews and the Holocaust:

> Clear-sighted witness, apostle of Christian self-exposure to the secular world and himself martyr to his cause, Bonhoeffer nevertheless failed wholly to grasp . . . the monstrous evil of the actual world about him. This painful truth, in retrospect inescapable, cannot escape his Jewish reader. In a concentration camp filled with Jews subjected to every imaginable form of torture, Bonhoeffer writes that Protestants must learn about suffering from Catholics. No mention is made in the *Letters and Papers from Prison* of Jewish martyrdom.[6]

In a long note appearing in a subsequent version of this essay, Fackenheim acknowledged Eberhard Bethge's objection to the preceding paragraph: that Bonhoeffer's letters had made no mention of Jewish suffering so as not to attract the attention of prison censors. Fackenheim also confessed ignorance of the "tremendous development" in Bonhoeffer's attitude toward Jews between 1933 and 1944. But he further alleged, as Schwarzschild had done two years earlier, that "in 1933 Bonhoeffer confined his opposition to Nazi Aryan legislation to its application to converted Jews" and quoted the notorious passage from "The Church and the Jewish Question" that describes the curse borne by the Jewish people for killing Christ.[7]

The 1970s

Fackenheim later recalled that when it became widely known in the 1960s that Bonhoeffer had not hesitated to invoke the ancient Christian charge of deicide, he and other Jewish thinkers "pressed Bonhoeffer scholars and followers to investigate whether Bonhoeffer's brave personal struggle against Nazism, in the years after 1933, was matched by a comparable theological struggle against Christian anti-Judaism, his own included."[8] In 1975 Eva Fleischner articulated the response to Fackenheim's question that had been adopted by many Jewish scholars. Of "The Church and the Jewish Question" she wrote that "one could hardly find a more graphical illustration of how deeply the 'teaching of contempt' had taken root" in the German mind. "It is true that Bonhoeffer wrote these lines early in the Nazi rise to power," Fleischner acknowledged. "Yet, despite his consistent and heroic opposition to Nazism, which ultimately cost him his life, there is no evidence that he ever repudiated the notion of a divine curse hanging over the Jewish people."[9]

In a study titled "Bonhoeffer und das Judentum" published in 1979, Pinchas E. Lapide presented Bonhoeffer's theology with considerably more generosity than either Fackenheim or Fleischner.[10] If Fleischner based her characterization of Bonhoeffer's theology on "The Church and the Jewish Question," Lapide charitably neglected to mention the essay. He acknowledged that "various statements of Bonhoeffer often appear to us today contradictory, unclear and ambiguous," but explained that because Bonhoeffer "was not capable of completely harmonizing the following of Christ with his Lutheran heritage" his image of Judaism is "an unfinished symphony."[11] But heritage was not destiny for the young theologian. Following his arrest Bonhoeffer turned away from the abstract theology of New York, London, and Berlin. "In prison and in camp," Lapide argued, "he wrote a 'De profundis' with a Jewish pen containing Jewish thoughts like those we have acquired by the thousands from Bergen-Belsen, from Auschwitz, and from Treblinka."[12] Lapide extolled Bonhoeffer's deeds as well, calling his decision to join the anti-Hitler conspiracy an act worthy of "Torah-true Judaism" and comparing him to the Hebrew prophets who "risked their lives for the divine law."[13] This "exemplary man of God" became "a blood witness for the God of Abraham, Isaac and Jacob."[14]

Lapide placed Bonhoeffer in a long line of exemplary Christians who, during times of spiritual crisis, have rediscovered the God of Israel:

Just as in the famous night of fire in 1645 the Hebrew Bible led the way for Blaise Pascal from the God of the philosophers back to the God of Abraham, Isaac and Jacob, in the dungeon of Tegel Bonhoeffer arrived at the insight that it was necessary to rethink and reinterpret the concepts of penitence, faith, righteousness, rebirth and sanctification in the Old Testament sense.[15]

But Lapide went further, declaring that in the process of rediscovering the Hebrew Scriptures, Bonhoeffer found the taproot of rabbinic Judaism. Lapide emphasized "the growing Hebraisation of the young theologian's thought structures," noting "rabbinic parallels" to Bonhoeffer's letters and referring to the German theologian as "Rabbi Bonhoeffer."[16] How Jewish does Bonhoeffer appear to Lapide? "If Eberhard Bethge had not assured us that Bonhoeffer's bookcase in prison was of exceedingly humble dimensions," Lapide wrote, "I might have fostered the suspicion that he read the *Mishnah*—not only read, but deeply absorbed and spiritually digested it."[17]

Lapide's article was not devoid of criticism. It noted, for instance, that as late as 1937 Bonhoeffer read the Old Testament christocentrically, just as the church fathers had done. For Lapide, however, not even Bonhoeffer's devotion to Christ represents a barrier to Christian-Jewish rapprochement. Because the "Rabbi of Nazareth" is "a pious Jew" whose Sermon on the Mount represents the "primordially Jewish core" (*urjüdischen Kernstück*) of his teaching, Lapide can understand Bonhoeffer as simultaneously "Jesus-like and deeply Jewish" (*jesuanisch und zutiefst jüdisch*).

Given that Lapide has become famous for acknowledging the essential Jewishness of Jesus, for emphasizing the common heritage of Jews and Christians, and for being willing to engage in dialogue with Christian theologians, his benevolent analysis of Bonhoeffer's theology is not surprising. But the contested status of Bonhoeffer's relationship to "the Jews" has meant that Lapide's embrace of the German theologian is frequently invoked by non-Jewish scholars.

The 1980s

In an article published in 1981 in *The Journal of Ecumenical Studies*, Stanley R. Rosenbaum made it clear that Lapide's take on Bonhoeffer did not represent anything like a Jewish consensus. Despite appreciation for Bonhoeffer's bravery, which made him "the outstanding candidate for Protestant sainthood during the Holocaust," Rosenbaum questioned whether Bonhoeffer's 1933 conception of "Nazi oppression as somehow congruent of Israel's historic curse" had undergone significant change during the subsequent twelve years. As evidence that it had not, Rosenbaum read "The Church and the Jewish Question" in light of passages from *Communio Sanctorum* and *Nachfolge (Discipleship)* and claimed that even during 1935 "neither Bonhoeffer nor his colleagues regard[ed] Judaism as a subject for discussion."[18]

While conceding that *Kristallnacht* had been a personal watershed for Bonhoeffer, Rosenbaum judged from scripture references cited in the pogrom's wake that "the clearly desired effect of *Kristallnacht* in Bonhoeffer's mind is as always to draw some Jews to accept Christianity."[19] Rosenbaum also found fault with Bonhoeffer's limited knowledge of Hebrew and rabbinic literature, his lack of close friendships with Jews, and his ignorance of German Jewish contemporaries such as Martin Buber, Franz Rosenzweig, and Leo Baeck. It is sad, Rosenbaum wrote, to search Bonhoeffer's works in vain for references to Jews that are not "ignorantly patronizing or dogmatically conversionist."[20] Rosenbaum reckoned that since Bonhoeffer assumed "Judaism died giving birth to Christianity," it is "painfully apparent that the only interest a Bonhoeffer Christian can have in Judaism is the individual conversion of its erstwhile adherents."[21] Rosenbaum's sobering conclusion was that "for a Jew . . . it is apparent that Bonhoeffer is no saint," but "the best of a bad lot," a tragic victim of "millennial Christian polemics against Jews."[22]

In 1987 Rabbi James A. Rudin of the American Jewish Committee presented a paper titled "Dietrich Bonhoeffer: A Jewish Perspective" at the Evangelische Akademie Nordelbien in Hamburg, Germany.[23] Rudin's focus was Bonhoeffer's influence on American Jewish thinking, particularly among those engaged in interreligious dialogue. This influence had been profound, according to Rudin. Bonhoeffer's personal heroism "touch[es] us deeply"; "we read with admiration" his 1933 attack on the Aryan Paragraph, as well as his famous declaration following *Kristallnacht* that "only the person who cries out for the Jews may sing Gregorian chants"; one is "deeply moved" by Bonhoeffer's decision to join the conspiracy as he "bravely and tragically moved into direct political action against Hitler and the Nazis."[24]

This is the Bonhoeffer who "has resonated within the Jewish community," Rudin observed. But there is another side to the Bonhoeffer coin, to which Rudin refers by rehearsing some of the problems with Bonhoeffer's essay "The Church and the Jewish Question" and claiming that, even when Bonhoeffer "turned to the Hebrew Scriptures for strength and comfort, [he] always saw those Scriptures as a prelude to the coming of Jesus, the Christ."[25] If Rosenbam sought to illumine the plainly anti-Jewish aspects of Bonhoeffer's theology, Rudin's contribution to the "Jewish perspective" on Bonhoeffer was the light he shed on the "ambiguities and ambivalences" that attend Bonhoeffer's reflections on the Jewish people:

> Traditionally, Christian thinkers have maintained two polarized views of the Jewish people. The first is that the Jews are "the brethren of Jesus Christ," and those Jews who have been baptized in the true faith have, in theological parlance, "come home" to Christianity.
>
> The opposing polar view is that the Jews represent the "Judas figure," the "people who nailed the redeemer of the world to the cross." In this theological construction, the Jews are cursed and punished by God, condemned to be the perpetual outsider, the universal pariah people. . . . Bonhoeffer reflects both of these extreme views.[26]

With this analysis, Rudin clarified Bonhoeffer's debt to the Christian tradition of reflection on "Israel," a debt that will be explored in depth in subsequent chapters.

Rudin's overall conclusion was that Bonhoeffer is a "transition figure," one who consistently expressed the "traditional Lutheran views of his time and place about Jews and Judaism," but appeared toward the end of his life to transcend the teachings of his church and embark on a path of Christian universalism. "He was thwarted in his attempt to fashion a new Christian understanding of Jews and Judaism," Rudin wrote, by the gangster state in which he lived. The ambiguities that remain have limited his influence within the American Jewish community; while widely respected, he is "not looked to as a major thinker in building bridges" between Christians and Jews.[27]

In 1988 Albert H. Friedlander addressed the Fifth International Bonhoeffer Congress in Amsterdam on the topic "Israel and Europe." Examining Bonhoeffer's sermon "The Church of Moses and the Church of Aaron" (May 1933), Friedlander commented on "seeing the Hebrew Scriptures re-emerge out of [his] profoundly Christian sermons." He also expressed admiration for the awareness of Jewish suffering in Bonhoeffer, who "understood the suffering God, as he had come to understand the suffering of Israel."[28] Friedlander accepted Bethge's claim that Bonhoeffer's theology contains "signposts" for a theology after Auschwitz, and was even able to construe Bonhoeffer's failings in a positive light:

> That there were flaws in Bonhoeffer's perception of the Jews and Judaism has been noted clearly over the years. These flaws are important and helpful to us, first, because it is much harder to work with saints than with decent, imperfect human beings, and second, because we cannot advocate sainthood toward one another as the hope for resolving ancient problems. It is the growth and development of Bonhoeffer, his acknowledgment of wrong perceptions, which is our greatest instruction.[29]

In an earlier essay, Friedlander had taken up a theme Andreas Pangritz would later pursue from the Christian side: the intriguing parallels between Bonhoeffer and his German Jewish contemporary Leo Baeck. But Friedlander warned that if we turn to these men after the Holocaust, it is because "of their humanity which faltered and erred but nevertheless endured in a time of darkness." Both men, Friedlander lamented, had been obscured by mythologies, the Bonhoeffer myth "created because the Church wanted reassurance that it, the Institution, was not a sinner."[30]

The published reflections on Bonhoeffer and "the Jews" by Richard L. Rubenstein are noteworthy not only because of Rubenstein's standing as a scholar of the Holocaust, but because his assessment of Bonhoeffer's significance for Christian-Jewish relations has steadily evolved. This is evident when we compare the first and second editions of *Approaches to Auschwitz* (1987; 2003), the more recent of which includes a section titled "The Special Case of Dietrich Bonhoeffer" that seeks to clarify Rosenbaum's memorable description of Bonhoeffer as "the best of a bad lot."[31] Rubenstein too takes Bonhoeffer to task for indifference to contemporary Judaism;[32] yet he reminds us that as objectionable as we may find Bonhoeffer's supersessionism, "without it he would have had no Archimedean point with which to transcend his culture and oppose Hitler and National Socialism. Regrettably, that faith was a seamless garment that included a harshly negative evaluation of Jews and Judaism."[33]

Like Rosenbaum, Rubenstein concludes that Bonhoeffer was unable to extricate himself from conventional Christian views of Jews and Judaism, and thus was a victim of the tradition he inherited; nevertheless, he "rose above the time and culture that produced him to do what only a handful of his fellow Germans were prepared to do, risk and finally sacrifice his life in the struggle to bring to an end the terrible evil that had overtaken his people."[34] Rubenstein's relatively charitable posture toward Bonhoeffer is reflected in his unequivocal assertion that Bonhoeffer merits the Righteous Gentile moniker that Yad Vashem has to this point denied him.

The 1990s

Addressing the Sixth International Bonhoeffer Congress in New York in 1992, Rabbi Irving Greenberg related that as a young yeshiva student "sometime in the early '60s," he picked up Bonhoeffer's *Letters and Papers from Prison*. Caught up in the optimism of the 1960s while attempting to assimilate the Holocaust's effects on the Jewish people, Greenberg found the book resonated in his soul. According to Greenberg, it was the words written on April 30, 1944, predicting the movement toward a completely religionless time, that "leaped off the page" at him.[35] Like previous Jewish interpreters (particularly Schwarzschild, Fackenheim, and Rosenbaum), Greenberg charged that Bonhoeffer's moving protest on behalf of Jews in 1933 had been limited to "Jews who converted to Christianity"; and he was troubled by the implication in Bonhoeffer's theology that "there is no way to God except through Christ." Still, he wanted to believe

> that had Bonhoeffer lived he would have continued to be theologically influenced by his encounter with reality and that he too would have given up the imperialist Christian claim, or Christ claim, as another example of letting go in favor of an appreciation of the presence of God in the presence and the midst of a life of Joy and of others as well. My proof . . . was the way in which [his] appreciation of what he called the Old Testament and I call Hebrew Scriptures grew in the last period, the breakthrough period, of [his] history.[36]

While not offering a full-scale examination of Bonhoeffer's thought, Greenberg did credit Bonhoeffer with "seeding [his] thinking," convincing him of the legitimacy of Jewish-Christian dialogue, and stimulating his reflections on the relationship of human and divine power.

As this survey indicates, the Jewish engagement with Bonhoeffer echoes with appreciation for his martyrdom and the decisions that precipitated it, as well as caution concerning certain aspects of his theological legacy. Attracted mainly by his resistance to National Socialism, the earliest Jewish responses to Bonhoeffer were content to characterize his theology with vague phrases such as "Hebraic inspiration" (Fackenheim) and "marks of kinship with basic Jewish orientation" (Schwarzschild). But as his writings became better known in the mid-1960s, difficult questions began to be asked and Jewish endorsements of Bonhoeffer became more tentative. Pinchas Lapide and Stanley Rosenbaum demonstrate that by 1980 the pendulum of Jewish sentiment could swing widely in either direction. A. James Rudin and Richard Rubenstein represent a centrist position rooted in the conclusion that Bonhoeffer's theology contains ambiguities that he had neither time nor opportunity to overcome. Overall, the response to Bonhoeffer among Jewish scholars combines acknowledgment that he towered above most Christians in Nazi Germany with disappointment that he evinced typical Christian approaches to Judaism.

Christian Perspectives

The 1960s

Among the earliest attempts to interpret Bonhoeffer in light of post-Holocaust Christian-Jewish relations was Walter Harrelson's "Bonhoeffer and the Bible," published in 1962.[37] Examining Bible studies, sermons, and letters from throughout Bonhoeffer's professional career, Harrelson was critical of Bonhoeffer's exegetical method, particularly his habit of interpreting the entire Bible christologically and locating its unity in Jesus Christ. Furthermore, Harrelson alleged, during the 1930s Bonhoeffer persisted in "portraying Judaism in New Testament times in a way which is patently erroneous," and which is part and parcel of the ancient "teaching of contempt."[38]

Assessing the implications of Bonhoeffer's exegesis for Christian-Jewish relations, Harrelson charged that often Bonhoeffer "remove[d] the Bible of the Jews from their hands." He noted that "if the Old

Testament has no meaning for faith apart from its meaning in Jesus Christ, then those who—in faith—do not declare Jesus to be the Messiah are simply left without their Scripture, are they not?"[39] Harrelson's damning conclusion was that Bonhoeffer did "not assign much meaning to the faith and hope of Israel *for Israel,* or for the Jewish people today." Linking Bonhoeffer's exegesis to the fate of Jews under Nazism, Harrelson found it "intolerable to maintain that the Jews who went to their death in Buchenwald and Dachau were in any less favorable position to comprehend the meaning of God's redemptive love, witnessed to in their Scripture, than were Bonhoeffer and his fellow Christian martyrs."[40]

The 1970s

While these charges hung in the air like a cloud over Bonhoeffer studies, a decade passed before the appearance of another scholarly work by a non-Jew devoted to the topic. At the First International Bonhoeffer Congress in Düsseldorf-Kaiserwerth, West Germany, in 1971, William Jay Peck presented a paper that was revised and published two years later as "From Cain to the Death Camps: An Essay on Bonhoeffer and Judaism." Peck's thesis was that Bonhoeffer's relation to "the Jews" was far more important than most commentators had perceived, that it occupied, in fact, "a decisive place in his theology, his political decisions, and his concept of religion."[41]

Peck's analysis went beyond deeds and occasional writings to explore "the mythic dimension in Bonhoeffer's theology and life." He detected a "definite parallelism" in Bonhoeffer's writings between Judaism and the modern secular world. "The decisive parallel," Peck wrote, "is the tension between Jesus Christ and the secular man, and between Jesus Christ and the Jew."[42] Significantly, Peck noted, it was only after the Jewish deportations were in full swing in 1942 that Bonhoeffer wrote about his rejection of religion. Peck even explained Bonhoeffer's failure to mention Jews from prison as a result of "the ineffability of the name of God" Bonhoeffer discovered in the Old Testament.[43]

Peck's ambitious project, though hampered by a less-than-clear distinction between mythological and mythical elements in Bonhoeffer's theology,[44] did provide openings for subsequent research. Peck observed, for instance, that Bonhoeffer's essay "The Church and the Jewish Question" linked the plight of Jews with Bonhoeffer's eventual decision to join the resistance movement, a connection largely overlooked to that point. Peck's article also represented an early attempt to view Bonhoeffer in the shadow of the Holocaust, reflecting growing consciousness of the "latent anti-Semitism within Christianity" and Christian responsibility for the death camps.[45]

In 1974 Ruth Zerner addressed the issue of Bonhoeffer's relationship to "the Jews" before the annual Scholars' Conference on the Church Struggle and the Holocaust.[46] Readily acknowledging that Bonhoeffer's writings "include problematic passages, ambiguities and contractions," Zerner set out to demonstrate that Bonhoeffer was "to some extent a victim of his background and perspectives."[47] Thus she argued, in contrast to Peck, that with regard to Jews our focus should be Bonhoeffer's actions rather than his theology. Accordingly, Zerner perceived in Bonhoeffer's "personal actions and private comments" a more reliable gauge of Bonhoeffer's concern for Jews' plight.

Zerner did not ignore the "thoughts" about Jews expressed in Bonhoeffer's writings, including "several equivocal and problematical paragraphs" in "The Church and the Jewish Question" that are "typical of pre-Holocaust, pre-Vatican II, Christian thinking."[48] She also corroborated Harrelson's assessment that "Bonhoeffer constantly interpreted the Old Testament in terms of Jesus Christ," adding that this christological focus is found throughout his writings.[49] Zerner's conclusion, however, was that, in the end, Bonhoeffer's theology was not a barrier to heroic action:

> While retaining certain traditional Christian images of the cursed Jews, Bonhoeffer refused to allow them to reinforce any fear of action. His thinking on Jews and their Bible may appear to us ambiguous, problematic and tentative in the light of post-Holocaust Christian re-thinking of theology regarding the Jews, but his final actions were unmistakably heroic.[50]

It is significant that although her focus was Bonhoeffer's actions, Zerner made a signal contribution to comprehending his theology of Israel by emphasizing its ambivalence toward Jews. "Despite his increasingly positive attitude towards Old Testament 'this-worldliness,' ambivalence about the Jews and the Hebrew Bible survived as a persistent feature of Bonhoeffer's thinking, even in *Letters and Papers from Prison*," she wrote.[51] As we shall see, this unresolved tension between conflicting images of Jews in the Christian imagination has been overlooked or downplayed by subsequent interpreters.

The 1980s

Around 1980 Eberhard Bethge produced a series of presentations and publications on "Bonhoeffer and the Jews" that had a perceptible influence on subsequent research.[52] Bethge's decision to explore this topic was induced by Emil Fackenheim's request for help, delivered before the English Language Section of the International Bonhoeffer Society in 1979, in determining the post-Holocaust significance of Bonhoeffer "the theologian." Bethge's conclusion was that although Bonhoeffer himself had not explicitly begun to formulate a "theology after the Holocaust," he was "among the earliest and strongest on the Christian side to break fresh ground in that direction" and that "something like a hermeneutic of the Holocaust became existentially and linguistically effective" in him.[53]

Bethge began his lengthy article "Dietrich Bonhoeffer and the Jews" by reviewing studies of the topic by Eva Fleischner, William Jay Peck, Ruth Zerner, and Pinchas Lapide that had appeared during the 1970s. He then discussed the presuppositions Bonhoeffer brought to the crisis of 1933—the ways his cultural milieu predisposed him to view German Jews, his inattention to the Jewish Renaissance of the 1920s (due in part to his fascination with dialectical theology and his disinterest in Berlin's ethos of theological liberalism),[54] and a Barthian concept of revelation predicated on the view that "the God of the Jews is also the God of the New Testament."[55] Bethge emphasized that Bonhoeffer's "emphatic adherence to the whole of scripture was, historically, an act of confession, that at that time was understood on every side as an active intercession for the Jews." As evidence for this claim Bethge cited SS journalist Friedrich Imholz's derisive response to Bonhoeffer's Bible study titled "King David" (1936), which closed with the affirmation that "the people of Israel will remain the people of God, in eternity, the only people who will not perish, because God has become their Lord, God has made His dwelling in their midst and built His house."[56]

Turning to Bonhoeffer's April 1933 essay titled "The Church and the Jewish Question," Bethge examined the various ways this article had been interpreted since its rediscovery and publication in the 1960s.

While the essay may appear to reveal "a thoroughly unenlightened proponent of that theology which assumes that Christians replace Jews as the chosen people, and, worse yet, that Jews should suffer under a punitive curse," Bethge insisted that these uncritical notions are "definitely not the central theme of the paper and that they are already in the process of being transcended."[57] Bethge contrasted Bonhoeffer's approach to the Jewish Question with that of other "confessors" by alluding to a parallel document by Walter Künneth, director of the Center for Apologetics in Berlin, who endorsed "lawful measures to protect the German people from foreign contamination" and "elimination of the Jews as a foreign body from the nation's life."[58] Dissenting from Jewish readings of the essay, Bethge stressed that "The Church and the Jewish Question" demonstrates Bonhoeffer's concern with Jews as such, rather than with baptized non-Aryans. Furthermore, according to Bethge, while the essay offered no "theology of the Holocaust," it did contain "small but significant signs of change."[59]

Bethge next considered the *Bethel Confession* and its section titled "The Church and the Jews," drafted jointly by Bonhoeffer and Wilhelm Vischer. Here Bethge perceived the juxtaposition of sharp anti–German-Christian formulations with anti-Jewish "theological views which we can scarcely read without second thoughts."[60] Nevertheless, Bethge observed in *Bethel* a path leading ultimately to solidarity with Jews, a path marked by Bonhoeffer's rediscovery of Romans 9–11 ("God wills to complete the salvation of the world, which he began with the election of Israel, through these self-same Jews") and use of traditional disinheritance theory against German Christians rather than against Jews ("The place of the Old Testament people of the covenant was not taken by another nation, but by the Christian church called out of and living among all nations"). Overall, Bethge discerned in *Bethel* a "new theological quality" in relation to living Jews that emphasized God's faithfulness to Israel and Israel's indestructibility—"both formulations which endangered those who subscribed to them."[61]

Bethge then directed his attention to the "decisions" that guided Bonhoeffer's path following his departure from Germany in late 1933—including his use of the phrase "open thy mouth for the dumb" (Prov. 31:8, KJV), aid he rendered to German emigrants, conversations with his students, the funeral sermon he preached for his grandmother Julie Bonhoeffer, his famous statement (traced to 1935, though never recorded in writing) that "only he who cries out for the Jews may sing Gregorian chants," and his responses to *Kristallnacht* (including notations in his Bible and his statement that "when today the synagogues are set afire tomorrow the churches will burn"). According to Bethge, references to Psalm 74, Zechariah 2, and Romans 11 in a circular letter to former Finkenwaldians dated November 20, 1938, "reveal a new, deeper expression of solidarity with persecuted Israel, with its suffering, and a sense of awe in the contemplation of God's election."[62]

Regarding Bonhoeffer's role in the anti-Hitler conspiracy, Bethge proffered an interpretation that was subsequently adopted by a majority of scholars: "There is no doubt that Bonhoeffer's primary motivation for entering active political conspiracy was the treatment of the Jews by the Third Reich."[63] In Bonhoeffer's posthumously published *Ethics*, Bethge identified "completely new statements," including a reference to "expulsion" of the Jews and of guilt for the "deaths of the weakest and most defenseless brothers of Jesus Christ" penned in the fall of 1940. He asserted that although Bonhoeffer did not say "*our* brothers," with the words "brothers of Jesus Christ"—the first reference in the circles of the Confessing Church to Jews (in general) as brothers in the full sense—he entered into "deep solidarity" with the victims of the Holocaust.[64]

Bethge went on to discuss reports compiled by Bonhoeffer in response to deportations of Jews from Berlin in October 1941 (which show a "premonition, even at this time, of a final escalation of the atrocities, even though certainly nothing was yet known about a 'Wannsee Conference' or about the technology of the gas chambers");[65] his involvement in "Operation-7"; his harsh treatment of a Nazi official in prison who voiced anti-Semitic sentiments in Bonhoeffer's presence; and the Tegel letters' connection of God's suffering in and through the world "with the Old Testament, and even more so with the presence of suffering Jews."[66] Bethge maintained, finally, that the summary of Bonhoeffer's Tegel theology appearing in "Outline for a Book" reveals the extent to which he "was affected by the crisis in his church caused by the Holocaust."

It is significant that while claiming that Bonhoeffer "established some presuppositions for new approaches to a post-Holocaust theology," Bethge ultimately returned to deeds when assessing Bonhoeffer's legacy: "What Bonhoeffer finally achieved was his identification with the persecuted and murdered Jews in a deed which has left an indelible impression."[67] Bonhoeffer's contribution to the Jewish-Christian dialogue, Bethge declared, was made in Flossenbürg.

In 1987 Robert E. Willis authored a comparative study of Bonhoeffer and Karl Barth focused on their responses to Jewish suffering. Ironically, given that Barth had considerably more opportunity for theological reflection and for assimilating the reality of the Holocaust, Willis argued that Bonhoeffer's more occasional theology actually allowed him to "see Jews as fellow humans for whom Christians were also responsible."[68] Responding to a view expressed by several Jewish scholars, Willis emphasized the rapidity with which Bonhoeffer realized that concern for the Nazis' Jewish victims could not be limited to converts. Bonhoeffer's awareness of Jews' vulnerability, according to Willis, moved against the stream in both the Confessing Church and German society and could "be traced directly to his theology."[69] As support for this claim, Willis invoked passages from *Discipleship* (where Bonhoeffer wrote that "any attack even on the least of men is an attack on Christ") and *Letters and Papers from Prison* (where he affirmed that "Jesus is there only for others").[70]

For Willis, the underlying unity of Bonhoeffer's thought was to be found in a persistent theology of the cross and the corollary of "unlimited action on behalf of the neighbor." Bonhoeffer was able "to enter into the reality of Jewish suffering and maintain solidarity with it"; and this was accompanied by a "gradual softening, virtually to the point of elimination" of Christian anti-Judaism.[71] While Willis acknowledged the "remorseless abstractness" attributed to Jewish destiny in "The Church and the Jewish Question," he maintained that references to the divine curse were morally neutralized in that essay by Bonhoeffer's emphasis on binding victims' wounds and protesting state-sanctioned injustice. Willis concluded that

> the centrality of Christ "for us" in Bonhoeffer's theology and the corollary that flowed from that point, the binding of those who live in Christ in the neighbor, overshadowed his occasional employment of the anti-Semitic strand within Christian theology and enabled him to reach out to the Jewish neighbor—whether converted or not— during those dark years when the *Endlösung* was carried out.[72]

Remarkably, Willis regarded Bonhoeffer's significance as lying precisely in his success at overcoming the theological apprehension of Jews that clung to Barth's theology and caused the reality of Jewish suffering to constantly elude his vision.[73] In contrast, according to Willis, Bonhoeffer's published writings are distinguished by a growing emphasis on "the concreteness of the requirement of neighbor-love, which permits the Jewish neighbor, especially, to be encountered largely apart from a prior theological scheme that undertakes to 'place' Judaism and the Jewish people in relation to the church."[74]

The Remembering for the Future conference at Oxford in 1988 featured presentations on Bonhoeffer and "the Jews" by Edwin Robertson and James Patrick Kelley, both of which appeared in the conference proceedings.[75] Robertson's study concentrated on the fateful period between January and April 1933, the phase of Bonhoeffer's initial responses to the Nazi revolution and the German Christians' bid for power in the church. Robertson maintained that the Jewish Question was very near to Bonhoeffer's thinking throughout the early months of 1933, not only in his radio broadcast on the "leadership principle" (*Führerprinzip*), but in his preaching and conversations with friends. With regard to "The Church and the Jewish Question," Robertson paid particular attention to the context in which it appeared (the general tone of the church and its leaders on the Jewish Question makes the essay "all the more impressive," he wrote) and Bonhoeffer's background ("As we read it we must recall that this young theologian was 27 and that he was a Lutheran").[76]

Robertson's article was particularly valuable for elucidating Bonhoeffer's treatment of Luther in "The Church and the Jewish Question." With the 450th anniversary of Luther's birth approaching that November and the Nazis seeking to portray Luther as a "*völkisch* prophet of the German people," Robertson observed, Bonhoeffer's Luther epigraphs were "carefully chosen" to subvert the popular image of Luther as an incorrigible anti-Semite.[77] Robertson's guidance for reading this essay reflected two aspects of what would become a standard interpretive strategy for minimizing Bonhoeffer's anti-Judaism. To Bethge's tactic of claiming that the essay's positive features outweighed any anti-Judaism it might contain, Robertson added assignment of the article's offensive ideas to the broader Christian tradition:

> In attempting to deal with the "quite special context of the church,"
> [Bonhoeffer] writes an unfortunate paragraph based upon Luther's
> "Table Talk." He repeats the old medieval teaching of the "curse"
> upon the Jews for crucifying Christ. This is indefensible . . . but
> it should not lead us to disregard this remarkable document of a
> Lutheran theologian helping the Protestant Church to find its way
> out of an impasse. His theology at this point is based upon Paul's
> vision of the "grafting of the vinestock back into the vine from
> which it was broken off"—and that is more important for him than
> the medieval "curse." Jews may rightly be offended at Paul's and
> Bonhoeffer's theology of the conversation [*sic*] of the Jews, but few
> can doubt the sincerity of his vision and his deep respect for what he
> would call God's ancient people the Jews.[78]

Whether or not this argument is convincing, it introduced an important insight into Bonhoeffer's theology of Israel—the acknowledgment
that the curse invoked by Bonhoeffer in 1933 is not only "medieval"
but Pauline as well, and that the theological tradition invoked here by
Bonhoeffer paradoxically combines respect for God's ancient people
with the notions of displacement and suffering. As we shall see in the
next chapter, these are characteristic features of the witness-people tradition Bonhoeffer relies upon in "The Church and the Jewish Question" to interpret Jewish destiny.

James Patrick Kelley's contribution to Remembering for the Future,
titled "The Best of the German Gentiles," examined two of Bonhoeffer's
earliest responses to the Nazi accession to power—his "Führer" essay
and "The Church and the Jewish Question." The latter Kelley identified
as Bonhoeffer's "first direct, specific treatment of the rights of German
Jews." While conceding that parts of the essay are "quite consistent" with
Luther's theological anti-Semitism, Kelley perceived "at least some first
hints of a less exclusively-antisemitic [*sic*] understanding of the relationship between the church and Israel, one that will be stressed in some
portions of Bonhoeffer's later, incomplete work on *Ethics*."[79] Like other
interpreters, Kelley held up Bonhoeffer's reference to the church's judgment in "The Church and the Jewish Question" ("As it looks at the
rejected people, it humbly recognizes itself as a church continually
unfaithful to its Lord") as evidence that the traditional model of Israel's
displacement was being nuanced, a process he saw extended in *Ethics*.

Kelley's article helpfully elucidated the influence of Bonhoeffer's brother-in-law Gerhard Leibholz on his political analysis of the Nazi "legal revolution," which, had it become persuasive for more Christians, might have destabilized the Hitler state and averted the Final Solution. "This is true," Kelley asserted, "in spite of Bonhoeffer's continuing to hold at this period to some 'theological antisemitism.'"[80] Kelley confidently concluded his article by noting that in light of his analysis it should no longer be possible to claim (as Fackenheim, Rosenbaum, and others had done) that Bonhoeffer was better than his theology because he fought only for the rights of non-Aryan Christians.

The 1990s and Beyond

The most in-depth treatment of "Bonhoeffer and the Jews" to date appeared in 1990 in a book-length study titled *Dietrich Bonhoeffer's Struggle against National-Socialist Persecution and Destruction of the Jews* by Christine-Ruth Müller.[81] Since commenting on Müller's entire volume is beyond the scope of this chapter, I will focus on its analysis of Bonhoeffer's resistance to the Aryan Paragraph between June and September 1933, that is, after he wrote "The Church and the Jewish Question."

Müller's study was characterized by attention to some of Bonhoeffer's less-known pronouncements, including an address delivered June 22, 1933, in which Bonhoeffer used Paul's image of the weak and strong in 1 Corinthians, characterizing as "weak in faith" those who would not tolerate the presence of Jewish Christians in the church. Müller also reviewed Bonhoeffer's summer Christology lectures, citing his emphasis on the uniqueness of Israel, "which stands apart from all people," and his scandalous claim that "Israel is the place where God fulfills his promise." In these addresses, Müller perceived an "openness toward the essence and meaning of Israel" that represents the "development of an Israel theology."[82]

Müller also discussed a pamphlet prepared by Bonhoeffer before the 1933 summer church elections in which he outlined an uncompromising rejection of the Aryan Paragraph and encouraged members of the "Gospel and Church" group to reject all distinctions between Jews and Germans in the church. She compared Bonhoeffer's position on the Jewish Question favorably with that of Martin Niemöller and suggested that the declaration that marked the founding of the Pastor's

Emergency League was probably Bonhoeffer's work.[83] In fact, Müller credited Bonhoeffer with pushing Niemöller to an uncompromising position on the Aryan Paragraph.

Müller paid particular attention to September 1933, when Bonhoeffer attended a series of ecumenical meetings as well as the National Synod in Wittenberg. She showed that at each of these gatherings Bonhoeffer tirelessly pushed to get the Jewish Question and anti-Jewish violence on the agenda. Thus she carefully substantiated the claims of Heinz-Eduard Tödt that the Jewish Question was the ground upon which Bonhoeffer first came into direct conflict with the Nazis.

Since the late 1980s, periodic treatments of "Bonhoeffer and the Jews" have been heard at international conferences—particularly the annual Scholars' Conference on the Holocaust and the Churches and the quadrennial International Bonhoeffer Congress.[84] The proceedings of the 1996 Congress in Cape Town contain an article by Alejandro Zorzin that revisits Bonhoeffer's early response to Nazism from the perspective of Latin American Protestantism's reaction to political oppression since the 1970s.[85] Zorzin's primary contribution to our topic is an extensive comparison between "The Church and the Jewish Question" and notes on the Jewish Question by Walter Künneth that were circulating at the time, which Zorzin surmises Bonhoeffer may have been responding to.

Künneth's notes on the Jewish Question, which were also discussed by Bethge in his seminal article titled "Bonhoeffer and the Jews," gave credence to racial definitions of non-Aryans and to the notion of a disproportionately high number of Jews in the German professions. For decades, Künneth wrote, there had been "such a proliferation of the Jewish influence, that the risk has arisen of an overgrowth of German intellectual life and a domination by foreign influences of the public sphere."[86] In general, Künneth's approach to *die Judenfrage* was to cater to Germans' racial consciousness and their fears of Jewish influence, while counseling partial acceptance of the Aryan Paragraph in the church. The special witness of the church, according to Künneth, was to ensure that "the elimination of the Jewish influence on the life of the people occurs in such a way . . . that it does not contradict the Christian ethos."[87]

Zorzin pointed out that while Bonhoeffer agreed with Künneth that the state had a right to regulate *die Judenfrage*, his approach differed in fundamental ways. Specifically, he rejected the state's racial-ethnic definition of "non-Aryans"; he included all victims of state actions in the church's purview; he rejected on principle the Aryan Paragraph's introduction in the church; he avoided much of the prejudicial content that attached itself to discussions of the Jewish Question in church circles; and he refused to countenance the violation of civil rights, even in exchange for a highly desired social "good" such as the "elimination of . . . Jewish influence."

In concurrence with Heinz-Eduard Tödt and over against Klaus Scholder, Zorzin argued that Bonhoeffer and Franz Hildebrandt represented a group in the Confessing Church that, from the beginning, clearly grasped the scope of National Socialist anti-Semitism and the centrality of opposition to the Aryan Paragraph to the church's identity. In this sense, Zorzin declared, Bonhoeffer's essay can serve as a guide for the church's response to a state that fails to perform the function of "God's order of preservation in a godless world."[88] In order to avoid Christian shortsightedness with regard to basic civil rights, Zorzin concluded, we should "continue searching out the clues that [Bonhoeffer] gives us in his early essay on the 'Jewish question.'"[89]

In his contribution to the Cape Town Bonhoeffer Congress, Andreas Pangritz explored Bonhoeffer's decision to join the German resistance in light of his developing theology of Israel.[90] In a subsequent essay appearing in *European Judaism* in 1997, Pangritz observed that although Bonhoeffer seemed scarcely aware of his Jewish contemporaries, it is possible to discern "substantive links between the Jewish thinking of the 1920s and 1930s and Bonhoeffer's renewal of Protestant theology."[91] In particular, Pangritz surmised what Bonhoeffer might have learned from Leo Baeck had he been aware of him.[92] The "great substantive contiguity" between the two thinkers suggests to Pangritz that during the Weimar period "more 'cultural osmosis' was possible than we have been willing to believe since the Holocaust."[93]

Reflections on Bonhoeffer: Essays in Honor of F. Burton Nelson, an anthology published in 1999, included two articles on Bonhoeffer and "the Jews." In ". . . They Burned All the Meeting Places of God in the Land," Jane Pejsa argued that in memorializing sites associated with Bonhoeffer's life and ministry, we ought to recall the destruction of *Kristallnacht*, "which turned out to be God's urgent call to his servant Dietrich Bonhoeffer."[94] Pesja rehearsed the responses to *Kristallnacht* noted by Bethge in his seminal article on the subject, and echoed him in calling the event "the critical turn in Bonhoeffer's life journey," after which he began to view his own fate as intertwined with that of German Jews. Pesja opined that amid the frenzy of memorializing that began in the mid-1990s, "Bonhoeffer himself would judge it grossly inadequate to remember him without simultaneously acknowledging those of God's people whose plight first opened his eyes."[95]

The same volume contained a long article by Geffrey B. Kelly titled "Bonhoeffer and the Jews: Implications for Jewish-Christian Relations." Kelly's essay covered much the same ground traversed by Bethge and others over the previous two decades, while answering criticism of Bonhoeffer's early response to Nazism by Stanley Rosenbaum and Stephen Ray. While Kelly admitted that "The Church and the Jewish Question" is "tinged with unfair characterizations of the Jews" and thus "somewhat problematic," he suggested that "we separate the predictable, theologically tainted assertions about the Jews" from Bonhoeffer's suggestions about how the church should react to the Aryan Paragraph. Our focus, according to Kelly, should be the essential point of Bonhoeffer's essay — the daring course he outlines for the church with regard to state action.[96] No other theologian of the time, Kelly reminded readers, was able to view the state's actions as victimizing a distinct minority. Among the other features of Bonhoeffer's theology and witness highlighted by Kelly are his repeated references to Proverbs 31:8 ("Open thy mouth for the dumb," KJV), and his analysis of Bonhoeffer's role in "Operation-7." This discussion concludes in a critique of Yad Vashem's decision to deny Bonhoeffer recognition as a Righteous Gentile, which, according to Kelly, cannot diminish the "value of his example and writings for the future of the Jewish-Christian dialogue and a fuller reconciliation of Jews and Christians."[97]

The most recent scholarly exploration of our topic appeared in the journal *Dialog* in 2004. In "Reclaiming Bonhoeffer after Auschwitz," Robert O. Smith sought to defend the German theologian from the critiques of "Jewish Holocaust thinkers" such as Fackenheim and Rubenstein while gauging his significance for the future of Christian-Jewish relations. Like Bethge and other advocates of the post-Holocaust Bonhoeffer, Smith perceived a "commitment to alleviating and redressing Jewish suffering" in Bonhoeffer's invocation of Proverbs 31:8; in his dictum that "only he who cries out for the Jews may sing Gregorian chants"; in his warning to his students in 1938 that "if the synagogues burn today, the churches will be on fire tomorrow"; and in his statements in *Ethics* that "Jesus Christ was a Jew" and that the church "is guilty of the deaths of the weakest and most defenseless brothers of Jesus Christ."

In *Letters and Papers from Prison*, Smith claimed to uncover "veiled references" to Jewish suffering and a "paradigmatic corrective to Christian anti-Jewish supersessionism."[98] Beyond this, according to Smith, Bonhoeffer's post-Holocaust significance lies in the fact that

> one can glean from Bonhoeffer's writings concerning Jews a series of specific commitments concerning Christianity's responsibility to the world, commitments drawn from his engagement with biblical Judaism (especially the prophetic) and the contemporary reality of Jewish suffering, a suffering tolerated by even his closest coreligionists.[99]

Realizing that Bonhoeffer's post-Holocaust relevance depends in part on a repudiation of his early anti-Jewish sentiments, Smith emphasized that it is impossible to "consider Bonhoeffer's corpus and find no effort to overcome the implicitly anti-Jewish presumptions of his context, as some have claimed."[100] Whether or not scholars will agree, Smith's article is a reminder of what is at stake for post-Holocaust Christianity in the ongoing process of interpreting Bonhoeffer's writings and actions.

Our survey suggests that before 1980 Christian examinations of Bonhoeffer's relationship to Jews and Judaism oscillated between the view that Bonhoeffer perpetuated the Christian "teaching of contempt" (Harrelson), the claim that Bonhoeffer's mature theology evinced "parallelism" with Judaism (Peck), and the attempt to distinguish Bonhoeffer's theology from his deeds (Zerner). In the wake of Bethge's seminal article of 1980, however, Christian perspectives on "Bonhoeffer and the Jews" begin to reveal consensus on several points: that Jewish persecution was Bonhoeffer's primary motivation for entering the conspiracy;[101] that anti-Judaism was a marginal theme in "The Church and the Jewish Question"; that in any case Bonhoeffer repudiated anti-Judaism in his response to *Kristallnacht*; and that he was "among the earliest and strongest on the Christian side to break fresh ground" in the direction of a "theology after the Holocaust."[102]

Observations

As we have seen, a relatively abrupt coming to light of "the Jews" in Bonhoeffer studies in the mid-1960s has been followed by a steady process of analysis and assimilation. While this process has not produced a scholarly consensus, it is has won widespread acceptance for the view that understanding Bonhoeffer's attitude toward Jews is crucial for interpreting his legacy. Before moving on, we should note some of the recurring themes in this literature.

First, there has been sharp disagreement—though little debate—on a fundamental point of interpretation associated with Bonhoeffer's initial response to Nazism. For some—including Jewish scholars Schwarzschild, Fackenheim, and Greenberg—Bonhoeffer's bold opposition to the German Christians is diminished by his apparently exclusive concern for baptized Jews. For others—including Christian scholars Bethge, Willis, Kelley, and Wolfgang Gerlach[103]—it is precisely Bonhoeffer's inclusion of Jews *as Jews* in the church's realm of obligation that distinguishes his contribution to the Church Struggle. Advocating this perspective, Clifford Green writes that "one of the redeeming features of Bonhoeffer's problematic essay on the church and the Jews in April 1933 is that he was concerned with the danger to *all* Jews, not just his co-religionists; this put him a step ahead of the Confessing church which focused on Christians of Jewish ancestry."[104] Dissenters, including those responsible for evaluating Bonhoeffer's candidacy for the honor of Righteous Gentile, remain unmoved by such arguments, maintaining the need for "the articulation of a clear-cut and public position with regard to Nazi measures against Jews, without distinction between baptized and non-baptized ones."[105]

The issue remains contested in part because the evidence is susceptible to various interpretations; indeed, even Bethge's biography can be read to support both positions. In speaking of "The Church and the Jewish Question," Bethge emphasizes that the essay's subject "was the Jewish question as such, not merely the church membership of Christians of Jewish descent." A few pages later, however, Bethge writes that in 1933 Bonhoeffer's "energies were wholly consumed in the fight against the Aryan clause," that is, with the fate of Jewish Christians in the church.[106] By September 1935, in the wake of the Nuremberg Laws, Bonhoeffer seems to have been convinced that the church's battle had to be waged on the Jewish Question rather than on the Aryan Paragraph. Yet upon his return to Finkenwalde from the Steglitz synod, discussion with his ordinands focused on Romans 9–11, Paul's reflections on the meaning of the Messiah's rejection by Jews.[107] The fairest conclusion seems to be that while Bonhoeffer was *more* concerned with the Jewish Question than most of his fellow confessors, his *main* preoccupation was the integrity of the church's response to the Aryan Paragraph, and that even in 1935 he never considered the Jewish Question apart from a theological context.

One also detects in this literature, particularly on the part of Christian scholars, an inclination to downplay the anti-Jewish sentiments in Bonhoeffer's writings. It is perhaps predictable that brief synopses of Bonhoeffer's life would tend to ignore the ambiguities of his early writings on the Jewish Question.[108] But one expects scholars to address such issues unflinchingly. Some admit that Bonhoeffer's April 1933 essay is "tinged with stereotypical assertions about the Jews" and move on to analyze what is truly "significant" in the text;[109] others regard the tract's anti-Judaism as reflecting a theological tradition Bonhoeffer inherited but eventually repudiated—either through silence, expressions of solidarity with suffering Jews, or opposition to the Nazi regime. Bethge locates Bonhoeffer's renunciation of anti-Judaism in his response to *Kristallnacht*, which he argues "reveals a new, deeper expression of solidarity with persecuted Israel." Smith concurs, asserting that "the inconsistencies of 1933 are put to rest in the formative event of *Kristallnacht*," Bonhoeffer's response to which represents "a clear repudiation of traditional Christian supersessionism."[110] As we will see, however, a "clear repudiation" of the troubling theological notions Bonhoeffer expressed in 1933 is difficult to verify.[111]

The penchant for viewing the glass as half-full is understandable, given scholars' desire to defend Bonhoeffer from criticism they believe is unfair or misguided. It is not dishonesty that underlies the motivation to "get past" Bonhoeffer's anti-Judaism, but the genuine desire to elucidate what was unique in Bonhoeffer's witness—in 1933 and afterward. But the cost of failing to take seriously Bonhoeffer's unfortunate and, frankly, embarrassing comments about Jewish destiny is inability to discern the continuities in his theology of Israel, and thus also failure to rightly gauge the prospects in Bonhoeffer for post-Holocaust theology.

Finally, it is critical to observe that while the scholars surveyed believe that on balance Bonhoeffer's life and work represent promising resources for Christian-Jewish rapprochement, many concerned with the phenomenon of anti-Judaism more generally place Bonhoeffer on the negative side of the ledger. In fact, although the scholarship reviewed here is both prominent and voluminous, it has not dislodged perceptions of Bonhoeffer as a leading exemplar of Christian anti-Judaism. Eva Fleischner, as we have seen, cites Bonhoeffer as an example of how deeply the "teaching of contempt" had penetrated the German theological imagination prior to the Holocaust. In *Anti-Judaism in Christian Theology*, Charlotte Klein invokes Bonhoeffer for a similar purpose. Analyzing the deicide charge in the writings of German theologians and biblical scholars, Klein notes that "in this connection it is not easy to quote so honourable a Christian martyr under National Socialism as Dietrich Bonhoeffer. But he cannot be left out, since what he says proves once again how deep are the roots struck by anti-Jewish prejudice even in the best of Christian theologians."[112]

Geoffrey Wigoder contends that Bonhoeffer "never ceased to see the Jews as accursed, although he was to suppress such sentiments during the war when he expressed his identification with Jewish suffering."[113] Franklin Littell, after rehearsing a litany of Bonhoeffer's brave actions on behalf of Jews, laments that he accepted the myth of supersessionism and affirmed the deicide charge.[114] Sidney G. Hall III cites "The Church and the Jewish Question" as evidence of the paradoxical attitudes of neoorthodox thinkers toward Jews.[115] William Nicholls compares Bonhoeffer unfavorably with Bernard Lichtenberg, perhaps the "one prominent churchman [who] openly stood up for the Jews," and claims that Bonhoeffer did not speak for Jews outside the church or take account of Hitler's aim of exterminating them.[116] And Clarke Williamson, a respected interpreter of Christian perceptions of the Jewish people, concludes that "Hitler and Bonhoeffer were united in seeking a world without Jews. One would extinguish them physically; the other would convert them—eliminate them religiously. The choice was between spiritual and physical genocide."[117]

In order to avoid the impression that such charges have evaporated in the light of recent scholarship, we should note Stephen Ray's *Do No Harm: Social Sin and Christian Responsibility*, published in 2003. Ray's book includes a chapter on Bonhoeffer's "The Church and the

Jewish Question," which he presents as an example of the way Christian "sin-talk" can inflict unintentional harm on a marginalized community by giving unwitting legitimacy to an oppressive cultural "common sense."[118] As background for understanding "The Church and the Jewish Question," Ray highlights the "discursive economies" that structure the "linguistic social context" in which Bonhoeffer lived and wrote.[119] According to Ray, because Bonhoeffer misread the important shift in his own context by which Jewish difference became identified with defilement, he tacitly accepted a discursive economy that legitimated Jewish essentialization. Seemingly unaware of the "anti-Semitic language loop" in which he was trapped, Bonhoeffer failed to challenge "the operative truism that *the Jew* really was different."[120]

Ray's judgment on "The Church and the Jewish Question" may be unfair since he ignores the essay's positive dimensions. But he succeeds in identifying a troubling paradox in Bonhoeffer's early response to Nazi encroachment in the ecclesiastical realm. Ray faults Bonhoeffer for missing the "wholly negative way that Jewish difference was being mediated in his context":[121]

> Bonhoeffer sought to challenge the racial claims of his opposition by reducing Jewish difference to the level of culture and religion. What he did not recognize was that these differences could be construed as being as profoundly essential as biological difference. For Bonhoeffer to have reached the goal he intended for this essay—a convincing theological challenge to the exclusionary legislation *and* its rationale—he would have had to reject the idea of Jewish difference altogether.[122]

It is significant, of course, that these negative assessments of Bonhoeffer's theology by Fleischner, Klein, Wigoder, Littell, Hall, Nicholls, Williamson, and Ray focus overwhelmingly on his writings during the early months of 1933. This means that they could be neutralized to some degree by evidence that Bonhoeffer recognized his involvement in the perpetuation of Christian anti-Judaism and took steps to compensate for it. This evidence will be reviewed in chapter 5.

THE GERMAN CHURCH STRUGGLE IN POST-HOLOCAUST PERSPECTIVE

As we have seen, much of the criticism directed at Bonhoeffer by those concerned with post-Holocaust Christian-Jewish relations concerns statements he made during the spring of 1933 at the height of the German Church Struggle. Furthermore, those who maintain that Bonhoeffer never repudiated these views regard him as illustrative of the enduring problem of Christian anti-Judaism. Charlotte Klein speaks for these scholars, writing that it is "not possible to find anything in the later works" to contradict the opinion that Bonhoeffer represents the deep roots of "anti-Jewish prejudice even in the best of Christian theologians." If a Bonhoeffer can speak in this way, she laments, "then we cannot be surprised that the Church generally was a silent onlooker during the years 1933–45."[1]

Those who regard Bonhoeffer's relationship with the Jewish people in a more positive light acknowledge his early failures yet insist that he later overcame them in ways that are instructive for the church. One goal of this book is to set aside these disagreements long enough to engage in a careful examination of Bonhoeffer's views within the social and religious contexts in which they were expressed. As preparation for doing so in the next chapter, we will explore the rhetorical and theological backgrounds against which Bonhoeffer's early response to Nazism must be interpreted.

Establishing Context

Contextualizing Bonhoeffer's response to the Jewish Question is a complex undertaking, one that remains incomplete despite many important contributions to the task. As was indicated in the previous chapter, the project of contextualization has been aided by scholars who contrast Bonhoeffer's approach to the Jewish Question with that of his contemporaries, German Christians and confessors alike.

Christine-Ruth Müller concludes her discussion of Bonhoeffer's opposition to the Aryan Paragraph by observing how astounding it is that Bonhoeffer overcame the restraints of the Lutheran tradition to develop new approaches to solidarity with persecuted Jewish citizens.[2] Richard L. Rubenstein notes that, despite the resonance of "The Church and the Jewish Question" with "older, hostile, supersessionary Christian stereotypes," it must be remembered that

> neither political nor humanitarian arguments could have convinced the majority of [Bonhoeffer's] fellow pastors of the inadmissibility of excluding pastors of Jewish origin. Luther's advice to "gladly accept them as brothers if they accepted Christ" was another matter. It was arguably one of the strongest theological arguments available to Bonhoeffer at the time. . . . Let us not forget where Bonhoeffer was coming from, the time in which he wrote, or the nature of his audience.[3]

Geffrey B. Kelly agrees, insisting that despite repeating ages-old Christian stereotypes, Bonhoeffer succeeded in drawing the attention of his fellow clergymen to issues—"admonition of a state, help to the victims regardless of their religious affiliation, and possibly jamming the spokes of the wheel of state"—the more conservative and order-loving among the ministers would have preferred to ignore.[4]

Alejandro Zorzin contrasts reflections on *die Judenfrage* by Walter Künneth with Bonhoeffer's principled rejection of racism and his uncompromising attack on the Aryan Paragraph. Heinz-Eduard Tödt asserts that Bonhoeffer was "the only one who considered solidarity with the Jews, especially with non-Christian Jews, to be a matter of such importance as to obligate the Christian churches to risk a massive conflict with that state—a state which could threaten their very existence."[5] Ruth Zerner concurs, observing that by September 1933, when he attended a World Alliance conference in Sofia, Bulgaria, Bonhoeffer made clear his uncompromising stand of Christian solidarity with all German Jews, baptized or not.[6] Andreas Pangritz reminds us that in the Barmen Declaration of May 1934, the Jewish Question would not be mentioned at all.[7] And Robert O. Smith writes that Bonhoeffer, merely twenty-seven in 1933, "was the first and, at the time, only Christian theologian either willing or able to speak to the theological and ecclesiological problems precipitated by this political crisis."[8]

These portrayals of Bonhoeffer's response to Nazi anti-Semitism, which underscore the ways he stood out from his peers inside and outside the Confessing Church, are crucial for interpreting the significance of his early writings. But a clear picture of the challenges facing his later theology requires a post-Holocaust analysis of the German Church Struggle that clarifies what Bonhoeffer had in *common* with other spokespersons for Christianity.

The Church Struggle and Anti-Jewish Discourse

The so-called German Church Struggle (*Kirchenkampf*) has been a subject of scholarly study and popular interest for decades. For obvious reasons, the minority of Germans who opposed the Nazis in word or in deed remain compelling symbols of courage, human reminders of the auspicious role faith can play in situations of political crisis. Rarely, however, has the discourse of anti-Nazi resistance been analyzed on the basis of its underlying assumptions about Jews, their role in German society, and their God-ordained destiny. When these assumptions are examined, it becomes apparent that despite their opposition to National Socialism and its encroachment in church affairs, Christian resisters to Nazism often affirmed views of Jews and Judaism that exacerbated the anti-Semitic environment in interwar Germany.

In order to appreciate the dynamics of anti-Nazi religious discourse, it is necessary to reconstruct the background against which Christian responses to National Socialism played out. One aspect of this background involves images of Jews that were part and parcel of the Christian theological tradition; another concerns recurring rhetorical patterns in interwar German religious debates. Establishing the theological and rhetorical contexts for religious resistance in the Nazi period reveals that in many ways resisters unwittingly increased Jewish vulnerability to Nazi assault.

The Theological Background

Christians in Germany who were led to reflect on the Nazis' systematic persecution of Jews relied on a rich theological tradition that extended back through reformers and church fathers to the pages of the New Testament. Across the centuries, Christians had perceived Jewish existence as unassailable proof of God's existence and immanence; Jewish history as a unique witness to divine providence; and the Jews' destiny as a mystery comprehensible only in the light of divine election and reprobation. Particularly when Jewish survival was at stake, Christians relied on these foundational ideas to explain what they perceived as God's mysterious dealings with this chosen but disobedient people.

Elsewhere I have described Jews' role in the Christian imagination with the phrase "witness people."[9] The Christian witness-people myth, whose content and structure were finalized by the early fifth century C.E., incorporates positive and negative judgments upon "Jews" and "Judaism" while infusing both with profound ambiguity. Augustine of Hippo (354–430 C.E.) maintained that after the death of Christ, Jews exist as living witnesses to God's sovereignty. For Augustine, and for the generations of subsequent believers who embraced his solution to the problem of Jewish existence *post Christum*, God wills Jewish survival "in unbelief" as mundane testimony to the transcendent realities of grace and punishment. Embodying reprobation and preservation simultaneously, the Jews are unique witnesses to God's mysterious providence.

In Augustine's paradoxical portrayal of the witness people, Jews are killers of Christ yet remain the people of God; their religion is superseded, yet they are not "cast off"; they are dispersed but carry "books" (the Christian "Old Testament") that "testify to Christ"; they are witnesses to divine judgment who nevertheless disseminate awareness of God's sovereignty; they are adherents of a lifeless religion whose tragic ignorance will be redeemed when they convert to Christ en masse in the eschatological future. Although never officially adopted by the church, witness-people theology animated Christian discourse for fifteen hundred years after the death of Augustine and was quite in evidence at the dawn of the Nazi era.

In a sermon preached in 1933, for instance, Basel theology professor Adolf Köberle illustrated the ongoing theological function of Augustine's witness people. On one hand, Köberle noted, persecution of Jews was predictable as people sought to protect themselves against their "corrosive influence." Such maltreatment fulfills "the eerie words that the Jewish people took upon itself long ago on Good Friday . . . 'His blood be upon ourselves and our children!'" On the other hand, according to Köberle, Christians "should tremble before the serious judgmental path of God toward the mysterious fate of this people."[10] The same year, Old Testament scholar Wilhelm Vischer proclaimed that the Jews "cannot become one nation like the other nations, even after the Crucifixion of Jesus. The history of the Jews is a special mystery of God."[11]

In 1935 Hans Dannenbaum, director of the Berlin City Mission, offered these musings on Jewish existence:

> God saves this people for a last, and one of the greatest, deeds of world history. Purified in the oven of suffering—and who knows through what bloody tribulations anti-Semitism will yet hound this people!!—it becomes ripe for conversion. And if this people, standing under the curse, still has such capability, then how marvelous must be its blessing for the world when it once again will be received by God in grace! And the day will come someday.[12]

Two years later, theologian Alfred de Quervain opined that while apostasy was the cause of the Jews' misfortune, "Israel is given to the congregation as a warning, so that it might not follow the path of Israel; . . . Israel remains as the scandal, and the church cannot simply explain, discuss, and clear this scandal away."[13]

This sort of reflection on the fate of Jews was by no means limited to those who embraced Nazi anti-Semitism. A Confessing Church pastor wrote that Nazi racial laws had "illuminated, like a bolt of lightning, a section of [the Jews'] thorny path through the world."[14] Even those who explicitly rejected racial concepts could affirm the unique identity of the Jewish people on theological grounds. A 1937 article in *Deutsche Kirche (German Church)* claimed that baptism "nullifies all racial origin," for the Teuton as much as for the Jew. However, the article's author continued, "Christianity knows only one people and race that matters before God. The Jewish people!" God made a covenant with Israel, and thus "all other peoples and races are of subordinate rank."[15] Far from normalizing Jewish existence, such apprehensions led many

Christians to assume that Jews would be the focus of Gentile resentments. One Confessing Church leader declared that "this people must go its own way until God Himself solves the Jewish question."[16]

Kristallnacht appears only to have heightened the tendency of confessing Christians in Germany to perceive the state's persecution of Jews in theological terms. Concerned that the *Bekennende Kirche* did not recognize the November pogrom as "the sign that it obviously [had] been," Karl Barth asked: "How is it possible that our Christian ears do not ring, considering the significance of this misery and wickedness? What would we be, what are we then, without Israel?" As in previous centuries, however, Jewish "misery" was seen as pointing inexorably to Christ: "Whoever rejects and persecutes the Jew, rejects and persecutes the one who died for the sins of the Jews and only *thereby* for our sins."[17]

To the end of the war, Christian opponents of the Nazi regime reiterated these aspects of the witness-people tradition. The Lempp Circle memorandum, written under the leadership of Württemberg Confessing pastor Hermann Diem, affirmed that "the church must witness to this salvation-historical significance of Israel before the *state* and resist to the utmost every attempt to 'solve' the Jewish question according to a self-made political gospel."[18] And the so-called Freiburg Circle memorandum, intended as a basis for church life after the fall of Nazism, warned that other peoples have no right to feel superior "if God punishes one people in his wrath." The Christian duty to bring all nations to the Gospel, according to the memorandum, exists also "with respect to the Jewish people, whose decisive guilt is that it resists the revelation of God in Jesus Christ, up to the present day."[19]

Thus, even when they imagined Christian-Jewish relations in a post-Nazi world, many confessors found it difficult to escape the gravitational pull of the witness-people tradition. The persistence of witness-people theology was particularly evident in post-war acknowledgments of guilt on the part of German Protestants. In 1947 the Oldenberg Church Council maintained in a letter to its clergy that because the people of Israel had rejected its Messiah, it was "an example of the divine judgment. . . ." The following year the Reich Council of Brethren of the Evangelical Church of Germany wrote that "by crucifying the Messiah, Israel rejected its election and intended purpose" and that as a result "God's judgment follows Israel up to the present day

[as] a sign of His forbearance." Reflecting the conviction that even in the Holocaust Jews had been reluctant witnesses to Christian truth, the council opined that this judgment is "the mute sermon of the Jewish fate, for us a warning and for the Jews an admonition."[20]

An instinctive propensity for mythological interpretations of Jewish experience contributed to a notable characteristic of the German Church Struggle: with respect to Jews and Judaism, leading Nazis and their sworn enemies often spoke the same language. Gerhard Kittel averred that "authentic Judaism abides by the symbol of the stranger wandering restless and homeless on the face of the earth," while confessor Martin Niemöller preached that a "dark mystery . . . envelopes [sic] the sinister history of this people which can neither live nor die, because it is under a curse which forbids it to do either."[21]

The Rhetorical Background

To appreciate the rhetorical background against which religious resistance in Nazi Germany played out, we must bear several things in mind. First, authors address issues of social, political, or religious concern in order to persuade their readers or hearers to adopt their own perceptions of these matters. Second, consciously or not, authors employ arguments they believe members of their audience will find compelling. Third, in oral and written discourse alike, the art of persuasion is in part the art of portraying one's opponents negatively—through outright vilification, association with undesirable images, or identification with unfortunate or unforeseen implications. Thus, in investigating the discourse of anti-Nazi resistance, we wish to ascertain how particular words, phrases, and arguments functioned in German religious rhetoric generally, what writers intended to say when they employed them, and, finally, what readers or hearers were likely to understand.

In his widely discussed study of National Socialist Germany, Daniel Goldhagen illustrates the anti-Jewish rhetorical environment that was both inherited and exploited by the Nazis. Goldhagen observes that by the late nineteenth century, "declaring the Jews to be one's enemy or declaring one's enemy to be beholden to the Jews was so effective for winning adherents that it became a standard part of the political and social repertoire."[22] Are these strategies discernible in religious discourse during the Nazi era? Several recent studies elucidate the rhetorical milieu in which the theological debates of the 1930s took place. In an article titled "Catholics, Protestants, and Antisemitism in Nazi Germany," Doris L. Bergen explores the interaction between anti-Semitism and confessional divisions in Nazi Germany. She notes that, like hostility between Catholics and Protestants, the use of anti-Jewish images in intra-Christian diatribes dates back to the sixteenth century. As the Catholic hierarchy denounced Luther and his followers as "Jews," Luther returned the insult.[23]

Bergen demonstrates that the same rhetorical strategy was in evidence four centuries later under Hitler:

> Like Communists and capitalists who blamed the Jews for each other's existence, Catholics and Protestants invoked anti-Jewish images against each other as well. Catholics denounced godlessness, immorality, and liberalism, traits associated with Protestants and Communists, but also with Jews. Protestants disparaged Catholics as dogmatic, divisive, and international in their orientation—terms typically invoked against Jews.[24]

In addition to expressing contempt for each other in a "Jewish" idiom, Catholics and Protestants used anti-Semitism as "a significant theological and tactical common ground" in their responses to National Socialism. Wishing to capitalize on the Nazi revolution while repudiating the regime's anti-Christian sentiments, spokesmen for both confessions made "tactical use of anti-Jewish language and associations."[25] According to Bergen, Catholics and Protestants alike responded to Nazi and neopagan charges that Christianity was "Jewish" with assertions "of their own 'true' Christianity as thoroughly German and utterly anti-Jewish."[26] This approach was particularly favored by members of the German Christian movement, who

> used notions of "Jewishness" as the antithesis of their own purported "Aryanism." With the words *Jew, Jewish* or *Judaism* they referred to diverse and contradictory qualities, but in every case, Jewishness represented the foil to their concept of Germanness. . . . If race, as the German Christians believed, was the fundamental principle of human life, then racial slurs provided the most effective form of

derision possible. German Christians tarred all opponents with the brush of Jewishness.[27]

Bergen's conclusion is noteworthy: while anti-Semitism did not bring Christians closer together, it did aggravate the circumstances of Jews.

In several studies of German Lutherans of an anti-Nazi bent, Uriel Tal has established that Christian opposition to National Socialism did not imply support for German Jews. Tal argues, in fact, that many who contended against nazification of the German churches did so by linking Jewish and Nazi attitudes toward Christianity. For example, in a public rejoinder to Nazi ideologue Alfred Rosenberg, Walter Künneth denied that the apostle Paul held a racial conception of Israel's election, countering that although Jews and Nazis emphasize a racial understanding of the Jewish people, in fact Israel's election is by grace and not works.[28] In another response to Rosenberg, Rudolph Homann situated the seeds of modern racism in the Old Testament, where, he argued, national religion (*Volkreligion*) existed side by side with the prophetic faith that gave birth to Christianity. Prophetic religion, furthermore, opposes the "idolatrous cult of the forces of nature and of blood" characteristic of both Jews and Nazis. In National Socialism and Israelite monarchy alike, Homann located a "natural religion based on race."[29]

In a subsequent study, Tal examined the Weimar period for the seeds of this German Lutheran tendency to compare and even equate "Judaism with the *Völkisch* movement, including National Socialism."[30] He found that, beginning in the early 1920s, influential Lutherans who would later join the Confessing Church conceptually linked Judaism and *völkisch* thinking. Typical was Hans Hofer, who described worship of one's nation as "a falling down to the low levels of Judaism."[31] Similarly, pastors and theologians such as Ernst Moering, Heinrich Frick, and Willy Stärk coupled Jewish nationalism and National Socialism, both of which they contrasted with the spiritual values of Christianity. In 1928 pastor Eduard Lamparter lamented that Judaism and Nazism alike distorted the meaning of *Heilsgeschichte* (salvation history) by misconstruing the millennial metaphor of Revelation.

Tal shows that during the late '20s and early '30s German Lutherans increasingly condemned Jews and the "new pagans" for their political messianism and "secular eschatology." According to Friedrich Niebergall, professor of pastoral theology at Heidelberg, "the very errors made by the *Völkisch* new pagans have their archetypal origins in the materialism, the self-sufficiency and self-righteousness, the narrow nationalistic ethnicity and the haughty resistance to salvation through faith and in Christ—so symptomatic of Judaism."[32]

This conceptual bond between Judaism and Nazism forged by German Lutherans during the 1920s was subsequently adopted by leading members of the Confessing Church, including Helmuth Schriner, Walter Künneth, Ernst Wolf, Heinrich Vogel, Hans Asmussen, Horst Stephan, Rudolf Homann, Christian Stoll, and Georg Merz. As the Church Struggle raged, these men compared their Nazi enemies with "Jews." Both "secular religions," they declared, proclaimed humanity's self-redemption through works rather than faith; both rejected Jesus as Messiah and sought to establish an earthly kingdom; both perpetuated the "disintegrating powers" that undermined traditional authority; and both fostered national particularism and racism by identifying themselves in terms of "blood."[33]

Tal regards as a puzzling phenomenon "those Lutherans who resolutely opposed racial antisemitism, and yet drew a common denominator between the Jew and the racist."[34] How do we explain, he asks, the equation of Judaism and Nazism "by a religious movement that will certainly be recorded by historians as a significant force of resistance to the evil of dictatorship?" As a tentative answer, Tal points to the Protestant churches' disestablishment under the Weimar Constitution and the resulting necessity for Protestants to compete with *völkisch* groups for popular support. As the Republic strained under the social and political changes of the late '20s and early '30s, Tal contends, conservative Lutherans who sensed a threat in the secular religion of Nazism combined two well-worn rhetorical traditions: the Christian antagonism toward the "Jew" and Martin Luther's dual struggle against Jew and pagan.[35]

Tal may be correct in identifying a social explanation for this phenomenon; we are concerned, however, with its rhetorical significance. If a leading characteristic of interwar religious discourse is its penchant for stigmatizing the Nazi enemy with a "Jewish" stain, then we must conclude that anti-Nazi authors knew instinctively that making National Socialism synonymous with "Jewishness" would strengthen their case with the average German. Of course, anti-Jewish rhetoric among pro-Nazi Christians may be interpreted as opportunism or capitulation to Nazi-think. But when employed by opponents of Nazi racism, the same anti-Jewish images and arguments should be understood as part of a rhetorical effort to establish intellectual and emotional common ground with moderate audiences. If, as Tal and Bergen indicate, "the anti-Jewish language of derision" was ubiquitous in interwar Germany—animating conflicts among Christians, as well as between Christians and Nazis—then the documents of the German Church Struggle need to be interpreted against this background.

Other studies supplement this ambiguous portrait of anti-Nazi religious resistance. Kenneth Barnes's work on Protestant social thought in Germany and Great Britain between the wars problematizes the standard portrayal of the Church Struggle in terms "of two adversarial groups, heroes and villains." Barnes emphasizes that "both Confessing Christians and national church spokesmen had been preaching the same message before 1933, a nationalistic, antisocialistic, antiliberal message that was conducive to the victory of Nazism regardless of the dissent some would later display."[36] And in a groundbreaking book only translated into English in 2000, Wolfgang Gerlach analyzes the statements and activities of Confessing Church leaders to reveal a "less than heroic" witness characterized mainly by silence. Gerlach concludes that, contrary to popular belief, loyal support for the Nazi state came not only from German Christians and the church's political "middle," but from members of the Confessing Church as well. He concludes on the basis of extensive archival research that the *Bekennende Kirche* "regarded the Jewish question as annoying and burdensome and treated it dilatorily," thus encouraging anti-Jewish persecution.[37]

Two dimensions of the rhetorical background for Bonhoeffer's early response to Nazism require further illumination: common understandings of the Jewish Question and use of "Jew" and "Jewish" as terms of derision.

The "Jewish Question"

One of the understudied features of the German Church Struggle is the extent to which Christians in both camps assumed that Germany faced a *Judenfrage* ("Jewish Question"), a matter the government was responsible for addressing with the help of privileged insight from the church.

Scholars in a number of fields offer assistance in clarifying the German concept of *die Judenfrage*. Sociologist Ronald J. Berger places the Jewish Question and its Nazi Final Solution in the context of "social problems constructionism," "a perspective that treats social problems not as a condition but as an activity that identifies and defines problems, persuades others that something must be done about them, and generates practical programs of remedial action."[38] Central to Berger's social problems approach to the Holocaust is the notion of "collective representations," simplified schemes of interpretation used to view heterogeneous groups of people as homogeneous and to construct them as problems warranting certain kinds of treatment. According to Berger, the Nazis built upon a long-standing collective representation of Jews that typified them as "persons who victimized others, who were morally unworthy of sympathy, and whose continued presence constituted a problem that needed solution."[39] This collective representation placed Jews and Germans in "complementary opposition," casting them as mutually exclusive and diametrically opposed entities.

Social problems claimsmaking entails assignment of responsibility for societal problems. In the case of Europe's Jews, these problems had traditionally included Christ's betrayal and murder, the kidnapping of Christian children, and the poisoning of wells. According to Berger, Martin Luther was a "pathbreaking claimsmaker concerning the Jewish problem, a key progenitor of the view . . . that Jews were a 'foreign nation' that lived symbiotically within German society."[40] As Paul Lawrence Rose explains, the passage from Luther to Hitler in German perceptions of the Jewish Question was complex. Modern German discussions of *die Judenfrage* had their historical point of departure in Andreas Eisenmenger's *Entdecktes Judentum (Judaism Uncovered)*, published in 1700. In Eisenmenger's view, Jews were an utterly foreign people who held contempt for others and were a threat to their hosts.[41]

The Jewish Question became a particularly pressing concern for German thought in the late eighteenth century. Between the eras of Immanuel Kant and Richard Wagner, the time-honored notion of the Jew as religiously alien was replaced by the conviction that it was actually Jewish "national character" that was alien to German life. In the late nineteenth century, as national character increasingly became conceptualized in terms of race, the Jewish Question began to connote the problems associated with this people of foreign essence who could not be assimilated without harm to the German nation.[42] During the Second Reich, *die Judenfrage* combined Jews' putative religious and racial distinctiveness with "universal, political, sociopolitical, and moral-religious" concerns.[43]

The liberal German mind might advocate "*Assimilierung, Germanisierung, und Christianisierung*" (Assimilation, Germanization, and Christianization), as professor Karl Wacker put it in 1893, but the question begged for a "solution" of some kind.[44] Meanwhile, radical responses were outlined by influential anti-Semites such as Eugen Dühring, who asserted in *The Jewish Question as Racial, Moral and Cultural Question* (1881) that Jews comprised a unique species incapable of assimilation into German culture. Extreme answers to the Jewish Question continued to be advocated during the Weimar period. In 1920 Bavarian minister president Gustav von Kahr received an urgent report titled "Recommendations for the Solution to the Jewish Question," which included many of the plans later formulated at the Wannsee Conference.[45]

Of the Jewish Question's connotations in post–World War I Germany, Daniel Goldhagen notes that across the social spectrum it was regarded as a compelling reality: even people who objected to physical violence "assumed as a matter of course that a 'Jewish Problem' did indeed exist, that the Jews were an evildoing tribe that had harmed Germany, and that a 'solution' must be found whereby their corrosive presence would be greatly reduced and their influence eliminated."[46] Thus, between 1700 and 1933 Germans of many persuasions had engaged in an ongoing conversation regarding the Jewish Question:

> The Enlighteners wanted to "improve the Jews" so that they could become good citizens, the romantic nationalists wanted them to convert to the values of the German *Volk*, to its *volksgeist*; the liberal assimilationists counseled intermarriage and pledging higher allegiance to universal human values than to Judaic religion, family or ethnic community; and *völkisch* nationalists of the late nineteenth century wanted to drive them back into their ghettos, strip them of their civil rights, or even exterminate them.[47]

Whatever solution might be advocated, there was universal agreement that the Jewish Question concerned the challenge of integrating an utterly foreign minority into the German *Volk* and strategies for limiting its corruptive influence in the meantime.

Like most Germans on the eve of the Nazi revolution, members of the Evangelical Church were convinced that Germany faced a serious Jewish Question whose most conspicuous symptoms were Jews' "excessive" influence in journalism, universities, the arts, and the professions, and their threat to Christian faith and family life.[48] As Hermann Strathmann, dean of the Erlangen Theological faculty, noted in 1933, Germans' "reawakened *völkisch* self-assurance" led them to regard the Jewish people "not just as a foreign element in our midst, but also, because of its notoriously corruptive influence on the thought, will, and morale of our *Volk*, as a danger threatening its very nature and life."[49] Such views were only partly attributable to the influence of National Socialism. Indeed, prior to 1930 perceptions of the Jewish Question in the church had already begun to shift from theological to sociological and ethnological.[50]

Following Hitler's seizure of power, Christian leaders on both sides of the Church Struggle were weighing in on the Jewish Question. Naturally, many members of the German Christian movement took a hard line. Notable in this regard is a June 1933 address by pro-Nazi New Testament scholar Gerhard Kittel, subsequently published as *Die Judenfrage*. In exploring "what shall become of Jewry," Kittel considered what he regarded as the only realistic options for solving the Jewish Question—extermination, Zionism, assimilation, and guest status.[51] Since the first three possible solutions were plagued by serious problems, Kittel maintained that only guest status would retain a distinction between Jews and Germans while encouraging Jews to "return to the religion of their fathers, and accept the role of alien as God's judgment on the Jewish people for their disobedience, the 'God-willed tragedy' which they as pious Jews must affirm."[52]

In general, members of the confessional opposition sought to address the Jewish Question while steering clear of the "aggressive anti-Semitism" they associated with Nazism. In 1933 some spiritualized the issue, insisting, with Wilhelm Vischer, that it was "not a racial question, but a question about God."[53] Others tried to mitigate the hardships resulting from state policies. An ecclesiastical document from 1933 identified the church's responsibility in the Jewish Question as demonstrating "complete brotherly love and compassion toward those among our members who are willing to assimilate themselves to the German national character, that is, in accordance with *Volk* and race." In return, these "foreign brothers and sisters in the faith [will] seriously attempt to discard those qualities inherited from their fathers that are foreign to what is German."[54] A religious periodical published the same year declared that "there is no biblical objection against containing the Jewish influence and assessing it as non-German," as long as the legitimate struggle against the Jewish community does not become inhumane.[55]

But the confessors never allowed these theological or moral reservations to obscure the Jewish Question's practical implications. In short, the prospect of a church and nation that were *Judenfrei* (free of Jews) held emotional appeal for the majority of Christians in Germany, regardless of their stand on church politics. As a result, Protestant church spokesmen—even those in the opposition—addressed the Jewish Question with the same underlying thought process that would guide perpetrators of genocide against Jewish civilians a decade later: Anti-Jewish measures were essentially "protective . . . for the safeguarding of the German *Volk*."[56]

Again and again, leaders in the church opposition indicated how closely their thinking coincided with broad German conceptions of the Jewish Question. In a radio broadcast, Bishop Otto Dibelius defended the Nazi boycott of Jewish businesses in April 1933 as necessary for curtailing Jewish influence on German public life;[57] the Pastor's Emergency League proclaimed it was prepared "to guard the ministry against 'Jewish foreign infiltration'";[58] and Martin Niemöller wrote that Germans had had "much to bear under the influence of the Jewish people, so that the wish to be freed from this demand is understandable."[59] In the wake of *Kristallnacht*, Bishop Theophil Wurm of Württemberg reiterated these sentiments, writing that he "in no way . . . dispute[d] the right of the state to resist Judaism as a dangerous element."[60]

Such attitudes echoed through the Christian churches even as the Final Solution was under way. In December 1941, when the German Evangelical Church Chancellery issued a decree noting "the elimination of Jews from the community of us Germans," Bishop Wurm cited the "dangers of alien Jewish infiltration" and pointed out that "no Evangelical church has denied the state the right to implement racial legislation for the purpose of maintaining the purity of the German *Volk*."[61] In a memorandum finalized in late 1942, members of the Freiburg

Circle lamented the insolubility of the Jewish Question, which they conceived in racial terms. "The existence of a numerically significant body of Jews within a people simply constitutes a problem that must lead to recurrent difficulties if it is not subjected to a fundamental and large-scale arrangement."[62]

Even after the war, confessing leaders affirmed the necessity of defending the German *Volk* against the Jewish menace. Bishop August Marahrens, for instance, acknowledged that the church should have done more to protect the Jews, even though "a number of them may have brought severe harm upon our people."[63]

"Jew" and "Jewish" as Terms of Derision

As we have seen, in interwar Germany authors of all stripes — Catholics and Protestants, pro-Nazis and anti-Nazis, traditionalists and neopagans — attempted to sully one another with the stain of "Judaism." In what ways is this strategy evident in the rhetorical skirmishes of the Church Struggle?

From the German Christian side, opponents in the Confessing Church were identified with Nazism and Judaism, the *Bekennende Kirche* compared to *Der Stürmer* (the Nazi propaganda newspaper) and the confessors accused of hostility toward Christ "the anti-Jew."[64] The *Deutsche Christen* (German Christian) party slogan in the 1937 elections — "We fight for the Jew-free German Evangelical Reich Church" — applied not just to "racial Jews or Jewish half-breeds," but to any who "can be considered, according to their inner attitude, as completely Judaized."[65] According to the German Christian leadership, because they insisted on Israel's chosenness, the confessors were Jews' "accomplices." "It is indisputable," wrote Wilhelm Kube, "that the Jew has his theologically disguised bodyguard in the confessional front."[66]

These charges were countered with comparable rhetoric from the other side. According to Wolfgang Gerlach, by 1934 the focus of the Confessing Church moved from resisting the Aryan Paragraph to counteracting contempt for the Old Testament. But the confessors were careful lest their defensive efforts be perceived as "too Jewish." In an article opposing the aryanization of Jesus, the *Deutsches Pfarrefblatt*

(German Ministers' Sheet) asserted that to refer to the Bible as a "Jew-ish book" was to defame not the Jews, but the Bible itself.[67] Gerhard Schmidt, meanwhile, wrote that Luther did not "reject the Old Testa-ment because of the Jews, but rather the other way around: Because of the Old Testament, he reject[ed] the Jews."[68]

In a variety of ways, confessors conveyed the accusation that pro-Nazi Christians behaved "Jewishly." In a church election pamphlet, Bonhoeffer's friend and colleague Franz Hildebrandt applied to the German Christians Jesus' warning that "you must not be like the hypo-crites; for they love to stand and pray in the synagogues and at the street corners, that they may be seen by men (Mt. 21:13; 6:5)."[69] And in 1935 Tübingen New Testament professor Adolf Schaltter alleged that Judaism was an ally of the Nazi state in its struggle against Christianity. "It cannot be denied that, in the German Reich, the situation for [the Jews'] ideology was never so favorable as now." Schlatter went on to liken Judaism to both "Nordic racism" and notions of community based in "the compulsion of the blood."[70]

One of the more clever attempts to paint Nazism with a "Jewish" brush appeared in a 1937 sermon by Martin Niemöller, who attacked the Nazi concept of "positive Christianity" by linking it to Judaism: "I cannot help saying quite harshly and bluntly," Niemöller wrote, "that the Jewish people came to grief and disgrace because of its positive Christianity. . . . Here positive Christianity, which the Jewish people wanted, clashed with negative Christianity, as Jesus himself represented it; the pious will of man came into conflict with the will of God."[71] The strategy of charging nazified Christians with "Jewish" behavior continued into the war years. In response to a December 1941 state-ment of the German Evangelical Church Chancellery that sought to remove baptized non-Aryans from their congregations, the Provisional Church Administration of the Confessing Church asked: "By what right do we desire to exclude, for racial reasons, Christian non-Aryans from our worship services? Do we want to be like the Pharisees . . . ?"[72]

While depicting Nazis and their Christian sympathizers with Jewish images, confessors strenuously repudiated the charge that they them-selves were "slaves of the Jews." Bishop Wurm bragged that "there is hardly any class that has kept itself so free of the specifically Jewish character . . . as the Protestant pastorate."[73] When the Nazi govern-ment sought to push all non-Aryan children into Jewish schools, the

Provisional Church Administration of the Confessing Church expressed its "serious misgivings from a confessional point of view" concerning "the Jewish spiritual or religious attitude that prevails in these schools [and] is incompatible with the Christian attitude."[74] Similarly, when confessors protested against the requirement that all non-Aryans wear the Jewish star, the complaint was that the decree would affect people who "have never had anything to do with the Jewish religion."[75] Wilhelm Halfmann, spiritual director of the Confessing Church in Schleswig-Holstein, charged that the Nazi enemies of Christ were "mired in the most terrible accusation that has ever slandered Christianity in Germany: Christianity is in bondage to the Jews."[76] Thus, while opposing overt German Christian attempts to de-Judaize the faith, the confessors were eager to prove their reliability in the church's defensive "struggle against Judaism."[77]

It might be supposed that the church's rhetoric became less stridently anti-Jewish once the extreme persecution of the Jews under Nazism began to be revealed. Yet even after *Kristallnacht* "Jewishness" functioned as the aspersion of choice among warring Christian rhetoricians. This is evident in the controversy over the infamous Gotesberg Declaration of 1939, a German Christian document that maintained that "the Christian faith is the insurmountable religious antithesis of Judaism." In response, the Confessing Church wrote that while Christianity "stands in insurmountable religious opposition to Judaism," this Judaism exists "not just among the Jews, but in all aspirations for a national church as well."[78] Another response charged the *Deutsche Christen* with turning the church into a "pharisaical sect." Even in 1943, when Bishop Wurm finally protested state actions against Jews, he was careful to point out that his challenge to the "policy of extermination conducted against Jewry" did not arise from "any predisposition for Jewry" or "any kind of philosemitic tendencies."[79]

The exercise in discourse analysis undertaken in this chapter yields some sobering lessons. Chief among them is that the ambivalence regarding Jews that has characterized the Christian mind since the time of Paul also pervaded the discourse of anti-Nazi resistance. In the next chapter this lesson will be applied to an interpretation of the early anti-Nazi writings of Dietrich Bonhoeffer. Elucidating the theological and rhetorical backgrounds of the German Church Struggle will help clarify how Bonhoeffer's attacks on his German Christian opponents both reflected and capitalized on an anti-Jewish intellectual environment.

BONHOEFFER'S EARLY ANTI-NAZI WRITINGS IN POST-HOLOCAUST PERSPECTIVE

"The Church and the Jewish Question" in Context

Defenders and critics of Bonhoeffer agree that his essay "The Church and the Jewish Question" of April 1933 represents his principal theological contribution to the German Church Struggle. As a carefully conceived model for theological resistance to the state, it evinces Bonhoeffer's prescience in recognizing the nature of Nazism and its threat to the German people, as well as his courage in challenging aspects of the Lutheran tradition that might impede this resistance. These features of the essay have invited readers to interpret it as an enticing preview of Bonhoeffer's own path in the struggle with Nazism. As Konrad Raiser writes, it "foreshadows the way which Bonhoeffer was going to be led himself."[1]

But reading "The Church and the Jewish Question" apart from what Bonhoeffer says about *Jews*—tempting as this is for Christians in a post-Holocaust environment—obscures the historical and theological contexts in which the essay was written. Having highlighted these backgrounds in the previous chapter, we now apply them to an analysis of Bonhoeffer's language and arguments.

The "Jewish Question"

In the rare cases where *die Judenfrage* is analyzed with respect to Bonhoeffer's writings, it is almost always done poorly.[2] Stephen G. Ray

Jr. is the lonely exception here. Noting that in Germany at the time the term indicated that "the Jewish presence was understood to be so corrosive that its very existence threaten[ed] the destruction of society," Ray faults Bonhoeffer for failing to challenge the reality of this "question." According to Ray, Bonhoeffer was insufficiently attentive to the fact that "'*der Jude*' (the Jew) and its presumed referent—Jewish persons—had an exclusively negative connotation in German communal discourse."[3] It is regrettable that Ray, who is not strictly speaking a Bonhoeffer scholar, is the lone researcher to focus on this basic aspect of the essay.

Bonhoeffer writes in "The Church and the Jewish Question" that "without doubt the Jewish question is one of the historical problems which our state must deal with, and without doubt the state is justified in adopting new methods here."[4] His words are remarkably similar to those of a *Gutachten* (professional opinion) issued by the theological faculty of the University of Erlangen the following September, which acknowledged that "today more than ever . . . the church must acknowledge the fundamental right of the state to such legislative measures."[5] Significantly, Bonhoeffer adds that "each new attempt to 'solve the Jewish problem' comes to nothing on the saving-historical significance of this people; nevertheless such attempts must continually be made."[6] Thus, like other Protestant theologians at the time, Bonhoeffer concedes the state's responsibility for dealing with the "historical problem" of the Jews' presence in Germany, while claiming for the church special insight into their destiny.

The fact that Bonhoeffer invokes a term widely employed to denote an acute social concern requires us to ask how he understood it. At the time, there was a virtual consensus that the German nation faced a serious *Judenfrage* in the form of alien Jews who posed an internal threat to society. If Bonhoeffer did not share this view of the Jews' presence in Germany, why did he adopt without comment a term that implied as much? At the very least, his failure to clarify his use of *die Judenfrage* invited misunderstanding. And because he wrote in an environment where Nazis and their Christian collaborators were speaking of the Jewish Question as a pressing task of the state, his lack of care could only increase the vulnerability of German Jews.

As we have seen, in 1933 Bonhoeffer's contemporary Gerhard Kittel published a study in which he concluded that guest status was the only viable "solution" to the Jewish Question facing Germany. Given how little Bonhoeffer had in common with Kittel theologically and politically, it is striking that they would rely upon such similar language to describe Jews' presence in Germany. Indeed, it is disconcerting to realize that despite questioning his readers' assumptions with regard to church-state relations, Bonhoeffer fails to subvert the popular notion that Germany confronted a Jewish Question that necessitated government intervention. Bonhoeffer's use of this highly charged term, coupled with his claim that the church exists wherever *Jew* and *German* "stand together under the Word of God," gave unwitting credence to a conviction widespread in his day, namely, that "Jews" were an alien people whose very existence posed a threat to ethnic Germans.[7]

"Jewish Christianity"

A subtler species of anti-Jewish rhetoric appears in the second section of "The Church and the Jewish Question," where Bonhoeffer denounces the German Christian obsession with maintaining racial purity in the church. Turning the tables on those who would label the Confessing Church and its ecclesiology "Jewish,"[8] Bonhoeffer attacks the *Deutsche Christen* with deadly accuracy using weapons honed by biblical and historical insight. "From the point of view of the church," Bonhoeffer writes, "it is not baptized Christians of Jewish race who are Jewish Christians; in the church's view the Jewish Christian is the man who lets membership of the people of God, of the church of Christ, be determined by the observance of a divine law."[9]

In effect, Bonhoeffer argues that it is German Christians, not the defenders of baptized non-Aryans, who are behaving "Jewishly." Members of the *Deutsche Christen* party, Bonhoeffer alleges, are contemporary representatives of "the Jewish-Christian type" with its attendant "legalis[m]." The true church must resist the German Christian error, he contends, lest it proclaim a "religion based on law" and constitute itself as a modern "Jewish-Christian community." Bonhoeffer bases these distinctions in the seminal conflicts between Jewish Gentile Christians (e.g., Paul) and Gentile Jewish Christians (e.g., the "Judaizers" of Galatians) in the earliest decades of church history. In Bonhoeffer's view, the resolution of these first-century conflicts determined that "Jewish Christians" would always symbolize those who allow church membership to be determined by "a divine law."[10] A loose paraphrase of Bonhoeffer's argument may be useful in bringing its anti-Jewish dimension into focus:

> You call *us* "Jew-lovers," but in fact it is your brand of Christianity that is truly "Jewish." For you are infected by the legalism that was and is the essence of Judaism. Thus, you self-proclaimed "Aryans" are fighting on the "Jewish" side in that perennial struggle which first shook the church in the first century, and the "Jewish" root will always bear false fruit.

It is stunning how few interpreters have commented on this aspect of "The Church and the Jewish Question," though the essay is among the most analyzed in the Bonhoeffer corpus. Steven S. Schwarzschild was perhaps the first to note the deeply anti-Jewish nature of Bonhoeffer's argument and remains one of the very few. In 1960 he perceived that

> the height of the argument [in this essay] is the following thought, which to a Jew is really the most extraordinary conception: Nazi law means to exclude Christians of Jewish birth from church positions; this makes full church membership a matter of biology and law; to make religion a matter of biology and law is a characteristic of Judaism; therefore, the Nazis want to make the Christian church into a Judaizing sect, and Nazism and Judaism are really, at bottom, saying the same thing; this must be prevented.[11]

The only other interpreter of "The Church and the Jewish Question" to foreground this problem is Stephen Ray, who observes that for Bonhoeffer, Jewish Christianity "becomes a grammatical linkage that cannot be supported theologically and is thus inappropriate ecclesial discourse." Ray links this problem with Bonhoeffer's endorsement of the phrase *die Judenfrage*, writing that "precisely because Bonhoeffer argued the first section of his essay within a framework that gives legitimacy to the concept of the Jewish problem, he brings to any usage of the expression Jewish Christianity a contaminated term."[12]

Bonhoeffer's subversion of arguments advanced by his ecclesiastical opponents was often brilliant. In response to the contention that the offense of racial nonconformity in the church could be removed for the sake of "the weak in faith," Bonhoeffer countered at a university meeting titled "The Struggle for the Church" that "those who were weak in faith, who wanted to set up a law like the Aryan clause before the doorway to the church, had to be borne by those who were strong in faith, as stated in Romans 14."[13] Such biblical-theological rebuttals of his Nazi-leaning contemporaries became Bonhoeffer's trademark. But it appears that the virtuosity of Bonhoeffer's rhetorical assault on the *Deutsche Christen* in "The Church and the Jewish Question" has obscured the extent to which it is steeped in anti-Judaism.

Despite the minimal attention it has received, this aspect of the essay is vital to our contextual analysis. For, as we have seen, describing as "Jewish" the ecclesiology of one's opponents was a strategy regularly adopted by Protestant polemicists. In 1934 *Junge Kirche (Young Church)*, the journal of the church opposition, published a list of "principles" condemning the Aryan Paragraph as "false doctrine" and calling a church that adopts it "a Judaistic, *völkisch* sect [that] will share the fate of all Judaistic sects: disintegration and relapse into sub-Christian piety, that is, paganism."[14] And in the midst of the 1937 church elections, a German Christian spokesman suggested that his opponents advocated a "new Jewish-Christian church."[15]

Like Bonhoeffer, the authors of these statements exploited and perpetuated an anti-Jewish cultural ethos in order to discredit their ecclesiastical enemies. Whatever their other merits, examples of Christian discourse from this period that feature "Jewish" as the adjective of derision par excellence could only increase the vulnerability of German Jews.

Witness-People Theology

Half a century ago, Stephen Schwarzschild wondered if Bonhoeffer's "peculiar view of Israel may be only one ramification of an Occidental background many share with him and which has not yet been sufficiently analyzed."[16] Unfortunately, the theological dimension of Bonhoeffer's anti-Judaism has yet to receive the scrutiny it deserves. In a letter penned just before he completed "The Church and the Jewish Question," Bonhoeffer wrote that "the Church is in great trouble with the Jewish question, which has caused the most sensible people to lose their heads and forget their Bible."[17] For his part, Bonhoeffer was determined not to forget his Bible or the clues to Israel's fate he believed it contained.

The paragraphs most often cited as evidence of Bonhoeffer's "peculiar view of Israel" appear toward the end of the essay's first section:

> Now the measures of the state towards Judaism in addition stand in a quite special context for the church. The church of Christ has never lost sight of the thought that the "chosen people," who nailed the redeemer of the world to the cross, must bear the curse for its action through a long history of suffering [quotation from Martin Luther's *Table Talk* on the scattered and insecure state of the Jews]. . . . But the history of the suffering of this people, loved and punished by God, stands under the sign of the final homecoming of the people of Israel to its God. And this homecoming happens in the conversion of Israel to Christ [quotation from S. Mencken on the church's hope that at the end of time Israel will penitently depart "from the sins of its fathers to which it has clung with fearful stubbornness to this day"]. The conversion of Israel, that is to be the end of the people's period of suffering. From here the Christian church sees the history of the people of Israel with trembling as God's own, free, fearful way with his people. It knows that no nation of the world can be finished with this mysterious people, because God is not yet finished with it. Each new attempt to "solve the Jewish problem" comes to nothing on the saving-historical significance of this people; nevertheless, such attempts must continually be made. This consciousness on the part of the church of the curse that bears down upon this people, raises it far above any cheap moralizing; instead, as it looks at the rejected people, it humbly recognizes itself as a church continually unfaithful to its Lord and looks full of hope to those of the people of Israel who have come home, to those who have come to believe in the one true God in Christ, and knows itself to be bound to them in brotherhood.[18]

Robert Willis's comments on this section of the essay are unusually candid: "All the ingredients of traditional Christian Antisemitism are present in that passage: the charge of deicide, suffering as divine punishment for that crime, the conversion of the Jewish people as the denouement of the lengthy 'dispute' between church and syna-gogue."[19] Yet if we consider the passage in light of the witness-people myth described in the previous chapter, we can perceive much more than "Christian Antisemitism."

Among the features of the passage that bring to mind the witness-people tradition are its style, structure, and tone. The *style* of this excerpt invests an aura of mythic unreality to Bonhoeffer's description of the "chosen people," a personified theological abstraction[20] whose import is to be gauged solely on this people's "saving-historical signifi-cance." This distinctive style is particularly evident when the segment is contrasted with the rest of Bonhoeffer's tract, which is characterized by precise and sequential argumentation. The passage also evinces a paradoxical *structure*. The reprobationist and preservationist dimen-sions of witness-people theology that reach in parallel lines back to Augustine are juxtaposed in Bonhoeffer's description of "this people, loved and punished by God." From the perspective of the essay's par-ticipation in the witness-people myth, the crucial affirmation is not that Jews "bear the curse" (the matter that has tended to draw the attention of scholars), but that the church must view their "long history of suffering" through the paradoxical lens of reprobation and preserva-tion. They are, indeed, "the 'chosen people,' who nailed the redeemer of the world to the cross."

Finally, Bonhoeffer's paradoxical portrayal of Jewish destiny in "The Church and the Jewish Question" resonates with the *ambivalence* that is a leitmotif of the witness-people tradition, an ambivalence symbol-ized in the crucial "but" that serves as the passage's verbal hinge. Kenneth C. Barnes observes that of all Bonhoeffer's writings, this short essay has been the most scrutinized "by both his hagiographers, who wish to find in this essay the basis of a strong defense of the Jews, and his detractors, who find the essay anti-Jewish."[21] Barnes regards these varying assessments as testimony to the fact that Bonhoeffer "contra-dicts himself throughout the essay." But what Barnes judges to be a lack of consistency is actually a manifestation of deep ambivalence toward Jewish life, an ambivalence rooted in a theological tradition that casts Jews as a divine witness-people.

Bonhoeffer's reliance on these time-honored apprehensions of Jewish fate is understandable when we recall that the essay was composed in hasty response to the first wave of Nazi anti-Jewish persecutions, particularly the state-organized boycott of Jewish businesses on April 1. Eberhard Bethge notes that "in this situation of crisis [Bonhoeffer] searched about, more spontaneously than carefully, for a means of quick reaction, unprepared as he was for the rapidly escalating pressures on all sides."[22] In this moment of social upheaval, Bonhoeffer mined the resources of the Christian imagination. Straining to comprehend the mystery of Jewish existence, he invoked time-tested verities to assure Christians that Jewish suffering was a mysterious affirmation of God's providence. As we shall see, these mythological ideas resurfaced in discussions among Bonhoeffer's seminary students in the wake of *Kristallnacht*.[23]

The ambivalence concerning Jewish destiny that permeates "The Church and the Jewish Question" is communicated even in Bonhoeffer's reliance on Luther, who is cited four times in the essay. Prior to the excerpt from Luther's *Table Talk* ("Jews are . . . tossed to and fro, they are scattered here and there in all lands, they have no certain place where they could remain safely and must always be afraid that they will be driven out"),[24] Bonhoeffer prefaces his tract with two Lutheran epigraphs:

> *Luther* 1546: "We would still show them the Christian doctrine and ask them to turn and accept the Lord whom they should by rights have honoured before we did. . . . Where they repent, leave their usury, and accept Christ, we would gladly regard them as our brothers."
>
> *Luther* 1523: "If the Apostles, who also were Jews, had dealt with us Gentiles as we Gentiles deal with the Jews, there would have been no Christians among the Gentiles. But seeing that they have acted in such a brotherly way towards us, we in turn should act in a brotherly way towards the Jews in case we might convert some. For we ourselves are still not yet fully their equals, much less their superiors . . . But now we use force against them . . . what good will we do them with that? Similarly, how will we benefit them by forbidding them to live and work and have other human fellowship with us, thus driving them to practice usury?"[25]

These epigraphs bespeak a solidarity with Jews and a sympathy for their plight that was conspicuously absent among German Lutherans in

Bonhoeffer's day, which no doubt explains why he selected them. But even as they disclose a kinder, gentler Luther, these citations anticipate the ambivalence toward Jews Bonhoeffer will express in the body of the essay. The selection from Luther's *On the Jews and Their Lies* (1546) was a particularly bold choice in the midst of the Church Struggle, since this notoriously anti-Jewish tract was being appealed to as a Christian sanction for the harsh treatment of Jews. Bonhoeffer cites the work, however, to demonstrate that even at the end of his life Luther was prepared to embrace Jews as brothers if they would "repent, leave their usury, and accept Christ."

Nonetheless, it is difficult to predict the effect of quoting Luther as an authority on the Jewish Question in Germany during the spring of 1933. Even Bonhoeffer's carefully selected excerpts seem to confirm Paul Lawrence Rose's assertion that Luther personifies "the often contradictory nature of German antisemitism, which oscillates between a sort of suspicious benevolence and hatred."[26] This ambiguity is certainly apparent in the quotation from Luther's *Table Talk* included in the body of "The Church and the Jewish Question." Is it a plea for sympathy or an affirmation of Jews' abiding status as aliens? Even the Luther of the essay's epigraphs, who never relinquishes his hope in Jewish conversion, can be interpreted in more than one way. Was this Luther a genuine "friend of the Jews," or did he wish to redeem Judaism by destroying it?[27]

Based on "The Church and the Jewish Question," the same question could be asked of Bonhoeffer: Was his vision of Jewish redemption also a scenario for destruction? Bonhoeffer's statement that as the church "looks at the rejected people, it humbly recognizes itself as a church continually unfaithful to its Lord" (a sentence seized upon by scholars who argue that the passage predicts judgment upon the church as well) seems to imply that "the very presence of the Jewish community (Israel) is a constant reminder to the church of its unfaithfulness in the failure of its mission to Jews."[28] According to this reading, the church's unfaithfulness is displayed not in its mistreatment of Jews so much as in its failure to evangelize them.

This discussion illumines the complex relationship between the witness-people myth Bonhoeffer relied upon to interpret Jewish travail and the modern, racial anti-Semitism he was seeking to combat. The myth had always worked to ensure the preservation of Jewish life in

Christendom, yet it portrayed contemporary Judaism as a vestige of rebellion that would vanish when the Jews turned en masse to Christ. This conception of Jews as Christians-in-waiting gave credence to images of an alien people who were cursed, wandering, and destined to disappear—the very images that cluttered the minds of German anti-Semites. Indeed, Bonhoeffer's Jew, who existed between the times and awaited his "homecoming"[29] (perhaps in Christ's second advent), is not unlike *der Ewige Jude* ("the Eternal Jew") of Nazi propaganda, who was, after all, fabricated from the Wandering Jew of Christian legend. Bonhoeffer's Jew and the Nazis' Jew were not identical, but the similarities cannot be ignored.

The *Bethel Confession*

The mythological impulse in Bonhoeffer's reflections on the Jewish people so prominent in "The Church and the Jewish Question" is further manifest in the *Bethel Confession*'s section titled "The Church and the Jews." The confession merits special attention in part because of claims that its discussion of "Israel" represents a substantial improvement over "The Church and the Jewish Question."

Geffrey Kelly opines that, despite its "sticky religious stereotypes of Judaism," the confession is significant for Christian-Jewish relations because it expresses "new beginnings" in the church's attitude toward Jews.[30] Particularly significant, according to Kelly, is the confession's affirmation of God's choice of Israel and its insistence that God has not retracted that choice. "What is startling, given the long history of Christian invective against Jews," is the way *Bethel* emphasizes "God's continued fidelity to Israel and the indestructibility of the Jewish people."[31] Craig Slane says of Bonhoeffer's involvement at Bethel that it "reveals his firm grip on the Christian obligation toward Jews."[32] Edwin Robertson writes that "if Bonhoeffer's clear attitude [on the Jewish Question] had been maintained and his Bethel Draft used at Barmen in 1934, we would not have the shame of saying, 'Barmen was silent about the Jews.'"[33]

What was Bonhoeffer's contribution to the *Bethel Confession*, and how might it supplement our knowledge of his theology of Israel in 1933? According to Guy Christopher Carter's excellent study,

Bonhoeffer had a major role in the confession's working group, which included Georg Merz, Hermann Sasse, Gerhard Stratenwerth, Hans Fischer, and Wilhelm Vischer.[34] Bonhoeffer's contribution is reflected in the August draft of the *Bethel Confession* (lost until 1956), which is included in the German edition of his collected works, as well as in *No Rusty Swords*. This version of the confession includes these paragraphs in a section titled "The Church and the Jews":

> The church teaches that God chose Israel from among all the nations of the earth to be his people. He chose them solely in the power of his Word and for the sake of his loving-kindness, and not because they were in any way pre-eminent (Exod. 19.5–6; Deut. 7.7–11). The Sanhedrin and the Jewish people rejected Christ Jesus, promised by the Law and the Prophets, in accordance with Scripture. They wanted a national Messiah, who would bring them political freedom and the rule of the world. Jesus Christ was not this, and did not do this. He died at their hands and for their sakes. The barrier between Jew and Gentile has been broken down by the crucifixion and resurrection of Jesus Christ (Eph. 2). The place of the Old Testament people of the covenant was taken not by another nation, but by the Christian church, called out of and living among all nations.
>
> God abundantly shows his faithfulness by still keeping faith with Israel after the flesh, from whom was born Christ after the flesh, despite all their unfaithfulness, even after the crucifixion. It is his will to complete the salvation of the world, which he began with the election of Israel, through these selfsame Jews (Rom. 9–11). Therefore he continues to preserve a "holy remnant" of Israel after the flesh, which can neither be absorbed into another nation by emancipation and assimilation, nor become one nation among others as a result of the efforts of Zionist and other similar movements, nor be exterminated by Pharaoh-like measures. This "holy remnant" bears the indelible stamp of the chosen people. The church has received from its Lord the commission to call the Jews to repentance and to baptize those who believe on Jesus Christ to the forgiveness of sins (Matt. 10.5f; Acts 2.38ff; 3.19–26). A mission to the Jews which for cultural or political considerations refuses to baptize any more Jews at all is refusing to be obedient to its Lord. . . .

The community of those who belong to the church is not determined by blood and therefore not by race, but by the Holy Spirit and baptism.

We reject any attempt to identify or confuse the historical mission of any nation with Israel's commission in sacred history.

No nation can ever be commissioned to avenge on the Jews the murder at Golgotha. "Vengeance is mine, says the Lord" (Deut. 32.35; Heb. 10.30). We reject any attempt to misuse the miracle of God's especial faithfulness towards Israel after the flesh as an indication of the religious significance of the Jewish people or of another people.

We oppose the assertion that the faith of Jewish Christians is, as opposed to that of Gentile Christians, affected by their descent and is Judaistic heresy.

We oppose the attempt to deprive the German Evangelical church of its promise by the attempt to change it into a national church of Christians of Aryan descent. This would be to erect a racial barrier against entering the church and would make such a church itself a Jewish Christian community regulated by the Law. We therefore reject the forming of Jewish Christian communities, because the false presupposition for such action is the view that the special element in Jewish Christianity can be appropriately compared with, for example, the historically determined peculiarity of the communities of French refugees in Germany, and that Christians from Judaism must develop a form of Christianity appropriate to their character.

The special element in the Jewish Christian does not lie in his race or his character or his history, but in God's special faithfulness towards Israel after the flesh and in that alone. The way in which the Jewish Christian has a special position in the church which is not based on any legal ruling in itself makes him a living memorial of God's faithfulness within the church and is a sign that the barrier between Jew and Gentile has been broken down and that faith in Christ may not be perverted into a national religion or a racially-determined Christianity. It is the task of Christians who come from the Gentile world to expose themselves to persecution rather than to surrender, willingly or unwillingly, even in one single respect, their brotherhood with Jewish Christians in the church, founded on Word and Sacrament.[35]

Much could be said about the way the confession interprets the meaning of Jewish existence. Given our focus on Bonhoeffer's debt to the witness-people tradition, we should note that this section of the *Bethel Confession* expresses perfectly the paradoxical structure of the witness-people myth. The preservationist impulse is evident in affirmations of "brotherhood with Jewish Christians" and assertions that the Jews cannot be exterminated nor any nation commissioned to avenge their murder of Christ, while the reprobationist impulse appears in reiteration of the deicide charge, avowal of supersessionism, and support of mission to the Jews. Furthermore, the confession employs a number of stock witness-people images: Jews as a "sign"; Jewish Christians as a "living memorial of God's faithfulness"; the chosen people as marked by an "indelible stamp."

The confession recalls "The Church and the Jewish Question" not only in its paradoxical apprehension of Jewish destiny, but in its echoing of distinctive themes as well. Among the unmistakably Bonhoefferan arguments in this section of the confession is a clever rebuttal of the German Christian "assertion that the faith of Jewish Christians is . . . Judaistic heresy" by the counterclaim that a national church of Aryan Christians would constitute the real "Jewish Christian community regulated by the Law."[36] There is also a striking similarity between the declaration that "no nation can ever be commissioned to avenge on the Jews the murder at Golgotha" since vengeance belongs to the Lord and the corresponding passage in "The Church and the Jewish Question" that affirms that although the Jews must atone for their part in the crucifixion by bearing a curse and enduring "a long history of suffering," the church "knows that no nation of the world can be finished with this mysterious people, because God is not yet finished with it."[37]

Comparing these documents can be instructive if we allow what is clear in one to illumine what is obscure in the other. For instance, the discussion of Jewish evangelism in the August draft of the *Bethel Confession* seems to clarify Bonhoeffer's oblique reference to the topic in "The Church and the Jewish Question." There Bonhoeffer counseled that in looking at "the rejected people, [the church] humbly recognizes itself as a church continually unfaithful to its Lord and looks full of hope to those of the people of Israel who have come home, to those who have come to believe in the one true God in Christ."[38] Christian responsibility for Jewish evangelism is more transparent in *Bethel*, which affirms the church's "commission to call the Jews to repentance and to baptize those who believe on Jesus Christ to the forgiveness of sins."[39]

While most of the affirmations in the *Bethel Confession*'s section on "The Church and the Jews" are stated or implied in Bonhoeffer's April essay, there are a few prominent exceptions. These include the declaration that "the place of the Old Testament people of the covenant was taken" by the Christian church, the canard that Jesus was rejected in favor of a national messiah who would bring Jews "rule of the world," and the conviction that "Israel after the flesh" cannot be absorbed into another nation by assimilation or emancipation. But since nothing on this list is incompatible with Bonhoeffer's approach to the Jewish Question in his April essay, it is possible that he endorsed these views expressed in the August version of the confession. Whatever the case, such ideas did nothing to counteract Nazi fantasies of an alien *Volk* who were agents of a Judeo-Bolshevik conspiracy, or allegations that Jews could not be members of the German nation.

Although the Bonhoeffer-Sasse document that preceded the August edition of the *Bethel Confession* did not include a section on the church and the Jews, it nevertheless provides another window on Bonhoeffer's thinking about the Jewish people during the summer of 1933. In the section entitled "Of the Triune God," we find a declaration rejecting "the false doctrine, that the voice of the *Volk* is the voice of God, as a fanatical interpretation of history. 'Then they cried out one and all and said: not this one, but Barabbas instead.' 'Hosanna!-Crucify!'"[40] This paragraph, which was retained virtually without change in the August, November, and final recensions of the confession, reflects Bonhoeffer's penchant for stigmatizing German Christians through association with Jewish thought and behavior.

Happily, given the negative evaluation of the Jewish devotion to law in "The Church and the Jewish Question," the section titled "The Law" in the Bonhoeffer-Sasse draft of the *Bethel Confession* indicates a new dimension of Bonhoeffer's thinking on this topic:

> The Old Testament law distinguishes itself from the laws for living and orders of life of other peoples in that it was given to Israel as the people of God, as the people elected to the church. It is on

these grounds not the subject of comparison but rather the subject of proclamation.[41]

In the subsequent section, titled "Of Obedience to the Law and of Life in the Orders," Bonhoeffer and Sasse "reject the false doctrine that the orders of the peoples are one with the law of God. That only applies to the Old Testament law of the people of Israel. For Israel is simultaneously folk and church. It alone is elect."[42] Both passages were retained in later versions of the confession.

In the chapter "The Orders," Bonhoeffer and Sasse declare that "neither the Bible nor the Lutheran Confessions know anything about an order of race," a statement that was softened in later versions of the confession.[43] In "Of Christ," they unmistakably affirm the Jewishness of Jesus, rejecting the false doctrine "that the appearance of Jesus is an efflorescence of the Nordic race in the midst of a world tormented by manifestations of decomposition." Christ is, rather, "the radiance of the glory of God in the world and the Son of David, sent to the lost sheep of Israel."[44] A few paragraphs later, Bonhoeffer and Sasse record what was, for the time, a remarkable acknowledgment:

> We reject the false doctrine as though the crucifixion of Christ were the sole guilt of the Jewish people, as though other peoples and races did not crucify him. All peoples and races, even the most preeminent, are guilty of his death and make themselves daily guilty anew when they revile the Spirit of the grace of God (Hb. 10:29).[45]

Although this statement does not remove the guilt of deicide from the Jewish people, it diffuses it in a way few Christians were willing to contemplate at the time.

Because Bonhoeffer refused to endorse the version of the *Bethel Confession* that circulated in November 1933, some have sought to distance him from the document's statements on Jews. Yet because the confession's section titled "The Church and the Jews" was considerably shortened between the August and November versions, it is likely that Bonhoeffer objected to what the later recension did *not* say.[46] Indeed, several aspects of the November document related to Jews are not dissimilar from sentiments Bonhoeffer had expressed in his April essay. For instance, in the section titled "Of History and the

End of All Things," the confession asserts that God "chose Israel to be His people in order to awaken the Messiah in it. But Israel rejected the Christ. It lost the promise given to it and became a stranger among all peoples, marked by the curse of God. The church of Christ became its heir." For this reason, the confession continues, the life and history of a *Volk* is "rich and dangerous," since it "always stands in danger of going the way of Israel. It stands in danger of misusing the promise directed toward those within it who are within the church, the company of the 'chosen,' just as Israel misused it. . . ."[47] This section of the confession, it will be noted, traffics in images of Jews and German Christians that are prominent in "The Church and the Jewish Question": Jews are a cursed witness-people (rejecting Christ, Israel becomes "a stranger among all peoples, marked by the curse of God"), and German Christians threaten to take the church "the way of Israel."

The available evidence points to the conclusion that Bonhoeffer endorsed the perspectives on the Jewish Question communicated in the *Bethel Confession* even if he did not have sole responsibility for recording them in August 1933 and did not sanction their final expression in November of that year. At the very least, Bonhoeffer's role in the *Bethel Confession* indicates that the opinions regarding Jewish history and destiny he expressed in "The Church and the Jewish Question" were not fleeting thoughts, but deep, and possibly enduring, convictions.

Scholarly Spin Control

Having undertaken a thorough examination of Bonhoeffer's early responses to Nazism and its ecclesiastical allies, we cannot help but note the failure of scholarship to fathom the significance of the images and concepts Bonhoeffer used to interpret Jewish existence during the crucial year 1933. With regard to "The Church and the Jewish Question," few researchers hesitate to mention the essay's anti-Jewish tropes; but most fail to do them interpretive justice.

One scholar refers to Bonhoeffer's invocation of the curse that bears down on the Jews as "unfortunate" (Edwin H. Robertson); another asks that it be "mercifully forgotten" (Walter Harrelson); one argues that the paragraphs in which Bonhoeffer describes the "quite special context" for the church's interpretation of the state's measures toward

Judaism are "definitely not the central theme of the paper" (Eberhard Bethge); another concludes that, unfortunately, Bonhoeffer's initial observations on the Jews in Germany "repeated ages-old stereotypes" (Geffrey B. Kelly); one contends that although the passage contains "all the ingredients of traditional Christian Antisemitism," these are "morally . . . neutraliz[ed]" by Bonhoeffer's discussion of unjust state actions (Robert Willis); others claim that the essay's objectionable language can be separated from its primary thrust (Geffrey B. Kelly and F. Burton Nelson); and one laments that the trees of Bonhoeffer's "Christian anti-Jewishness" have obscured the "forest of [his] contribution to Christian political responsibility" (Robert O. Smith).[48]

Scholars who venture an explanation for the perplexing anti-Judaism in "The Church and the Jewish Question" are either vague—he was inexplicably "bound to a certain problematic view regarding Judaism" (Josiah Ulysses Young III); dismissive—his words represent "the all-pervasive anti-Semitism of his era" (Robert F. Koch); or misleading—he "recalled the scriptural curse in order to warn the church of his day against incurring a similar curse through its failure to oppose Hitler's racist policies" (Ann W. Astell).[49] To this latter category belongs the common explanation that Bonhoeffer's anti-Judaism is "predictable" since he was under the influence of traditional Lutheran theology (William Jay Peck, Stephen A. Wise, Geffrey B. Kelly, Stephen Plant, and David H. Jensen, among others). Edwin H. Robertson even claims that the paragraph in question was "based upon Luther's 'Table Talk.'"[50] Without doubt Bonhoeffer was deeply influenced by Martin Luther. But to refer to his invocation of anti-Jewish images and concepts as "Lutheran" ignores their deep roots in Christian theology and gives the mistaken impression that Bonhoeffer was appealing to a peculiarly Lutheran doctrine that can be identified and repudiated. Because Bonhoeffer alluded to a tradition that was much older than German Lutheranism, it is simply inadequate to blame his anti-Judaism on a failure "to recognize the anti-Jewish biases of his own Lutheran heritage."[51]

Undoubtedly, Victoria Barnett speaks for the majority of Bonhoeffer scholars when she warns that we should not "overlook the genuine offense and pain these words give to Jewish readers."[52] Yet the principal difficulty with the words analyzed in this chapter is not their affront to post-Holocaust sensibilities, but their mirroring of a mythological tradition that Christians have neither sufficiently understood nor fully repudiated. In other words, what ought to concern us is not Bonhoeffer's regrettable words so much as the images they propagate and the unconscious level at which they are communicated. Overall, scholarly analysis of "The Church and the Jewish Question" has encouraged us to view Bonhoeffer's appeal to the witness-people tradition as an excrescence of his main argument, to separate these "theologically tainted assertions" from the "specific core" of his essay, to "chip off" teachings of contempt toward Jews in order to uncover gleaming treasures.[53] But because Bonhoeffer's witness-people theology resonates so deeply in the Christian imagination, it simply will not be "neutralized"; rather, it threatens to distort the way Christian readers interpret the rest of Bonhoeffer's argument. His authorial voice may speak in favor of the rights of Jews; but this voice is in danger of being distorted by mythological speculation on the divine necessity of Jewish suffering.

A genuinely post-Holocaust perspective on Bonhoeffer will wrestle with the irony that, despite his early intention of opposing Nazism and defending the rights of Jews, in many ways Bonhoeffer communicated "the very attitudes and prejudices that made the Nazi party successful and the Holocaust possible."[54] It is paramount, of course, to ascertain the extent to which Bonhoeffer was able to overcome these attitudes in his developing opposition to the Nazi regime.

5.

BONHOEFFER AND POST-HOLOCAUST THEOLOGY

Few if any scholars regard Bonhoeffer's essay "The Church and the Jewish Question" as a promising foundation for Christian-Jewish rapprochement. Yet many argue that while Bonhoeffer's initial attempt to respond to Jewish persecution was a false start theologically, the remainder of his life represented a correction of this misstep as he blazed a path for post-Shoah Christianity. Advocates of the post-Holocaust Bonhoeffer insist that he recognized, resisted, and ultimately repudiated "traditional" apprehensions of the Jewish people.[1] In response to the unfolding of the Third Reich's campaign of terror against Jews, they contend, Bonhoeffer evolved a theology based in exemplary solidarity with Jews.

The present chapter evaluates claims for this post-Holocaust construal of "Bonhoeffer and the Jews" through a careful examination of his writings. Do we find that Bonhoeffer challenges traditional Christian habits of understanding that undermine respect for Jews or prevent appreciation of Judaism on its own terms? If so, he may be able to function as a guide for the post-Holocaust re-visioning of Jews in which Christians are engaged. Is the mythological dimension, so prominent in 1933, absent from his later references to the Jewish people? If so, we have substantial evidence of a fundamental change in Bonhoeffer's perception of Jews. However, if Bonhoeffer recapitulates the tradition in troublesome ways, or if formal aspects of the witness-people myth survive in his mature thought, our estimate of his contribution to post-Holocaust theology will have to be formed accordingly.

A Post-Holocaust Thinker?

Philosopher and Holocaust survivor Emil Fackenheim has judged, quite reasonably, that if Bonhoeffer did not reach radical conclusions related to Christian responsibility for the Holocaust, "this is hardly surprising in view of what little of the facts of the Holocaust he could have known."[2] Less cautious scholars, however, have not hesitated to place Bonhoeffer at the vanguard of a post-Holocaust theological reformation. Zealous to repair Christian-Jewish relations in the shadow of Auschwitz, they have interpreted Bonhoeffer's martyrdom, the actions that precipitated it, and the theological reflections that preceded it as partial redemption for the church's silent acquiescence in Jewish suffering.

Eberhard Bethge, whose portrayal of Bonhoeffer as laying "the foundations of a Christian theology after the Holocaust"[3] was reviewed in detail in chapter 2, is not the only interpreter to claim Bonhoeffer for post-Holocaust Christian theology. In various ways, other scholars have corroborated Bethge's optimistic assessment of "Bonhoeffer and the Jews" and his judgment that Bonhoeffer's theology "pointed out to us the beginning of a new path."[4] Douglas A. Huneke finds in Bonhoeffer's assertion that suffering and God are not contradictory "a beginning point for post-Shoah reformation." Along with Elie Wiesel, Huneke maintains, Bonhoeffer helps us comprehend "the nature of an empathic, suffering, living, just and present God."[5] Andreas Pangritz views Bonhoeffer's late theology—particularly the theme of "the secret discipline"—as a way to re-Hebraize Christianity after Auschwitz.[6] Douglas C. Bowman asks, "Would it not be possible to conclude that an outcome appropriate to the trend of Bonhoeffer's thinking would be a process of Judaizing Christianity?"[7]

Ruth Zerner argues that had Bonhoeffer survived he would have undertaken a radical rethinking of Christian attitudes toward Jews and refers to him as an "unconscious Jew."[8] Wayne Whitson Floyd Jr. perceives the German theologian as standing "on the brink of being able to imagine a theology beyond the Holocaust."[9] Geffrey Kelly recognizes in Bonhoeffer's thought "the presence of the 'suffering servant,' indeed of Jesus Christ himself, in the long lines of victims at gas chambers in Nazi death camps."[10] Larry Rasmussen compares Bonhoeffer's theology with that of Irving Greenberg, arguably the most influential

Jewish theologian in contemporary North America.[11] Robert O. Smith implores us to "reclaim . . . Bonhoeffer after Auschwitz";[12] and Craig Slane refers to Bonhoeffer as "a Holocaust . . . figure."[13]

Evidence and Counterevidence

How credible are these declarations of Bonhoeffer's relevance for re-imagining the relationship of Christianity and Judaism in the shadow of the Holocaust? Are they primarily symbols of respect for Bonhoeffer's courage and Christian theology's need for inspiring guides in its reassessment of Judaism? Evidence for a genuine opening to Jews in Bonhoeffer's theology must be given careful consideration, but we must remain alert to counterevidence as well. While a comprehensive analysis of Bonhoeffer's thought and action as they relate to the Jewish people is beyond the scope of this chapter, we will interrogate some of the texts scholars have offered as evidence of Bonhoeffer's seminal importance for post-Holocaust theological reflection.

Church Struggle

Adumbrations of a burgeoning appreciation for Jews and Judaism have been located in a number of Bonhoeffer's essays, addresses, university lectures, and publications during the early 1930s. In fact, many find evidence of a sea change in Bonhoeffer's relationship to Jews in 1935, particularly in his preparation for and reaction to confessional synods at Augsburg and Steglitz, where he hoped his church would directly address the Jewish Question. Geffrey Kelly notes that by this time Bonhoeffer's judgments of Confessing Church synods depended on whether their resolutions included a defense of the Jewish people.[14] Bethge concurs, observing that during the summer of 1935 it became clear to Bonhoeffer that "the Jew had to be helped and that you should not separate the question of Jews at large from the Aryan paragraph in the church."[15] Craig Slane argues for the centrality of Jews to Bonhoeffer's outlook during this period, claiming that at the root of his vision for Finkenwalde "there lay a concern for others, particularly Jews."[16]

How were these concerns and commitments reflected in Bonhoeffer's theology? As we learned in chapter 2, a number of scholars concerned with "Bonhoeffer and the Jews" make much of his growing affinity for the Old Testament. A prime example of this affinity is located in the Berlin lectures delivered during the winter term of 1932–33, published as *Creation and Fall*. In these addresses, which were dedicated to a Barthian "theological exposition" of Genesis 1–3, Bonhoeffer articulated his view that the Old Testament was to be "regarded as the book of the church and therefore to be read in light of its fulfillment in Christ."[17]

In the recently published critical edition of *Creation and Fall*, John W. de Gruchy commends Bonhoeffer's choice of Genesis as the focus of these lectures, noting that on the eve of the Nazi revolution, downplaying or denying the Old Testament as Scripture could only reinforce German anti-Semitism. A contemporary review of the book acknowledged the import of Bonhoeffer's decision to expound Genesis 1–3 and charged "anyone who is inclined to take cheap shots at the Old Testament" to let the book "introduce him or her to the profoundly serious character of this part of our Bible."[18] Yet de Gruchy, who applauds Bonhoeffer's inclusion of the Old Testament in the Christian canon, must also emphasize the "christocentric character" of his biblical interpretation in *Creation and Fall*.[19] Indeed, within these lectures a generous view of the Old Testament's revelatory power coexists with a thoroughgoing christocentrism, reminding us that while attention to the Old Testament as Scripture is crucial to maintaining Christian identity, this does not by itself represent an opening to Judaism.

In fact, Bonhoeffer's desire to give the Old Testament its due while maintaining a christocentric hermeneutic created tensions that were never resolved, at least not by 1936, when he updated the Lutheran catechism he had begun in 1931, drawing "upon the Old Testament for the purpose of relating the new 'Israel' to the present day."[20] The same year, Bonhoeffer claimed famously that "whoever knowingly separates himself from the Confessing Church in Germany separates himself from salvation," and wrote to Rüdiger Schleicher that "God is to be found in the cross of Christ and this is the message of the Bible, not only in the New but also in the Old Testament (Isaiah 53!) . . . with the cross of Jesus is the Scripture, that is, the Old Testament, fulfilled."[21]

All this suggests that despite his insistence on the Old Testament's centrality for Christian faith, Bonhoeffer's christological focus made it difficult for him to acknowledge any salvific quality in postbiblical Judaism. As James A. Rudin observes, when Bonhoeffer "turned to the Hebrew Scriptures for strength and comfort, [he] always saw those Scriptures as a prelude to the coming of Jesus, the Christ."[22] Irving Greenberg refers to this tendency as Bonhoeffer's "imperialist Christian claim."[23]

Martin Kuske's appraisal of Bonhoeffer's Old Testament interpretation demonstrates that the problem we are describing applies to writings from throughout the years of the Church Struggle. According to Kuske, Bonhoeffer had "a share in the new theological consideration of the Old Testament before and during the church struggle."[24] As evidence of Bonhoeffer's efforts to combat marginalization of the Old Testament, Kuske points to his study "King David" (published in the Confessing Church publication *Junge Kirche [Young Church]* in 1936), which provoked the indignation of a German Christian reader who called it "obnoxious, vulgar nonsense" that "offends the morality and ethic of the German race."[25] Bonhoeffer's study of King David is remarkable, argues Kuske, because it deems the testaments to be of equal value, inasmuch as both witness to Christ: "The God of the Old Testament is the Father of Jesus Christ. The God who appears in Jesus Christ is the God of the Old Testament. He is a triune God."[26] For Kuske the high point in Bonhoeffer's Old Testament interpretation is the dialogue in "King David" between the church in which he lived (riven by the Church Struggle), the crucified Lord, and the David stories—a dialogue that invested the Old Testament with new relevance for Christians in Germany.[27]

Keith W. Clements offers a similar analysis of Bonhoeffer's Old Testament exegesis. Opposing the conclusion of E. G. Wendel that for Bonhoeffer the Old Testament was simply an object for christocentric interpretation, Clements argues that Bonhoeffer was genuinely attracted to the Old Testament and allowed it to speak for itself. His sermons turned to the Old Testament at crucial moments in his life, Clements observes, a fact that evinces a "lifelong, increasingly personal and existential attachment" to this portion of Scripture. Clements observes that given the influence of Adolf von Harnack on Bonhoeffer and prevailing German attitudes toward the Old Testament, he could "almost have become a Marcionite." But the influences of Martin Luther and Karl Barth were stronger, and led Bonhoeffer to a view of Scripture that embraced the Old Testament as "a commentary on God's self-revelation in Christ." Bonhoeffer may have found Christ in the Old Testament, Clements writes, but he also found himself there, along with the crisis of his church and his country.[28]

In editorial comments in the critical edition of *Life Together,* Geffrey B. Kelly underscores the significance of Bonhoeffer's Christian claim on the Old Testament in an intensely anti-Jewish cultural environment. Remarking on Bonhoeffer's refusal to dismiss the psalms of vengeance as representing a "preliminary stage of religion," Kelly writes that Bonhoeffer was combating not only the tradition of Marcion but the views of his contemporary Emanuel Hirsch, "whose exegesis of portions of the Old Testament seemed tainted with Nazism's regnant anti-Jewish ideology."[29] Kelly's introduction to *Prayerbook of the Bible* underscores the same point: "In the context of Nazi Germany's bitter opposition to any manner of honoring of the Old Testament, this book, at the time of its publication, constituted an explosive declaration both politically and theologically."[30]

Kuske, Clements, and Kelly helpfully place Bonhoeffer's treatment of the Christian "Old Testament" in the context of struggles within the German church and his own life; but a post-Holocaust perspective must also attend carefully to the anti-Jewish implications of various modes of biblical interpretation. Bonhoeffer's conviction of the testaments' inseparability may appear to represent a pathway toward apprehending Judaism on its own terms. But his presupposition that God is the one God of the entire Bible, though it may have disturbed many Christians at the time, was conditioned by Luther's insistence that the person of Christ is revealed as much in the Old Testament as the New, as well as Barth's dictum that the God of the Bible is revealed exclusively in Jesus Christ. Thus Bonhoeffer's window on the Old Testament was unmistakably christological. Through this window he read the Old Testament in light of the incarnation and crucifixion, interpreted David typologically (a "shadow and prototype" of the crucified Messiah, important "only insofar as he is a witness of Christ"), and viewed God's choice to be encountered in the cross of Christ as the message of both testaments.[31]

Compared to those German Christians who impugned the Old Testament or sought to sever it from the Christian canon, Bonhoeffer's positive attention to the Hebrew Bible is notable. But viewed within the broad tradition of Old Testament interpretation in the church, there appears to be little that is new. Not only in Bonhoeffer's Bible studies "King David" and "Ezra and Nehemiah," but in *Life Together* (1938) and *Prayerbook of the Bible* (1940) as well, we encounter the classical interpretive schemes of typology and expectation/fulfillment.[32] These modes of Old Testament exegesis, dominant throughout Christian history, have been linked during the last half century to the Christian "teaching of contempt" that made the Holocaust possible. Bonhoeffer's debt to this tradition of anti-Jewish interpretation is symbolized in a marginal note to "King David," where he warns that failing to read the Old Testament in light of the incarnation and crucifixion would leave us "with the Jewish or heathen understanding."[33] However we understand these words, they do not appear to sanction the post-Holocaust imperative that Christians endeavor to interpret the Hebrew Bible on its own terms.

Discipleship

Given the book's popularity, it is surprising that relatively little has been written about *Discipleship*'s potential contributions to a post-Holocaust theology—especially since one's interpretation of Jesus' Sermon on the Mount can reveal quite a lot about one's view of Christianity's relationship to Judaism.

An element of *Discipleship* that seems to reflect Bonhoeffer's take on this relationship is his relatively positive construal of "the law," so unusual in the Lutheran tradition that it provoked accusations of "legalism" in the Confessing Church.[34] Indeed, in Bonhoeffer's insistence that "adherence to Christ also means adherence to the law of God," Bethge perceives the basis for a novel Christian appreciation of law to counteract "the traditional one-sidedness of the concept . . . with its fatal consequences in practice."[35]

Other scholars have detected in *Discipleship* significant references to Jewish suffering and the church's responsibility therein. In Bonhoeffer's statement that "whoever from now on attacks the least of these people attacks Christ, who took on human form and who in himself has restored the image of God for all who bear a human countenance," Kelly identifies an unmistakable allusion to the Jews, "employed at a time when explicit mention of the Jews could bring on the full wrath of the Nazi security forces."[36] Smith sees Bonhoeffer's commentary on Matthew 5:23-24—which includes the charge that "the community of Jesus' disciples ought to examine itself as to whether it is here and there at fault toward sisters and brothers, and whether, for the sake of the world, it has participated in hating, despising, and humiliating others"—as implicating the church in Jewish suffering in a way that prefigures the confession of guilt in *Ethics*.[37]

Bethge's point concerning Bonhoeffer's declaration that "the disciples are bound to the Old Testament law" is a valid one whose importance in a Lutheran context should not be underestimated. But Bonhoeffer's Christian refusal to relinquish the law does not ensure a positive assessment of its role in Judaism. For Bonhoeffer, Christ "alone understands the law as God's law," while "Israel misunderstood the law. Idolizing the law and legalizing God were Israel's sins. . . . When the Jews equated God and the law, they did it in order to get God into their power."[38] Far from representing the basis for a novel Christian appreciation of the law, as Bethge claims, this view contains the seeds of supersessionism ("misunderstanding . . . the law cut the Jews off from God") and is even linked in Bonhoeffer's logic to the deicide charge: "For the sake of God's true law, Jesus had to suffer at the hands of the advocates of the false law. Jesus died on the cross as a blasphemer, as a transgressor of the law, because he put into force the true law against the misunderstood, false, law."[39]

Kelly's interpretation of Bonhoeffer's warning that "whoever . . . attacks the least of these people attacks Christ" as referring to Jews is a credible reading. But it is not advanced by the editors of the critical edition of *Discipleship*, probably because the purported allusion to Jewish suffering is far from "unmistakable." Smith's claim—that in speaking of the disciples' responsibility to examine whether they are at fault toward "sisters and brothers," Bonhoeffer implicates the church in Jewish suffering—is supported by notes in the critical edition of *Discipleship*, which place Bonhoeffer's concern for those beyond the church community in the context of "the increasing Nazi mistreatment and murder of Jews."[40] The textual voice that would defend suffering Jews, however, must compete with the voice of traditional anti-Judaism, which claims in the same passage that "for the followers of Jesus, unlike the rabbis, service to God in worship can never be separated from service to sisters and brothers."[41]

Another prominent example of anti-Judaism in *Discipleship* has been noted by Walter Harrelson, Stanley Rosenbaum, and others:

> God's beloved people had been ill-treated and laid low and the guilt belonged to those who had failed to minister to them in the service of God. The Romans had not done this, but the chosen ministers of the Word, and their misuse of that Word. There were no longer any shepherds in Israel. No one led the flock to fresh waters to quench their thirst, no one protected them from the wolf. They were harassed, wounded and distraught under the dire rod of their shepherds, and lay prostrate on the ground. Such was the condition of the people when Jesus came.[42]

This description of Israel's spiritual condition in the first century reso-nates with the classical Christian "teaching of contempt" for Jews. In fact, the degenerate state of "late Judaism" implied in this passage was a potent ingredient in German theological anti-Judaism before the Holocaust.[43]

How shall we summarize Bonhoeffer's attitude toward Jews and Judaism during the years of the Church Struggle? In *Discipleship*, at least, we encounter the same paradoxical amalgamation that char-acterized "The Church and the Jewish Question" and the *Bethel Confession*. On one hand, we find expressions of solidarity with suffer-ing Jews and an implied obligation to respond that few if any Chris-tians in Germany were articulating at the time; on the other hand, we note the recirculation of some of the very anti-Jewish canards that were used to rationalize this suffering. What is offered to contempo-rary Jews is taken away from biblical Jews; and because the two are organically linked in the Christian imagination, Bonhoeffer's "Jew" is shrouded in ambiguity.[44]

Kristallnacht

Some scholars, obliged to concede Bonhoeffer's rather traditional posture toward Judaism and the Old Testament prior to 1938, perceive a marked change in the wake of *Kristallnacht*. In an article on Bonhoeffer's reaction to the pogrom of November 9–10, 1938, first published in 1991, Bethge contends that Bonhoeffer's response to *Kristallnacht* became the "decisive impetus in his life" and marked a "decisive point" in his thinking.[45] Bethge acknowledges that the change was revealed gradually in Bonhoeffer's actions but argues that he realized almost immediately that "this day of persecution might determine his vocation and his fate." Evidence for this claim includes pencil marks in Bonhoeffer's Bible, the more significant because they represent the only "note in his Bible giving a date or key word for something contemporary."[46]

Not all interpreters have been impressed by these notations in Bonhoeffer's Bible. Wolfgang Gerlach observes that it was probably during this period that Bonhoeffer famously remarked, "Only he who cries out for the Jews may also sing Gregorian chant." Yet, Gerlach complains, Bonhoeffer himself "did not cry out but only underlined Ps. 74:8 in the Bible that he used for prayer and meditation."[47] Even Bethge concedes that Bonhoeffer made no "public utterance," either during or after the fateful pogrom (in part because of his "illegal existence" at the time). However, a sentence inserted in a circular letter written by Bonhoeffer on November 20 suggests that the theologian was engaged in serious reflection in the wake of *Kristallnacht*: "During the last few days I have been thinking a great deal about Psalm 74, Zechariah 2:12 (2:8 'he who touches you touches the apple of his eye!'), Romans 9:3f (Israel, to whom belongs the sonship, the glory, the covenant, the law, the service, the promises), Romans 11:11–15. That takes us right into prayer."[48]

But is there evidence that Bonhoeffer's pensive response to widespread anti-Jewish violence was accompanied by qualitatively new perceptions of the Jewish people and their destiny? Referring to the citation from Romans 9, Bethge writes that in 1938 Bonhoeffer read and taught "about this text in order flatly to contradict the church's centuries-old teaching of the rejection of the Jews, being so moved that he asks how church teaching could so long have completely forgotten this statement from Paul about the continuing existence of Judaism."

As for Zechariah 2:8, Bethge notes that although less than a year earlier
Bonhoeffer had applied this text to the church's persecution, he now
interpreted it "unambiguously and exclusively in terms of its validity
for the Jews, leaving no room for a theology of punishment."[49] It is also
telling, Bethge and others argue, that after this time Bonhoeffer no
longer spoke or wrote of a divine curse hanging over the Jews.

There are problems, however, with maintaining that Bonhoeffer's
appropriation of these biblical passages in the aftermath of *Kristallnacht*
represents a departure from the theological outlook that had previously
determined Christian apprehensions of Jews. First, while the language
of divine punishment is happily absent from Bonhoeffer's reflections,
silence is weak evidence for substantive theological change when the
images and concepts in question are part of a mythological construct
that has inhabited the Christian mind for centuries. Second, Bethge's
attempt to demonstrate that in the wake of the November pogrom
Bonhoeffer was moving toward a new "theology of Israel" ironically
reinforces the view that he was unable to renounce the witness-people
myth.

Bethge makes much of the fact that the biblical passages alluded
to in the circular letter of November 20 do not appear in Bonhoeffer's
earlier writings, at least not in reference to Jews. But Romans 9–11
contains the very musings on the fate of "Israel" *post Christum* that
nurture the roots of the witness-people myth. Although possessing "the
adoption, the glory, the covenants, the giving of the law, the worship,
and the promises" (9:4), Israel has "stumbled over the stumbling stone"
(9:32). "Through their stumbling salvation has come to the Gentiles,
so as to make Israel jealous" (11:11). "They have a zeal for God, but it
is not enlightened. For, being ignorant of the righteousness that comes
from God, and seeking to establish their own, they have not submitted to God's righteousness" (10:2–3). "As regards the gospel they are
enemies of God . . . ; but as regards election they are beloved, for the
sake of their ancestors; for the gifts and the calling of God are irrevo-
cable" (11:28).

Similarly, Clements suggests that it was unusual for a Protestant
pastor "to be so familiar with the Old Testament as to be able to turn
to a specific text so readily and to read it as a direct commentary on
what was happening."[50] But this comment does not apply to texts that
describe the travail of Israel. In fact, throughout Christian history the

psalms had been treated as an unusually reliable source of inspiration for elucidating Israel's fate. Psalm 59, for instance, had been regarded as both prediction and justification of Jewish dispersion in the Christian era since at least the time of Augustine. Verse 11, which reads, "Do not kill them, or my people may forget; make them totter by your power, and bring them down, O Lord, our shield," was interpreted by Augustine as a prediction of the Jewish Diaspora.[51] Bernard of Clairvaux invoked the same text to convince marauding crusaders of their obligation to spare Jewish lives. "The Jews are not to be persecuted, killed or even put to flight," Bernard warned.

> Ask anyone who knows the sacred Scripture what he finds foretold of the Jews in the Psalms. "Nor for their destruction do I pray," it says (Ps. 59:12). The Jews are for us the living words of Scripture, for they remind us always of what our Lord suffered. They are dispersed all over the world so that by expiating their crime they may be everywhere the living witnesses of our redemption.

"If the Jews are utterly wiped out," Bernard insisted, "what will become of our hope for their promised salvation, their eventual conversion?"[52]

Thus, when Bonhoeffer turned to Israel's prayer book in order to comprehend the crisis of Jewish existence in his time, he was extending a venerable interpretive tradition. True, he was no longer construing statements about Israel to refer exclusively to the church; but when he read the Bible in the light of burning synagogues, he was doing so in order to clarify the Christian meaning of Jewish history. According to Bethge, what drew Bonhoeffer to Psalm 74 was the connection between "the shattering experience of abandonment felt by the desperate victims of the pogrom two-and-a-half millennia earlier, when the Babylonians laid waste the Temple and deported the people . . . [and] the acute and real cries of abandonment of that night in 1938."[53] This observation only confirms that Bonhoeffer's post-*Kristallnacht* apprehension of the Jewish people continued to reflect the witness-people tradition. Bonhoeffer's engagement with Psalm 74 may represent a "very important new stage in *his* interpretation," but its continuity with the Christian tradition is notable.[54]

While the Nazi pogrom may have pushed Bonhoeffer to explicitly reject the notion that a divine curse pursued the Jews through history, it does not appear to have dissuaded him from perceiving Jewish travail through the prism of salvation history. Apparently, the same was true of Bonhoeffer's students, at least one of whom made comments in the margins of his own Bible beside Psalm 74.[55] Indeed, the potency of the witness-people impulse in Christian readings of the psalms is evident in a published reminiscence by Gottfried Maltusch, who recalled that in the "great discussion" among Finkenwaldeans in the aftermath of *Kristallnacht*, Bonhoeffer "utterly refused to see . . . a fulfillment of the curse on the Jews," and added that "if the synagogues burn today, the churches will be on fire tomorrow."[56] These statements conceal a contradiction that is apparently lost on Maltusch: Bonhoeffer asserted that *Kristallnacht* was bereft of theological significance but used the event to draw a lesson for the church. Christine-Ruth Müller is more precise in calling Bonhoeffer's warning a "theological interpretation of the events."[57]

Ethics

It is *Ethics* to which the majority of scholars turn for literary evidence of a substantially new theological apprehension of Jewish life on Bonhoeffer's part. Noting that "the language of displacement theology, of punishment theology, of mission theology, seems nearly to have vanished" in the wake of *Kristallnacht*, Bethge contends that in *Ethics* Bonhoeffer achieved a "breakthrough for a coming theology after the Holocaust."[58] Kenneth C. Barnes declares that in this text Bonhoeffer for the first time perceives Jews as Jews rather than as potential Christians.[59] Geffrey Kelly writes that *Ethics* contains "some of the most remarkable statements of the need for Christian solidarity with the Jews."[60] Andreas Pangritz argues that Bonhoeffer returned to Germany in 1939 in order to share not the destiny of "his people" or even the destiny of the Confessing Church, but the destiny of the Jewish "brothers of Jesus Christ."[61] Even Pinchas Lapide has hinted that *Ethics* might provide the foundation for a new Christian theology of Judaism.[62]

Two passages from *Ethics* are commonly cited in this connection. In a section of the book titled "Heritage and Decay," Bonhoeffer writes:

> The historical Jesus Christ is the continuity of our history. Because Jesus Christ was the promised Messiah of the Israelite-Jewish people, the line of our forebears reaches back before the appearance of Jesus Christ into the people of Israel. Western history is by God's will inextricably bound up with the people of Israel, not only genetically but in an honest, unceasing encounter. The Jews keep open the question of Christ; they are the sign of God's free, gracious election and of God's rejecting wrath: "see the kindness and the severity of God" (Rom. 11:22). Driving out the Jew(s) from the West must result in driving out Christ with them, for Jesus Christ was a Jew.[63]

Many tout this passage as a gauge of the development in Bonhoeffer's "theology of Israel." William Jay Peck identifies Bonhoeffer's declaration that "Western history is . . . inextricably bound up with the people of Israel" as a major contribution to contemporary Jewish-Christian relations.[64] Kelly calls the excerpt "unique for its empathic linking up of Christ with Judaism and of Judaism with the fate of Christianity," and observes that it was composed during the massive deportations of Jews from Germany.[65] James Patrick Kelley regards these sentences as a repudiation of the theological anti-Semitism prominent in "The Church and the Jewish Question," and its replacement with "some kind of indissoluble solidarity between the two covenant peoples."[66]

A second *Ethics* excerpt regarded as evidence of a transformation in Bonhoeffer's "theology of Israel" appears in the midst of his confession of the church's guilt:

> The church confesses that it has witnessed the arbitrary use of brutal force, the suffering in body and soul of countless innocent people, that it has witnessed oppression, hatred, and murder without raising its voice for the victims and without finding ways of rushing to help them. It has become guilty of the lives of the weakest and most defenseless brothers and sisters of Jesus Christ.[67]

Bethge asserts that inasmuch as the language of displacement, punishment, and mission is conspicuously absent from this passage, it signifies a "cardinal point in the meaning of Bonhoeffer for Jewish-Christian relationships after the Holocaust." Perhaps at this point, he surmises, one sees "something like a breakthrough for a coming

theology after the Holocaust."[68] Commenting on Bonhoeffer's reference to "the weakest and most defenseless brothers and sisters of Jesus
Christ," Clifford Green writes that "so far as we know, Bonhoeffer is
the only theologian of the Confessing Church who referred to Jews
as 'brothers.'"[69] And Smith regards Bonhoeffer's confession of guilt as
providing "a sure foundation for the ongoing, critical conversation"
between Christians and Jews. In it, Smith avers, is laid "the ground-
work for a post-Holocaust Christian theology and . . . new possibilities
for Jewish-Christian relations."[70]

Before declaring that these passages mark the opening of a new path
for Christian-Jewish understanding, we must determine the extent to
which they are compatible with older perceptions. First, however, we
are obligated to observe that whatever the individual merits of these
passages, they can not be interpreted in isolation from the book's "faith
in the revelation of ultimate reality in Jesus Christ":[71]

> *In Jesus Christ the reality of God entered into the reality of this world.*
> The place where the questions about the reality of God and about
> the reality of the world are answered at the same time is charac-
> terized solely by the name: Jesus Christ. God and the world are
> enclosed in this name. In Christ all things exist (Col. 1:17). From
> now on we cannot speak rightly of either God or the world with-
> out speaking of Jesus Christ. All concepts of reality that ignore Jesus
> Christ are abstractions.[72]

And again: "The message of the church to the world can be none other
than the word of God to the world. This word is: Jesus Christ, and
salvation in this name. It is in Jesus Christ that God's relationship to
the world is determined." And, finally: "Faith in this Jesus Christ is the
single source of all good."[73]

These bold christological assertions lead us to speculate whether the
"fundamental theological perspective"[74] of *Ethics* will allow its author
to hear Jews testify to anything other than the rejection of a messiah
who is their only hope of salvation and only access to truth. If one
defines reality and morality in christological terms, in other words, can
one appreciate Judaism on its own terms? It is significant that theologians who have reflected on this question from a post-Holocaust perspective have developed "modest christologies" that defer confirmation

of Christ's identity to an eschatological horizon or stress that "Christian faithfulness to God in Christ must respect Jewish faithfulness to God through Torah."[75]

Also salient for evaluating the implications of Bonhoeffer's ethics for a Christian "theology of Israel" are the book's direct portrayals of Jews and Judaism. Particularly interesting are seventeen references to "Pharisees" or "pharisaism" that span six of the book's thirteen essays, most of them brief allusions in which "Pharisee" is shorthand for hypocrite, "pharisaism" for arrogance.[76] Clifford Green, editor of the critical edition of *Ethics*, seeks to mitigate any offense such usage might cause, noting that it "reflects the vernacular prejudices of [Bonhoeffer's] era."[77] But if Bonhoeffer was aware that "historically [the term] referred to a group of highly respectable pious Jews,"[78] why did he belabor the conventional usage? The answer seems to lie in the essay "God's Love and the Disintegration of the World," where Bonhoeffer presents a character study of "the Pharisee"—within Judaism and beyond.

In this section of *Ethics* Bonhoeffer employs the Pharisees of history to highlight Jesus' distinctive message and demonstrate "the contrast of the old and the new":[79]

> The knowledge of the Pharisees was dead and barren, the knowledge of Jesus, and of those bound to him, is loving and fertile; the knowledge of the Pharisee has a disintegrating effect, the knowledge of Jesus is redeeming and reconciling; the knowledge of the Pharisee destroys any genuine doing, the knowledge of Jesus and those who are his consists solely in doing.[80]

"The Pharisees and Jesus speak on completely different planes," Bonhoeffer emphasizes; "that is why they speak so curiously past each other." The Pharisee's doing "is pretense and hypocrisy, . . . aris[ing] out of a disunited existence."[81] They symbolize hypocrisy— "They say it and do not do it"—and Jesus' polemic against them is aimed at their "pseudo-doing, self-deception."[82] Here the Pharisee's exemplary functions—as emblem of Jewish opposition to Jesus and foil to authentic Christian existence—are the ones traditionally reserved for him in Christian theology. In fact, Bonhoeffer's portrait of the Pharisee resonates not only with the broader *adversos Judaeos* tradition, but with the specific anti-Jewish conventions of German theology.[83]

It is significant that in this section of *Ethics*, Bonhoeffer uses the term "Pharisee" to denote not only the Jewish contemporaries of Jesus, but also "generically to refer to a type of person dominated by the knowledge of good and evil."[84] In Bonhoeffer's words, Pharisees "are not an accidental historical phenomenon of Jesus' time, but human beings for whom nothing but the knowledge of good and evil has come to be important for their entire lives. The Pharisee is the epitome of the human being in the state of disunion."[85] This type of reasoning exhibits formal similarities with a rhetorical strategy Bonhoeffer favored during the Church Struggle—portraying his enemies as modern "Jewish Christians" who were "Jewish" not in ethnicity but in behavior and belief. Just as in 1933 German Christians represented the "Jewish-Christian type," in *Ethics* anyone obsessed with the knowledge of good and evil qualifies as a modern "Pharisee."[86]

Editor Green is of the opinion that Bonhoeffer's removal of "Pharisees" from first-century Palestine somehow alleviates the anti-Jewish propensity in their depiction. But that propensity is exacerbated when Jesus' flesh-and-blood Jewish opponents become abstract figures under the influence of supra-historical forces. We catch a glimpse of these forces in Bonhoeffer's description of the Pharisees' temptation of Jesus:

> What takes place between Jesus and the Pharisees is merely a repetition of that first temptation of Jesus, in which the devil tried to present him with a conflict in God's Word, and which Jesus overcame by his essential unity with God's Word. This temptation of Jesus in turn has its prelude in that question with which the serpent in paradise causes Adam and Eve to fall: "Did God really say . . . ?"[87]

Overall, the Pharisees' role in *Ethics* is much as it had been in Christian polemical literature throughout the ages—nameless, faceless Jews personifying a legalistic attitude toward life and tragically missing God despite their zeal for the law; well-intentioned men who unwittingly ally themselves with Satan.

Having considered Bonhoeffer's portrayal of the "Pharisee" (the only explicit mention of Jews in *Ethics*), we are in a better position to evaluate the statements (all oblique and requiring inference) believed to refer to Jews suffering under Nazi persecution. Bonhoeffer's confession that the church "has become guilty of the lives of the weakest and most defenseless brothers and sisters of Jesus Christ" does appear to be an indirect reference to the Jews[88] and is perhaps even a signal of Bonhoeffer's decision to enter the conspiracy and "take up for himself, as an act of *metanoia* [conversion], the protection of Jewish life."[89] More ambiguous are the declarations in the paragraph from "Heritage and Decay" regarding Jesus the Jew as "the promised Messiah of the Israelite-Jewish people," Western history as "inextricably bound up with the people of Israel," and the Jews as "keep[ing] open the question of Christ."

James Patrick Kelley considers this passage the basis for a Christian affirmation of Judaism's essential integrity apart from the church, Jewish rejection of Jesus' messiahship representing one side of a dialogue that makes authentic Christian faith possible.[90] Yet before we imagine how Bonhoeffer's words might be read in a pluralistic world shadowed by the Holocaust, we should consider them in light of the theology that made Jews so vulnerable to destruction in the ruins of Christendom.

At this point it should not be difficult to discern that the excerpt from "Heritage and Decay" reiterates a controlling assumption of witness-people theology—the conviction that God's providential action in history is transparent in the existence, wandering, and suffering of the Jewish people. Further, the reference to Paul's ruminations on Jewish existence *post Christum* in Romans 11, the affirmation that Jews simultaneously signify divine grace and divine wrath, and the claim that "the Jew . . . is sign" unmistakably echo the witness-people tradition. Bonhoeffer's reference to Israel as "sign" is a leitmotif of this tradition, one recovered by theologians such as Barth in their reflections on the travail of Israel under the Nazis.[91]

Finally, the declaration that "the Jew keeps open the question of Christ," while no doubt an expression of Bonhoeffer's "ongoing search for a theological foundation upon which to establish his racial-ethical concern for Jews,"[92] resonates with the functional view of Jewish survival that has characterized witness-people theology since the time of Augustine. In this tradition, Jewish persistence is both natural and special revelation. Jews' survival testifies to divine providence, while Jewish suffering following Jesus' crucifixion is a "sign" pointing to Christ. Bonhoeffer remains within the intellectual confines of this tradition, inasmuch as Jews "keep open the question of Christ" by bearing witness to the dialectic of grace and judgment it is their destiny to reflect. Even if we interpret Bonhoeffer's declaration that "driving out the Jew(s) from the West must result in driving out Christ with them" as an allusion to the deportation of German Jews and a reminder of the bond between Judaism and Christianity that was badly obscured during the Nazi era, his linkage of Jewish fate and Christian hope indicates that he continued to view Jewish suffering christologically.[93]

How much new ground was broken, then, in Bonhoeffer's reflections on Jewish fate in *Ethics*? To the extent that it manifests witness-people thinking, the relationship between Jews and Christians articulated in *Ethics* is formally continuous with the section titled "The Church and the Jewish Question" analyzed in chapter 4. In 1933 "the suffering of this people, loved and punished by God" is illumined by "the sign of [its] final homecoming"; in 1940, the Jew is a "sign of the free mercy-choice and of the repudiating wrath of God." Although intended to oppose the Nazi vision of a Jew-free (*Judenrein*) Europe, Bonhoeffer's image of the Jew as a mirror of election and judgment is rooted in the same mythological structure from which curse theology emerged.

It appears that Bonhoeffer's reflections on Jewish suffering in *Ethics*, reflections that are read by so many as marking a path to post-Holocaust Christianity, reflect the witness-people tradition in both tone and content. It is fair to ask why they could not have been written by Augustine, the early Luther, or Barth, all of whom believed that Jews survived as testimony to the messiah they rejected.

Letters and Papers from Prison

Many perceive in Bonhoeffer's prison writings an affinity for Jews only hinted at in *Ethics*.[94] This affinity is seen as expressing itself primarily in a reacquaintance with the Old Testament that left a profound mark on Bonhoeffer's surviving letters and papers. What insights did Bonhoeffer glean from his encounter with the Hebrew Bible? In a dozen or so letters from prison dated between May 1943 and July 1944, Bonhoeffer reflected on the distinctiveness of Israelite religion and the Hebrew conception of God.[95] These reflections are summarized in a letter dated December 5, 1943, which is cited more than any other in this connection:[96]

> My thoughts and feelings seem to be getting more and more like those of the Old Testament, and in recent months I have been reading the Old Testament much more than the New. It is only when one knows the unutterability of the name of God that one can utter the name of Jesus Christ; it is only when one loves life and the earth so much that without them everything seems to be over that one may believe in the resurrection and a new world; it is only when one submits to God's law that one may speak of grace; and it is only when God's wrath and vengeance are hanging as grim realities over the heads of one's enemies that something of what it means to love and forgive them can touch our hearts. In my opinion it is not Christian to want to take our thoughts and feelings too quickly and too directly from the New Testament. We have already talked about this several times, and every day confirms my opinion. One cannot and must not speak the last word before the last but one.

A few sentences later, Bonhoeffer poses a series of penetrating questions:

> Why is it that in the Old Testament men tell lies vigorously and often to the glory of God (I've now collected the passages), kill, deceive, rob, divorce, and even fornicate (see the genealogy of Jesus), doubt, blaspheme, and curse, whereas in the New Testament there is nothing of all this? "An earlier stage" of religion? That is a very naïve way out; it is one and the same God.[97]

Bonhoeffer's rediscovery of the Old Testament during his sojourn in prison was not only challenging, but theologically fruitful, as it informed his growing conviction of the "profound, this-worldliness of Christianity."[98] Many scholars, in fact, detect in his thoughts on the Old Testament the roots of the "new theology" Bonhoeffer strained toward in Tegel prison. Martin Kuske argues that the Old Testament's prophetic message of judgment was crucial in Bonhoeffer's formulation of the "world come of age."[99] Ruth Zerner and William Jay Peck connect Bonhoeffer's musings on "religionless Christianity" with his rediscovery of the Old Testament in prison. Francis I. Andersen predicts that had Bonhoeffer survived, he "would have made very extensive and altogether original use of the Old Testament in his programme for developing 'the non-religious interpretation of biblical concepts.'"[100] David Ford contends that Bonhoeffer's description from prison of the Christian life as "living unreservedly in life's duties, problems, successes and failures, experiences and perplexities" is "thoroughly Jewish in its main lines, and is essentially an outworking of the twofold imperative to love God and one's neighbor."[101]

A nontriumphalist view of the relationship between the Testaments is another resource for post-Holocaust theology believed to lie in Bonhoeffer's reflections from prison. In *The God of Israel and Christian Theology*, R. Kendall Soulen repeatedly invokes Bonhoeffer's prison letters as guides for identifying and correcting supersessionist strains in Christianity. Like other interpreters, he avers that Bonhoeffer's call for "religionless Christianity" was closely related to his "discovery of the Hebrew Scriptures as the indispensable context of the gospel."[102] But Soulen goes further in claiming a link between the doctrine of supersessionism and the weaknesses Bonhoeffer identified in traditional patterns of Christian thought—what Bonhoeffer calls "religious" interpretation of the gospel. Remarkably, Soulen regards the "false contextualization of the Bible identified by Bonhoeffer in his call for a worldly Christianity," elliptical though it is, as a firmer basis for conceiving a nonsupersessionist unity of the canon than the mature theologies of Barth or Karl Rahner.[103]

There is no doubt that Bonhoeffer's prison letters of 1943–44 reveal a new and growing appreciation for the portion of the Bible Christians traditionally call the "Old Testament" (he claims to have read through it two and a half times), as well as discomfort with a conception of Christian faith that "separates Christ from the Old Testament."[104] However, these letters possess elements that warn us against too quickly identifying them as unqualified resources for post-Holocaust theology. First, there are puzzling references that indicate the need for a good deal more theological work on the relationship between the covenants. These include the assertion that in the Old Testament "the *church* stands, not at the boundaries where human powers give out, but in the middle of the village," that the ground for recognizing God at the center of life "lies in the revelation of God in Jesus Christ," and that "*all* that we may rightly expect from God, and ask him for, is to be found in

Jesus Christ."[105] What is truly perplexing is that these references often appear in the very letters in which Bonhoeffer discusses the "new theology" inspired by his immersion in the Old Testament.

Second, these letters offer nothing to qualify Bonhoeffer's well-documented opinion that Christians must interpret the entire Bible christologically. In that sense at least, there is fundamental agreement between *Letters and Papers from Prison* and Bonhoeffer's earlier work on the Old Testament.[106] If there is a difference in the way Bonhoeffer reads the Old Testament after his arrest, it is captured by John W. de Gruchy's comment that in prison Bonhoeffer "preferred to read the New Testament from the perspective of the Hebrew Bible rather than the other way around." De Gruchy maintains that both approaches are appropriate;[107] yet as long as "reading the New Testament from the perspective of the Hebrew Bible" remains a christocentric enterprise, this hermeneutic will be susceptible to post-Holocaust critique.

This leads to a third observation, one made by Walter Harrelson in 1962 and still very relevant. In *Letters and Papers from Prison*, as in earlier comments on the Old Testament, Bonhoeffer fails to consider the possibility that the Hebrew Bible might be read on its own terms—fails, that is, to show any interest in how Jews might understand the text apart from Christ. Harrelson's sobering conclusion is that while Bonhoeffer's approach to the Old Testament enabled him to preserve it as Christian Scripture, he "rescued it for the Church by denying it to Israel."[108] This charge was reiterated by Zerner in 1974 and intensified by Rosenbaum in 1981, who wrote that even in 1944–45 Bonhoeffer assumed that Judaism had "died giving birth to Christianity."[109] These allegations have not been answered so much as forgotten in the wake of repeated claims for Bonhoeffer's "breakthrough" toward a new understanding of the Old Testament.

In the final analysis, how we regard Bonhoeffer's relationship to the Old Testament depends to a great extent on the context in which we view it. If we consider Bonhoeffer's reading of the Old Testament against the background of his time and place, in which forces inside and outside the church tempted Christians to belittle and marginalize this portion of the biblical canon, we can only applaud his firm opposition to neo-Marcionism. But if we judge it in light of post-Holocaust concerns, as Harrelson and others have attempted to do, it is clear that Bonhoeffer's perspective on the "Old Testament" is implicated in an interpretive tradition that casts Jews as adherents of a superseded religion who must learn from Christians how to interpret their own Scriptures.[110]

Bonhoeffer's witness to the unity of the Bible is certainly one leg upon which Christian-Jewish reconciliation must stand. But acknowledging the necessity for Christians to retain the Old Testament, to recognize its distinctive emphases, and to learn from it how to understand the revelation in Jesus Christ is not tantamount to appreciation for the Hebrew Bible, much less Judaism. To claim otherwise is to commit the classic error of identifying contemporary Judaism with ancient Israelite religion, making rabbinic Judaism a biblical faith on the model of Protestant Christianity. Charitable Jews have paid tribute to Bonhoeffer as one whose interest in the Old Testament led him to drink "from the same well from which Judaism is nourished."[111] But the well that nourishes Judaism is not the religion itself.

Persistent Ambivalence

If Bonhoeffer's response to the Jewish Question in 1933 has been the occasion for scholarly spin control, his subsequent publications have been the target of a great deal of hopeful interpretation. Passages that hint at sensitivity to Jewish suffering become proof texts, while demeaning references to Jews are ignored or downplayed. Bonhoeffer's legitimate fears of security police and prison censors encourage interpretive license.[112] Dubious allusions to the Holocaust are claimed.[113] Catchy statements touting Bonhoeffer's role in the "re-judaization" of Christianity are reprised again and again.

Perhaps it is not surprising that texts authored by an anti-Nazi resister and martyr, texts reputed to mark a path out of the morass of Christian anti-Judaism, would become the focus of wishful interpretation. If so, we are indebted to bold scholars like Ruth Zerner who remind us that Bonhoeffer's mature theology resonates with the ambivalence toward Jews so characteristic of his earlier reflection. Despite his "increasingly positive attitude towards Old Testament 'this-worldliness,'" Zerner concludes, "ambivalence about the Jews and the Hebrew Bible survived as a persistent feature of Bonhoeffer's thinking, even in *Letters and Papers from Prison.*"[114] As we have seen, this conclusion is supported by a careful evaluation of the textual evidence.

What are we to make of this ambivalence? The explanation hinted at throughout this chapter is that Bonhoeffer's theology of Israel reflects not only the cultural context in which he lived, but the contours of the witness-people tradition forged in Augustine's theology and embedded in the Christian imagination. Recall that in Augustine's paradoxical portrayal of the witness-people, Jews are killers of Christ yet remain the people of God; their religion is superseded, yet they are not "cast off"; they are dispersed but carry "books" (the Christian "Old Testament") that testify to Christ; they are witnesses to divine judgment who nevertheless disseminate knowledge of God; they are adherents of a lifeless religion whose tragic ignorance will be redeemed when they convert to Christ en masse at the end of history.

Now we are in a position to identify the paradoxical perceptions of Jews that animated Bonhoeffer's contemplation of "Israel" from 1933 through 1944.

Jews are the "chosen people." Bonhoeffer wrote in 1935 that "the people of Israel will remain the people of God, in eternity, the only people who will not perish, because God has become their Lord, God has made His dwelling in their midst and built His house"; in 1938 he reiterated that "the God of Abraham, Isaac, and Jacob is the God and Father of Jesus Christ and our God."[115] Following *Kristallnacht*, these affirmations were underscored by biblical references to Romans 9–11 and Zechariah 2:8 ("One who touches you touches the apple of my eye").

Yet they are also the "rejected people" who murdered God's Messiah and suffer under a divine curse as a result. Bonhoeffer wrote in 1933 that the Jews are "the 'chosen people,' who nailed the redeemer of the world to the cross." He never explicitly repudiated the deicide charge leveled in both "The Church and the Jewish Question" and the *Bethel Confession.* Even Bethge acknowledges that "there are no explicit corrections or recantations of the formulas about replacement, curse and mission in connection with Judaism."[116]

Christians cannot forget their organic link to the Jewish people, a link rooted in Christ and his Jewish identity. To emphasize this connection and the resulting obligation of solidarity with suffering Jews, Bonhoeffer referred to Jews as "brothers and sisters of Jesus Christ."

Yet Jewish religion is lifeless inasmuch as it is detached from God's revelation in Christ. The Old Testament is indispensable for Christians but primarily as a guide for understanding the promises that are fulfilled in Jesus Christ.

The church must take seriously its responsibility to evangelize Jews. As it "looks at the rejected people, it humbly recognizes itself as a church continually unfaithful to its Lord."[117]

Yet Jews are a mystery that cannot be removed. The Jews "are the sign of God's free, gracious election and of God's rejecting wrath."[118] Jewish suffering keeps open the question of Christ.

This method of describing Bonhoeffer's theology of Israel brings into focus the continuities in his thought while avoiding a snapshot approach that unfairly freezes it in the spring of 1933.[119] Because this approach effectively elucidates Bonhoeffer's thinking in the light of perennial Christian apprehensions of the Jew, it is useful in helping determine just what Bonhoeffer did and did not achieve theologically with regard to Jews and Judaism. Thus it allows us to evaluate persistent claims that Bonhoeffer can serve the Christian community as a "beginning point for a post-Shoah reformation."[120]

BONHOEFFER AND THE HOLOCAUST

A Different Post-Holocaust Perspective

In chapters 1 and 2 we noted that spokespersons for Yad Vashem and scholars concerned with identifying anti-Judaism among prominent Christian theologians have seized upon "The Church and the Jewish Question" as a reliable synopsis of Bonhoeffer's thinking on "the Jews." As a result, they overlook significant changes in his thought during the months and years following that essay. In chapters 4 and 5 we saw that those who advocate Bonhoeffer as a guide for post-Holocaust Christianity, while attentive to developments in his thinking, tend to diminish the continuities between "The Church and the Jewish Question" and Bonhoeffer's later writings. Thus, neither freezing him in time nor placing him beyond his time has proved a successful strategy for interpreting "Bonhoeffer and the Jews." In this chapter we seek a different post-Holocaust perspective on the Bonhoeffer legacy. Our focus shifts from Bonhoeffer to the Holocaust itself in the expectation that considering Bonhoeffer through the lens of the Shoah rather than vice versa will produce a more realistic image of the post-Holocaust Bonhoeffer.

There have been many attempts to link Bonhoeffer and the Holocaust, but even Bonhoeffer scholarship has been uneasy with the results. In 1989 F. Burton Nelson warned that if Bonhoeffer's connection with the Holocaust were to be taken seriously, scholars must "seek to bring together with *much* more precision, *much* more insight, and *much* more accuracy, the connecting links between his theology and the historic chronicle of shame that marked the Holocaust years."[1] Unfortunately,

Nelson's advice has gone largely unheeded, and scholars continue to make assertions about Bonhoeffer's association with the Holocaust that are misleading, imprecise, or misinformed.

Sidney G. Hall III declares that Bonhoeffer died "in the Holocaust," meeting his end "in a death camp."[2] R. Kendall Soulen maintains that Bonhoeffer's credibility as post-Holocaust theologian is based in his identity as one "who wrote from within the death camps of Nazi Germany."[3] Craig J. Slane avers that Bonhoeffer did theology in "the Holocaust context," that his life and death are "an interlocking piece" of the Shoah.[4] Ann W. Astell claims that Bonhoeffer read the Bible with a "Holocaust hermeneutic."[5] Larry L. Rasmussen suggests that Bonhoeffer understood Paul van Buren's charge that we must "learn to speak of Auschwitz from the perspective of the cross . . . by first learning to speak of the cross from the perspective of Auschwitz."[6] Geffrey B. Kelly asserts that a study of Bonhoeffer's theology "points to the presence of the 'suffering servant,' indeed, of Jesus Christ himself, in the long lines of victims at the gas chambers in Nazi death camps."[7]

Such claims focus the imagination on the death Bonhoeffer shared with millions of European Jews. But by associating him with death camps, gas chambers, and even Auschwitz, none of which he experienced, they distort history and perpetuate the anachronistic notion that Bonhoeffer was cognizant of what we call "the Holocaust." While Bonhoeffer possessed uncommon knowledge of Nazi anti-Jewish actions up to the deportation of German Jews, it is unlikely that he ever heard the name "Auschwitz" or had any idea of the methods or scale we associate with the phrase "Final Solution to the Jewish Question." Even Eberhard Bethge, who asserts that Bonhoeffer entered into "deep solidarity" with victims of the Holocaust in the fall of 1940 by alluding to the "expulsion" and "deaths" of Jews, concedes that these words were written "before the gas chambers were even built."[8] Thus, when Bethge and others speak of "Bonhoeffer's breakthrough to . . . a theology which recognizes the epochal character of [the Holocaust] for Jewish-Christian relations," we should keep in mind the historical factors that limited Bonhoeffer's awareness of, and thus response to, the Shoah.[9]

Perhaps during the last weeks of his life, when he sojourned in Buchenwald and encountered prisoners of wider experience in *l'univers concentrationnaire*, Bonhoeffer began to fathom the genocide of Jews under Hitler. But such speculation is the kind of wishful interpretation of Bonhoeffer's relevance for Christian-Jewish relations that was subjected to criticism at the end of chapter 5. Properly evaluating this relevance requires us to eschew historically dubious claims about Bonhoeffer's experience of the Holocaust in favor of an examination of his legacy through the critical lens of Holocaust studies. Such an examination will allow us to go beyond reading Bonhoeffer's life via the persecution of Jews (as novelists have done) or searching for glimpses of a new theology of Israel in Bonhoeffer's fragmentary writings (as scholars have done) in order to scrutinize Bonhoeffer's career under Nazism in view of what the Holocaust teaches us about human thought and behavior in situations of extremity.

A variety of resources may be employed to yield this sort of post-Holocaust perspective on Bonhoeffer. One of them—analysis of theological concepts that elucidate the subtlety and stubbornness of Christian perceptions of Jews—was utilized in chapters 4 and 5. Another is a typology scholars have developed to interpret the varieties of human action and response that define the Holocaust. This typology includes murderous Nazis and innocent Jews, as well as ordinary perpetrators, compliant victims, and—most important for our understanding of Bonhoeffer—bystanders, resisters, and rescuers.

Players in the Holocaust Drama

Thanks to Raul Hilberg and other scholars of the Final Solution, it has become customary to designate the characters in the drama orchestrated by the Nazis by the various roles they played. These include "victims," "perpetrators," "bystanders," and, of course, "resisters" and "rescuers." As was discussed in the preface, interpreting Bonhoeffer's relationship to the Holocaust by means of these roles has the advantage of privileging neither action nor thought, but combining both in a way that elucidates Bonhoeffer's similarities with those who occupied similar positions vis-à-vis the Shoah.

Approaching Bonhoeffer from this perspective need not diminish his singularity, for his uniqueness is accentuated when we recognize that at various times he occupied several of these categories of human agency. Furthermore, Bonhoeffer's story reveals something about the classifications themselves; namely, that while movement between them could occur, it was neither uncomplicated nor decisive. Because the roles of bystander, resister, rescuer, and victim overlap in Bonhoeffer's career, his story illumines the human complexity of the Nazi era as well as the inadequacy of any typology of human behavior that might be applied to it.

Bystander

When we think of Bonhoeffer's career under Nazi rule, "bystander" is not the first designation that comes to mind. Nonetheless, Bonhoeffer's role as temporary bystander before Nazi anti-Semitism is one scholars have come increasingly to acknowledge.[10] Kenneth C. Barnes describes Bonhoeffer's initial response to Jewish persecution as "hesitant and tentative, a far cry from the Bonhoeffer of later fame."[11] Even as staunch a defender of Bonhoeffer's reputation as Eberhard Bethge has intimated that during the early years of the Nazi regime Dietrich was a "silent bystander."[12] In Bethge's view, Bonhoeffer occupied this role through 1938, since even in the aftermath of *Kristallnacht* he failed to join the courageous few who decried anti-Jewish violence:

> On that day, Dietrich Bonhoeffer and we his colleagues were not like Pastor Julius van Jan, who immediately told the whole truth from his village pulpit in Württemberg and was threatened by demonstrators and reprimanded by his church leadership for it. We were not like Helmut Gollwitzer. Although he used more circumspect language, no one listening to his sermon from Niemöller's pulpit in Dahlem was in doubt about what now to think and to fear. We were not like Karl Immer, who said to his congregation in Wuppertal on November 13: "The question is, how deep do the roots of evil go?" It was clear to everyone who was meant.[13]

Yet even though it is endorsed by Bethge, the appellation "bystander" must be applied very carefully in Bonhoeffer's case. Because he eventually took a decisive stand on behalf of the Nazis' Jewish victims, Bonhoeffer appears more favorably in the light of post-Holocaust criticism than the vast majority of his co-religionists. Furthermore, long before he took action on behalf of threatened Jews, Bonhoeffer comprehended the theological dilemma that confronted the church in the form of the Aryan Paragraph. In fact, relative to other Christian interpreters of the Jewish Question in Nazi Germany, Bonhoeffer stands out for the rapidity of his recognition that the church could not limit its concern to "non-Aryan" converts.[14]

Nevertheless, as the Nazi anti-Jewish campaign began to unfold in the early months of 1933, Bonhoeffer showed himself to be more cautious bystander than effective resister. Two pieces of evidence support this conclusion. One is Bonhoeffer's decision against participating in a funeral service for the father of his twin sister's husband, who died April 11, 1933. According to Bethge, members of Dietrich's family encouraged him to conduct the service for this Jew, but he acceded to the wishes of his church superintendent in declining to do so. The decision to distance himself from a Jewish member of his extended family during the first wave of Nazi persecutions is the closest thing in Bonhoeffer's career to classic bystander behavior. Ruth Zerner refers to the decision as "far from heroic—rather cautious and perhaps cowardly."[15]

This assessment is one Bonhoeffer likely would have shared; for in a letter to his brother-in-law written just six months after the event, he asked, "How could I have been so much afraid at the time? . . . All I can do is to ask you to forgive my weakness then. I know now for certain that I ought to have behaved differently."[16] Bonhoeffer's opportunity to atone for his temporary failure of nerve came in January 1936 with the passing of his grandmother Julie Tafel Bonhoeffer. At her funeral, Dietrich spoke openly of the woman's deep empathy for German Jews. "Her last years were clouded," he recalled, "by the great sorrow she endured on account of the fate of the Jews among our people, a fate she bore and suffered in sympathy with them."[17]

A second indication of Bonhoeffer's brief identity as a bystander in the Nazi campaign against "non-Aryans" appears in his theological writings of 1933, primarily "The Church and the Jewish Question" but also the chapter of the *Bethel Confession* titled "The Church and the Jews." The former document is rightly regarded as a landmark of theologically based anti-Nazi resistance, for it openly broaches the prospect of direct action on behalf of the state's victims. According to

Bonhoeffer, one possibility for the church's action toward the state in the matter of the Jewish Question is

> not just to bandage the victims under the wheel, but to put a spoke in the wheel itself. Such action would be direct political action, and is only possible and desirable when the church sees the state fail in its function of creating law and order, i.e. when it sees the state unrestrainedly bring about too much or too little law and order. In both these cases it must see the existence of the state, and with it its own existence, threatened.[18]

However, by suggesting that Christians will naturally perceive Jews as "the 'chosen people,' who nailed the redeemer of the world to the cross" and should "tremble" before the terrible judgment manifest in Israel's unfolding history, "The Church and the Jewish Question" lends support to the bystander posture eschewed in the passage above. A similar conclusion may be drawn concerning the *Bethel Confession*, which also encourages Christians to view Jewish travail in the light of salvation history. The confession adamantly declares that "no nation can ever be commissioned to avenge on the Jews the murder of Golgotha"; yet its reminder that "vengeance" is the Lord's implies that the eyes of faith may perceive divine judgment in the flow of secular history.[19]

To the extent that these texts encouraged Christians to stand in awe before the mystery of Israel's anguish, they advocated a kind of theological bystanderism. Christians must expect Jews to endure a series of chastisements instigated by God, Bonhoeffer seems to argue, even though they are not authorized to participate in executing these judgments. Rather, as they observe God disciplining Jews in the historical realm, Christians must maintain a fearful humility and engage in quiet self-evaluation. Much to Bonhoeffer's eventual frustration, this very attitude reigned in the Confessing Church through the Nazi era.[20]

In the language of social psychology, Bonhoeffer's early comments on the Jewish Question reflect *just-world thinking*, the mental habit, typical of bystanders, of concluding that victims deserve their fate. Bonhoeffer's just-world outlook sought to reassure Christians that, tragic though Jewish suffering might be, it was to be expected given Jews' rebellion and God's relentless desire to reprove his chosen people. Just-world thinking is a natural psychological process, but as Ervin

Staub reminds us, as a chief method of devaluing minority groups and making them scapegoats for perceived societal problems, it represents an important step on the path toward genocide. Staub argues that bystanders can be moved toward passivity and silence when experts provide them with a definition of reality that normalizes what is going on around them. Such thoughts, in turn, affect behavior: "Even bystanders who do not become perpetrators, if they passively observe as innocent people are victimized, will come to devalue the victims and justify their own passivity."[21]

Another lens for viewing Christian expectations of Jewish suffering is provided by the concept of *killing as healing*, identified by Robert Jay Lifton as crucial to the functioning of German physicians who contributed to the Final Solution. To the extent that the Christian witness-people myth is predicated on the hope that Jewish affliction will bring a purified remnant of "Israel" to salvation, it represents what Lifton calls a "healing-killing paradox." The Nazi version of this paradox rationalized the killing of Jews as necessary for saving the Aryan race. The rationalizations of Christian theology and the justifications of Nazi perpetrators were often quite disparate, of course, but both ideologies had the effect of portraying Jewish misery as part of a holy and immortalizing vision.[22] Christians inherited from Jews the notion that God chastens God's children. As this interpretation of history impressed itself on the Christian mind, medical analogies were occasionally called upon to explain the chastising work of the divine Parent. In an example familiar to many Germans, Martin Luther called Christians to deliver a "severe mercy" upon Jews, one he likened to amputating a gangrenous limb in order to save a patient.

Both killing-as-healing ideology and witness-people theology, then, countenance suffering for the sake of rebirth. In the Christian tradition, the Jews' misfortune is interpreted under the sign of their "final homecoming," as Bonhoeffer puts it in "The Church and the Jewish Question." Similarly, as Lifton shows, many Nazi doctors maintained psychic balance in the camps by cultivating an ethos of revitalization that submerged the pain and death they dealt in a mystical vision of "biological renewal." Of course, Nazi doctors were developing a justification for committing premeditated bodily harm, while Christians who sought to comprehend God's ways with the Jew were seeking a theological rationale for bystanderism. Furthermore, the myth was not useful for validating direct attacks on Jews, as Bonhoeffer makes clear in his warning that Christians are not authorized to supplement God's curse with their own actions.

It is important to place Bonhoeffer's role as bystander in perspective. During the Nazi era, virtually every representative of the German church with a public voice was led by ingrained Christian prejudice to speak about Jews in ways that normalized or justified their persecution. If anything distinguishes Bonhoeffer from his contemporaries in this regard, it is the conspicuous absence of stridently anti-Jewish rhetoric from his writings after 1933. A useful comparison can be made with Bonhoeffer's theological mentor Karl Barth. When in early 1933 Bonhoeffer counseled the church to respond to the agony of the "rejected people" by humbly recognizing its own unfaithfulness, he was construing Jewish suffering as a reflection of the church's own sins. Bonhoeffer never spoke so cavalierly of Jewish misfortune again. Barth, however, continued to do so until at least 1950, when he described elect Israel as a "mirror" in which the church sees reflected "the primal revolt, the unbelief, the disobedience in which we are all engaged," that is, "who and what we all are, and how bad we all are."[23]

Resister

Even if his first public statements on the Jewish Question provided Christians with a theological rationale for remaining passive in the face of anti-Jewish persecution, Bonhoeffer himself could not do so for long. Very quickly he became one of the most vociferous advocates of resistance to the German Christian campaign of coordination (*Gleischschaltung*) with the Nazi state. But given the tendency to project "saints and villains" onto the history of the Third Reich, a portrait of Bonhoeffer informed by the Holocaust will depict his career as resister with painstaking accuracy.

On one hand, Bonhoeffer's resistance activities are prone to distortion by romantic projections based in the need for moral heroes. On the other hand, we are likely to *underestimate* the significance of Bonhoeffer's defiance of National Socialism if we fall prey to the larger myth of resistance in which many painful memories of the Nazi era have been repressed. This myth is perpetuated by notions that rebellion against Hitler and the Nazis was widespread, that the majority of Germans were silent victims of Nazi tyranny, and that millions of would-be resisters lived in thrall to the Nazi police state. From time to time, postwar German culture has been quite receptive to this illusion of pervasive opposition. As Claudia Koonz observes, it has even influenced historical scholarship:

> During the first decades after 1945, scholarship and memoirs about "the Resistance" (*Widerstand*) counterpoised the forces of good against massive evil. . . . In historical memory, the resisters' heroism and often martyrdom offset the dismal record of collaboration and obedience in nazified Europe. . . . Recently, however, the stark image of a monolithic "Resistance" has yielded (among Marxists and liberals) as the historical profession itself has shifted its perspectives. Oral histories, memoirs by victims, and local history projects have blurred sharp contrasts between resistance and collaboration. . . . [There has been a] collapse of clarity about the divisions between those who opposed and those who supported Nazi policies.[24]

Recognizing the attraction of the resistance myth and the reality it was invented to obscure will aid in clarifying Bonhoeffer's role as anti-Nazi resister.

For Bonhoeffer the journey from bystander to resister was a gradual one, as he struggled to overcome the elements in his background that predisposed him to quietism and anti-Judaism. Stirrings of resistance to the Nazi regime were evident already early in 1933—in his radio address on the "leadership principle" (February), in his essay "The Church and the Jewish Question" (April), and in his work on behalf of the Pastors' Emergency League. To call this phase of Bonhoeffer's resistance "ecclesiastical" is not to dispute James Patrick Kelly's claim that "The Church and the Jewish Question" contains a blueprint for what could have been a campaign of serious *political* resistance. It is only to recognize that at the time Bonhoeffer imagined that the church would be the agent of this resistance.

Bonhoeffer's movement from ecclesiastical to political resistance was neither quick nor smooth, but two sets of experiences seem to have been critical in making it possible. First, he was prepared for direct action by his earlier "pacifist resistance" that included opposition to military service and admonishment of European Christians against war and rearmament. Second, as he witnessed the Confessing Church's failure to acknowledge the theological either/or he had formulated with regard to the Aryan Paragraph in the spring of 1933, Bonhoeffer's faith in ecclesiastical resistance waned. He left for London in October 1933, disappointed by his inability to provoke recognition of the Jewish Question among his colleagues.

Upon returning to Germany in 1935, Bonhoeffer renewed his personal struggle with the leaders of the Confessing Church. In the wake of the Nazi Nuremburg Laws, he sought to make the church confront the issue of Jewish persecution at the Confessing Synod at Steglitz. When it failed to do so, Bonhoeffer broached with his students the possibility of political resistance.[25] By 1938, when the Confessing Church's quest for "legalization" led over 85 percent of its members to sign an oath of loyalty to the Führer, Bonhoeffer had concluded that there was no hope for effective resistance in the ecclesiastical realm. If it is possible to plot a point of no return in Bonhoeffer's progress toward political resistance, it may have been June 20, 1939—the day he made the fateful decision to return to Germany from New York City, despite the offer of employment in America.

Less clear than the timing of Bonhoeffer's decision to enlist in the resistance is its basis in his thinking. Andreas Pangritz contends that when Bonhoeffer wrote that he had decided to share the "destiny of Germany" and return to Europe, he was thinking not of "his people" or even of "brethren" in the Confessing Church, but of the destiny of the Jewish "brothers of Jesus Christ."[26] Other scholars agree that Bonhoeffer's entry into the conspiracy was a long-postponed response to Nazi persecution of German Jews.[27] However, John de Gruchy notes that

> there is little actual documentary proof that Nazi anti-Jewish policies were a driving motive for Bonhoeffer's action. Even Bonhoeffer's famous statement "Only the one who cries out for the Jews can sing Gregorian chant" may be apocryphal; it was never written down and none of his students, including Bethge, could definitively pinpoint the occasion, or even year, when he made it.[28]

Regarding Bonhoeffer's motivations for resistance against the Nazi state, it is important to acknowledge that not all who defied Nazi power did so out of concern for Jews. This is true even for resisters who were religiously motivated. An excellent example of the ambivalence that anti-Nazi resisters could harbor toward Jews appears in the second leaflet of "The White Rose," the Munich resistance cell led by Hans and Sophie Scholl:

> We do not want to discuss here the question of the Jews, nor do we want in this leaflet to compose a defense or apology. No, only by way of example do we want to cite the fact that since the conquest of Poland *three hundred thousand* Jews have been murdered in this country in the most bestial way. Here we see the most frightful crime against human dignity, a crime that is unparalleled in the whole of history. For, Jews, too, are human beings—no matter what position we take with respect to the Jewish question—and a crime of this dimension has been perpetrated against human beings.[29]

These lines, fashioned to incite the "better part of the nation" to rebellion, are not exactly a ringing endorsement of the civil and political rights of Jews. Indeed, the italicized "three hundred thousand" might be read as compensation for the fact that the victims were, after all, only Jews. The leaflet continues, "Someone may say that the Jews deserved their fate. This assertion would be a monstrous impertinence; but let us assume that someone said this—what position has he then taken toward the fact that the entire Polish aristocratic youth is being annihilated?"[30] Even if Jews have gotten what was coming to them, the authors imply, surely the same cannot be said about the decimation of the Polish nobility.

While no one would deny the bravery of the Scholls and their associates, their words reveal why we cannot make assumptions about resisters' attitudes toward Jews based solely on the fact that they opposed the Nazi regime.

Victim

It is not inappropriate to view Bonhoeffer through the lens of victimhood, for his death was the ultimate price of his decision to oppose the Nazi regime. But in the context of post-Holocaust Christian-Jewish relations, Bonhoeffer's identity as victim must be carefully conveyed. First and foremost, it is important to distinguish those who, like Bonhoeffer, *chose* victimhood by virtue of conspiring to resist the Nazis from those who were *made* racial enemies of the state with the stroke of a pen. The fact that in 1936 Bonhoeffer could produce an "Aryan certificate" in an effort to retain his teaching position makes this distinction unmistakably clear.[31]

Because he was racially privileged, Bonhoeffer enjoyed a range of moral choices considerably broader than that of "non-Aryans." Lawrence L. Langer has coined the term "choiceless choice" to describe the moral universe in which many Jewish victims of the Nazis were forced to exist. Langer writes that these unfortunate persons "were plunged into a crisis . . . where crucial decisions did not reflect options between life and death, but between one form of abnormal response and another, both imposed by a situation that was in no way of the victim's own choosing."[32] We are often reminded that Bonhoeffer's decision to return to Germany in 1939 was made before "the terrible alternative of either willing the defeat of [his] nation in order that Christian civilization may survive, or willing the victory of [his] nation and thereby destroying our civilization."[33] This was a terrible alternative indeed; but as Bonhoeffer himself realized, it was one he could have made "in security." Thus it should not be equated with the truly choiceless choices faced by many European Jews.

Jewish responses to Bonhoeffer have stressed this very point. In 1960 Steven Schwarzschild wrote that although Bonhoeffer was "a true blood-martyr to Nazism,"

> our debt to the unnumbered martyrs of Israel requires the acknowledgement . . . that a German Christian, a relative and colleague of prominent German aristocrats, was treated differently, almost as a human being, even during the hours of his final and excruciating agony, than were they. This must be remembered, with all the

profound sorrow that we feel for every victim of barbarism if only because of the danger that a few heroes like Bonhoeffer may be abused by German and Gentile apologists to outshout the weeping of the Jewish people for its dead.[34]

Over twenty-five years later, A. James Rudin reiterated this Jewish caveat regarding Bonhoeffer's "martyrdom":

Dietrich Bonhoeffer, a well born, well educated German Lutheran, was killed by the Nazis, but quite clearly he could have chosen another path that would have spared him a prison execution. He had a choice, and he consciously chose to do what he did with full knowledge of the consequences.

But it was not so for the Jews. The learned and the ignorant, the well born and the lowly, the scholars and the students, the atheists and the believers, and, of course, the baptized and the unbaptized, every Jew was a target for the Nazi murderers.[35]

To his credit, Eberhard Bethge recognizes the difficulty of singling out Bonhoeffer's "martyrdom" in the context of immense Jewish suffering. In Flossenbürg on April 9, 1945, writes Bethge, Bonhoeffer, "out of his free will, had entered into full solidarity with those total victims who had no choice to avoid being murdered."[36] More generally, Bethge claims that because "Jewish passion" reduces Christians to silence in the wake of the Shoah, the stories of those we wish to commemorate must "be related to this Jewish travail."[37] But other Christian interpreters have not been so careful. Geffrey B. Kelly, for example, writes that "Bonhoeffer became a victim of the Holocaust in solidarity with his Jewish brothers and sisters."[38] And Clifford Green describes Bonhoeffer as "shar[ing] the fate of the Jews in the Third Reich," calling him "a victim like the six million."[39] Such affirmations blur the distinction between Aryan and non-Aryan victims of the Nazi terror and make an accurate assessment of Bonhoeffer's post-Holocaust legacy more difficult.

A second reason Bonhoeffer's identity as victim must be carefully expressed is that the designations "victim" and "survivor" often have been misapplied to Germans who harbored anti-Nazi attitudes but in fact remained bystanders. Since the end of the Nazi era, Germany has repeatedly been symbolized as a nation of helpless victims over whom a gang of criminals inexplicably gained control. More than half a century after the war's end, the allure of this victimization myth remains quite strong. Alf Lüdtke, a scholar of the German resistance, describes a personal epiphany he experienced while reading the letters German soldiers sent to their employers during World War II. Particularly striking was "how intensely the authors of the letters seemed to identify with both the Nazi policy of utter contempt for 'peoples of the East' and the actual killing of 'enemies' at the front line or in the *Hinterland*." Such documents raise serious doubts, Lüdtke concludes, about the claim "that the 'masses' in Nazi Germany were completely subdued and thus made victims to the dominant cliques and bureaucracies of state and party."[40]

Expressions of the victimization myth are often quite subtle. First published in Germany in the late 1940s, Inge Scholl's *The White Rose: Munich 1942–1943* reflects a conception of the Nazi experience very compatible with the victimization myth. In the leaflets of "The White Rose," as well as in the movement's story as chronicled by Scholl, languages of imprisonment and enslavement predominate. Descriptions of Germany under Nazi rule traffic in images of a criminal regime crushing a tyrannized populace, a gang of thugs who control, enslave, steal from, and imprison innocent citizens, an invisible cancerous growth, a tyrannous yoke, a band of demons and monsters.[41] Without diminishing the heroism of Hans and Sophie Scholl or their collaborators, it is instructive to observe how compelling it has been in the years since World War II to imagine Germans as helpless victims of a tyrannical Nazi mob.

This discussion reminds us that care is required in referring to German Gentiles as Nazi victims. While Hitler and his henchmen created many non-Jewish victims, the vast majority of "Aryan" Germans were not among them. However, despite not being a direct casualty of the Nazi racial worldview, by the time of his imprisonment, Bonhoeffer had achieved an exemplary solidarity with suffering Jews. When we consider his glib pronouncement in 1933 that Jews were destined to endure a "long history of suffering," it is clear that only his own suffering made such solidarity possible.

What do we learn from surveying Bonhoeffer's life in categories established by scholars of the Holocaust? Our study not only elucidates various possible responses to Nazi rule and the way these affected the twisted path toward Auschwitz; it indicates the ways Bonhoeffer's responses are similar to those of other Germans and the ways they are unique. Finally, viewing Bonhoeffer's career in terms of these categories indicates that the journey from bystander to resister was a gradual and complicated one. Encouraged by these results, we now turn to a more detailed exploration of Bonhoeffer's role as rescuer.

BONHOEFFER AND CHRISTIAN RESCUE

Bonhoeffer as Rescuer

We do not know precisely why Bonhoeffer decided to join the conspiracy against Hitler, but we do know that after doing so he became involved in a secret Jewish rescue operation that led eventually to his arrest and imprisonment. Thus Bonhoeffer's martyrdom was related not only to political resistance, but to rescue as well.[1] While friends and supporters have been engaged in a twenty-year-long endeavor to have these facts acknowledged by Yad Vashem, the Holocaust Martyrs' and Heroes' Remembrance Authority in Jerusalem, Yad Vashem's refusal to honor Bonhoeffer as a "Righteous Gentile" has opened up a post-Holocaust perspective on his legacy that is both problematic and embarrassing. The controversy not only has cast unwelcome attention upon Bonhoeffer's early anti-Nazi writings, but has publicized the official judgment that "there is no proof that [Bonhoeffer] was involved in saving Jews."[2]

But the decisions of Yad Vashem need not discourage us from speaking of Bonhoeffer the rescuer. As we saw in chapter 6, such descriptions are not titles so much as heuristic devices that aid us in exploring the varieties of human behavior during the Holocaust. Furthermore, Bonhoeffer's identity as a Christian rescuer is firmly rooted in the historical record and in the popular imagination. Historically, it is indisputable that the Nazi authorities would have taken Bonhoeffer's role in "Operation-7" quite seriously had they known its full extent. And the function of Bonhoeffer's rescue activities in Christian memory is clear in the dozens of novels, films, and dramatic productions that have appeared in recent years. For now at least, Bonhoeffer may be denied official recognition as one of the "righteous among the nations," but history and memory place him in the company of those Christians who risked their lives to aid Jews in the midst of the Nazi scourge.

Resisting the temptation to dwell on the reasons Bonhoeffer ought to be commemorated in Yad Vashem's Garden of the Righteous, we will ask how rescue research illumines Bonhoeffer's career in the German resistance, and what he has to teach us about the phenomenon of Christian rescue. As we consider Bonhoeffer's post-Holocaust legacy in light of the vast body of research on the behavior and motivation of Christians who aided Jews in Nazi-occupied Europe, we will be guided by questions whose trajectories form a sort of hermeneutic circle: How does our knowledge of rescue during the Holocaust illumine our understanding of Bonhoeffer? And how can Bonhoeffer broaden our fledgling understanding of religiously motivated rescuers? The second movement in this hermeneutic circle holds particular promise, since rescuers with explicit religious motivations were a small minority about whom we know relatively little.[3]

From Rescue Research to Bonhoeffer

Over three decades of sociological research on rescue in Nazi Europe have given rise to a composite picture of the experiences, sociological variables, and personality factors that were characteristic of rescuers across Europe. What does this research suggest about what Bonhoeffer may have in common with the "typical" person who risked his or her life on behalf of Jews?

One of the more provocative findings of psychohistorical research on Holocaust rescuers concerns socialization patterns among persons who later aided Jews. Among the prevalent socializing factors linked to rescue are accepting, affectionate, and communicative parental relationships; child rearing that de-emphasizes blind obedience, uses reasoning discipline, and eschews physical punishment; intense identification with a parent who is a strong moralist; the valuing of tolerance; absence at home of negative stereotypes regarding Jews (but not, interestingly, the presence of positive ones); the teaching of values such as "inclusiveness" (or a universal application of moral values), independence, self-reliance, competence, and high self-esteem; and the experience of childhood loss.[4] Remarkably, these socialization factors appear to be stronger predictors of rescue behavior than variables such as age, gender, occupation, social class, health, or political affiliation.

Upbringing alone does not account for altruism, of course. Rescue behavior was a function of socialization combined with favorable situational factors—such as contact with Jewish friends or coworkers and opportunities to take action on behalf of threatened Jews. The interaction of socialization, knowledge, and opportunity in the experience of rescuers is summarized by researchers Samuel P. Oliner and Pearl M. Oliner:

> It begins in close family relationships in which parents model caring behavior and communicate caring values. . . . Securely rooted in their family relationships, they risk forming intimate relationships outside it. . . . More open to new experiences, they are more successful in meeting challenges. Each risk they surmount strengthens their abilities to confront further challenges and confirms their sense of potency in affecting external events. . . . Personal relationships with the victims themselves encourage early awareness and empathic reactions. . . . Already more accustomed to view social relationships in terms of generosity and care rather than reciprocity, they are less inclined to assess costs in time of crisis. Already more deeply and widely attached to others, they find it difficult to refrain from action.[5]

Anyone familiar with Bonhoeffer's biography will recognize that this portrait of the altruistic personality applies in many ways to Dietrich and his extended family. Indeed, while he cannot be part of a controlled study, Bonhoeffer appears to share many of the *experiences* and *traits* characteristic of rescuers.

For example, he knew childhood loss (World War I had taken his brother Walter, whose Bible Dietrich inherited), grew up in an environment of social tolerance and liberal ideas, and was exposed to an expanding range of new experiences while traveling and living outside Germany. The anti-Semitism prevalent in post–World War I Germany was not tolerated in the Bonhoeffer home,[6] his siblings had close Jewish friends, and his family associated "as a matter of course with Jews at the levels of friendship, vocation and education."[7] Further, Dietrich was influenced by a strong moral figure who resisted anti-Jewish social pressures—his maternal grandmother, Julie Tafel Bonhoeffer, with whom he lived while a student at Tübingen, and who at age ninety-one conspicuously violated the boycott of Jewish businesses organized by the SA on April 1, 1933.

Finally, Bonhoeffer gained personal insight into the vagaries of Jewish existence under Nazi rule through his brother-in-law Gerhard Leibholz and London roommate Franz Hildebrandt, both of whom were of Jewish background.[8] Edwin Robertson argues, in fact, that for Bonhoeffer the Jewish Question was inseparable from the future of his twin sister, Sabine, and her husband, Gerhard. When in 1938 it became clear to Bonhoeffer that the Leibholzes would be forced to emigrate,

> the flight of Sabine affected him deeply. He believed that twins had a special affinity and the departure of Sabine, with whom he had shared so much when they were together as children, and even later when they were apart, affected him greatly. . . . When he spoke out for the Jews, or battled to keep them from further humiliation, he was like a knight errant fighting for Sabine.[9]

Hildebrandt offers his own assessment of the Bonhoeffer family's role in Dietrich's decision to resist Nazism: "In the midst of the general capitulation on the part of the German intelligentsia, the Bonhoeffer family, his parents, brothers, sisters and the old grandmother, stood with unclouded vision and unshaken will; their house in Berlin-Grünewald, soon my second home by adoption and grace, was an oasis of freedom, fresh air and good humor."[10]

Another brother-in-law, Hans von Dohnanyi, was Bonhoeffer's source of information about Nazi plans. It was Dohnanyi who informed Dietrich of the impending publication of the "Aryan laws" of April 1933, the preparation of the Nuremberg Laws in 1935, and Hitler's plans to go to war. If Bonhoeffer's parents' home in Berlin was his "information center," it was in large part because Dohnanyi was nearby with "a constant close-up view of the Nazis' evil deeds."[11] James Patrick Kelley notes that the data that formed the basis for Bonhoeffer's early analysis of Nazism "had been supplied over the preceding two years by his family and friends, especially Gerhard Leibholz and Hans von Dohnanyi."[12]

Thus, while it may be true that "at Bonhoeffer's cradle, in his family, in his confessional and national traditions there was no preformed inclination toward resistance,"[13] the Bonhoeffers fit the broad social-ization profile that emerges from rescue research. Dietrich's extended family not only contributed to a pattern of socialization conforming to that of many rescuers; they brought him specific *knowledge* of Nazi anti-Jewish measures and the *opportunity* to combat them. Thus, although it remains customary to view Bonhoeffer's anti-Nazi resistance as the journey of a man bravely struggling to overcome his background, in many ways that background provided the foundation on which resis-tance was built.

Models of Moral Courage

To name the relational capacity associated with rescue behavior, Oliner and Oliner have coined the term "extensivity." Extensive persons possess not only a strong sense of attachment to other people, but "a feeling of responsibility for the welfare of others, including those outside their immediate familial or communal circles."[14] Conversely, "constricted" persons isolate themselves emotionally, encounter little in the way of diversity, and begin to fear what is unknown. "When a crisis occurs in which the lives of outsiders are at stake, they detach themselves still further from any association with its victims, preferring to know as little as possible about their fate," the Oliners explain.[15] How central is exten-sivity for understanding altruistic behavior during the Holocaust? Once the Oliners had isolated this variable, knowing only whether a subject had an "extensive" or "constricted" orientation toward others enabled them to predict with 70 percent certainty whether or not that person had been a rescuer.

As we have just seen, Bonhoeffer appears to fit the model of the "extensive" altruist. Still, many find compelling the image of an iso-lated resister motivated only by personal courage, walking alone along a path leading to a personal Golgotha.[16] As George W. Bush put it in a recent commencement address, Bonhoeffer teaches us that "work of lasting value can . . . be done by a solitary soul, condemned and stripped of all power."[17] Perhaps this image of the soul in exile has clung so tenaciously to Bonhoeffer because it corresponds to the reigning model of moral courage, which calls for a solitary hero to defy convention and move bravely into the dangerous unknown. Oliner and Oliner argue that this image has dominated social-scientific research on altruism since the appearance of Teodor Adorno's study of "the authoritarian personality" in 1950. In the shadow of Adorno's influential study, autonomy and independence have been the traits said to make people least susceptible to fascism and most prone to resistance.

In 1970 Jeremy London extended the autonomy paradigm to rescue behavior per se when he concluded that "adventurousness" was the dominant trait of rescuers of Jews in Nazi Europe. In the 1980s Nechama Tec designated social "marginality" the chief predictor of rescue behavior. In *When Light Pierced the Darkness: Christian Rescue of Jews in Nazi-Occupied Poland*, Tec drew attention to "autonomous altruists" sharing a number of interrelated traits, including individuality/separateness and independence/self-reliance.[18] Tec characterized the Polish rescuers she studied as persons who did not fit into their social milieus:

> The less integrated into a community people are, the less constrained and controlled they are by the community's norms and values. Thus freed of constraints people are more likely to resist the pressures of the community and act independently. A high level of independence, then, implies a greater amount of strength and freedom to act in accordance with personal inclinations and values.[19]

In war-time Poland, this social marginality allowed "independent individualists" to heed a personal imperative to "stand up for the needy."[20] Other researchers have followed London and Tec in targeting individuality, self-esteem, and separateness as key features in the rescuer personality.

Why has autonomy so dominated scholarly apprehensions of moral behavior in general and rescue in particular? According to Oliner and Oliner, this model of moral courage is inherently appealing, particularly for those influenced by the American myth of the marginal hero: "The emphasis on autonomous thought as the only real basis for morality continues to enjoy widespread acceptance. . . . The lonely rugged individualist, forsaking home and comfort and charting new paths in pursuit of a personal vision, is our heroic fantasy—perhaps more embraced by men than women but nonetheless a cultural ideal." The Oliners conclude with a sentence that seems to have been written with Bonhoeffer in mind: "His spiritual equivalent is the moral hero, arriving at his own conclusions regarding right and wrong after internal struggle, guided primarily by intellect and rationality."[21]

Oliner and Oliner's own definitive study of rescue behavior with more than four hundred subjects (including surviving rescuers, rescued Jews, and a control group of nonrescuers) caused them to eschew this conception of the heroic ideal in which "individuals behave virtuously because of autonomous contemplation of abstract principles." Instead, they argue for a paradigm shift in our view of the character "type" most likely to show altruism in situations of crisis. In contrast to the picture of rescuers as autonomous, adventurous loners, they draw a portrait of community-embedded persons, "extensive" human beings who are led by socialization and experience to empathize with others.

In contrast to the images of autonomy, independence, and marginality commonly associated with these persons, Oliner and Oliner found that nearly every rescuer in their sample was involved in some kind of supportive network and that some—persons they refer to as "normocentric" rescuers—took part in rescue action in conformity with an influential person or group, whether family, church, friends, resistance networks, neighbors, or community leaders. In their initial helping acts, 52 percent of rescuers responded to a normocentric expectation rooted in a feeling of obligation to a group rather than in a direct connection with the victim. Normocentric rescuers, in other words, were more likely to be motivated by the expectations of a reference group than by sympathy or affection.[22]

By portraying rescue as an activity nurtured by communities, Oliner and Oliner have set in motion a radical shift in our understanding of altruistic behavior in situations of social crisis, one with implications for our understanding of Bonhoeffer. For in his case the general appeal of the "John Wayne" model of moral courage is combined with the specific attraction of Bonhoeffer the Christian saint and martyr, the "lonely resister . . . having to decide against his own people, against his own church, against commonly held beliefs [in] an intense inward struggle."[23]

It is true, of course, that Bonhoeffer's bold stand on the Jewish Question virtually isolated him even in the Confessing Church, that as a result he was compelled, as he put it, "to go for a while into the desert" of Great Britain, that he experienced various forms of exile, and that he lived without a permanent residence from the closing of Finkenwalde until his death, a life he himself described as "nomadic."[24] Yet the exilic existence forced upon him by circumstances should not obscure the fact that from the time of his first public address following Hitler's appointment as chancellor to his fateful involvement in a plot on the Führer's life, Bonhoeffer worked in concert with others. Nor should we forget that throughout this period he received direction, stimulation, and inspiration from family members and friends,[25] from ecumenical contacts abroad,[26] from an older "mentor" in Bishop George Bell, and from participation in a secret community of resistance.

When we are alert to it, the role of fellowship in Bonhoeffer's struggle against the Nazis becomes quite apparent. Following Martin Niemöller's arrest in 1937, Bonhoeffer reflected, "I must learn again how fortunate I have been until now always to have been in the company of the brothers. And for the past two years Niemöller has been alone."[27] Eberhard Bethge confirms the function of communal identity in Bonhoeffer's resistance when he writes that "in 1932 Bonhoeffer moved into the community . . . within the church that protested publicly with him. Nineteen thirty-nine led him into an even more restricted circle of kindred spirits."[28] These statements appear to reflect just the sort of group identification that Oliner and Oliner had in mind when they coined the term "normocentric."

Oliner and Oliner's substitution of caring empathy for adventurous autonomy as the defining trait of the altruistic personality creates a rich context for our depiction of Bonhoeffer the resister. And it forces us to ask whether the tendency to link moral courage with independence has given rise to misleading portrayals of Bonhoeffer as a moral "lone ranger" who discovered the resources for resisting political tyranny in the quiet autonomy of his own soul; whether these portrayals obscure the facts that throughout his life Bonhoeffer was nurtured by the church, ecumenical relationships, his role in a large family, and his experience as a fraternal twin; and whether these aspects of his identity have been obscured by a need to identify a free-standing moral hero untainted by the forces of evil so pervasive in Nazi Germany.

In other words, how might our memories of Bonhoeffer—and the articles, books, sermons, and commencement addresses they inform— be different if we approached his career under Nazism with the assumption that "moral decisions arise as much out of affiliation as through autonomous reasoning"?[29] Oliner and Oliner conclude their study by observing that the sort of courage displayed by rescuers "is not only the province of the independent and intellectually superior thinkers but . . . is available to all through the virtues of connectedness, commitment, and the quality of relationships developed in ordinary human interactions."[30] Realizing that as many as 80 percent of former rescuers of Jews in Nazi-occupied Europe express a sense of belonging challenges us to highlight these aspects of Bonhoeffer's post-Holocaust legacy.

From Bonhoeffer to Rescue Research

Shifting the direction of our inquiry, we now ask how Bonhoeffer's path of resistance for the sake of Jews might contribute to our perception of the larger population of Gentile rescuers, particularly those who appear to have been motivated by Christian faith. One of the more basic questions raised by rescue research is also among the most elusive. Apart from the sociological variables, personality traits, experiences, knowledge, relationships, and social conditions that predisposed men and women toward rescue, what can be said about their conscious motivations?

Generally speaking, Gentiles who risked their lives to protect Jews during the Holocaust were motivated either by *universalism* (an inclusive perception of the Jew as a human being possessing inherent dignity and worth) or by *exceptionalism* (an exclusive perception of the Jew as uniquely dear to God and thus fundamentally distinct from others). Among Christians who sacrificed their personal safety to defend Jews, these dynamics can be described in terms of *Christian humanism* (a general theological conviction that all human beings are endowed with basic rights) and *Christian philosemitism* (a unique theological obligation based in the identity of those in danger). The idea that those who resisted Nazi racism must have been motivated by universalist sentiments has appealed to Christian authors in search of clues to a faith that transcends exclusivism.[31] Yet research indicates that in many notable cases Gentile rescuers were driven not by universalist ideals but by a religious philosemitism that coexisted with quite traditional notions regarding Jews and their destiny.

Universalism

The emphasis on universalism in anti-Nazi resistance goes back at least to the work of Adorno, whose ideal anti-fascist personality—the "genuine liberal"—perceived others as individuals rather than as examples of a human type, and thus was neither a "Jew lover" nor a "Jew hater."[32] In all studies of rescue, in fact, a majority of subjects are classified as "moral" rescuers driven by "humanitarian motives." While these persons embody what we might like to think of as "Christian" values, moral rescuers tend not to draw explicit connections between their religious identities and moral sensibilities. Typically, they claim to have sheltered Jews because it was the right thing to do—indeed, what anyone would have done in similar circumstances.

Tec, the first scholar to publish a book-length study of the rescue phenomenon, concluded that the chief motivating factors for Poles who aided Jewish neighbors and strangers were a sense of individuality and a moral commitment to stand up for the needy. Although overwhelmingly Catholic, Polish rescuers did not perceive Jews through the lens of Christian theology, Tec found, but in terms of "universalistic perceptions . . . that defined them as helpless beings and as totally dependent on the protection of others."[33] She concluded that even the most pious Polish rescuers "seemed to be religious in a special way. They were independent in their interpretation of religious values, and this independence prevented them from blindly following the teachings of the Church." It is moral conviction, in other words, not religiosity per se, that is crucial to understanding them as rescuers.[34]

Tec stressed, in fact, that the moral imperative heeded by Polish rescuers was *humanistic* in the broadest sense—"help was to be offered to anyone in need, regardless of who they were."[35] The pivotal role played by this sort of humanism in Polish rescue was Tec's main finding:

> The fact that everything except the dependence of those who were aided seems to have faded into the background suggests that these helpers saw their obligations in the broadest terms—in applying the idea of man's obligations to help his fellow man. Moreover, the strength of this moral imperative, together with its universal quality, may in part explain why these Poles were willing to risk their lives for strangers and why they insisted that they did not see Jews as Jews but only as haunted, persecuted human beings in desperate need of aid.[36]

Oliner and Oliner's definitive study of rescue across Europe confirms the function of universalism as a motivating ideology, as almost half of rescuers in their sample cited a "universalistic obligation" among their reasons for rescue. In fact, one scale on which the parents of rescuers in their sample differed significantly from those of nonrescuers was their greater inclination to assess Jews as individuals as opposed to members of a group. "I did not help them because they were Jews," and "For us, people were just people," are comments that denote this inclination. Echoing Tec, Oliner and Oliner observe that where rescuers differed from others *religiously* was in their "interpretation of religious teaching and religious commitment, which emphasized the common humanity of all people and therefore supported efforts to help Jews."[37] They cite several rescuers whose comments are emblematic of such thinking:

> We all have the right to live. It was plain murder, and I couldn't stand that. I would help a Mohammendan just as well as a Jew.
>
> These people just had the right to live like other people—not just Christian people. Jewish people are the same—all people are the same.
>
> Jewish people had as much right to live as I did.
>
> It just happened to be Jewish people who were persecuted—it could have been anyone.
>
> We had to give our help to these people in order to save them. Not because they were Jewish, but because every persecuted human needs some help, just as my father found help when the Turks killed the Armenians.[38]

Not surprisingly, Oliner and Oliner found that rescuers were significantly more inclusive than nonrescuers in noting the groups to whom they felt an ethical obligation and more likely to emphasize that ethical values are to be applied universally. For those who believed strongly in justice, "the ethnic identity of the persecuted was irrelevant; what mattered was their innocence." Oliner and Oliner conclude that, at least for most rescuers, helping Jews was an "expression of ethical principles that extended to all humanity."[39] Eva Fogelman corroborates the notion that rescuers were often motivated by the opinion that Jews "were human beings . . . not something 'other.'" She too highlights the stories of rescuers like Theresa Weerstra, who looked at a little Jewish girl and saw "no difference between her and any of her own three children." For Fogelman, Weerstra represents the many rescuers who believed in a "common, caring kinship of humankind under God."[40]

In reviewing the literature, David Gushee delineates three sorts of moral-humanitarian motivation found among rescuers of Jews. Some acted nonreflectively on the basis of an emotional empathy for those who suffered, while more reflective rescuers employed either a language of "care" or "an inclusive, principled moral commitment to justice and human rights."[41] Gushee observes that among Christian rescuers, moral-humanitarian motivation often expressed itself in a conviction of the preciousness of every human life rooted in the doctrine of creation. In support of this view, he cites a French bishop who proclaimed that "all men [and women], Aryan or non-Aryan, are brothers [and sisters], because they are created by the same God." "Our Lord had created the Jew just as he had created me," said a Dutch rescuer. "Jews are men and women. Foreigners are men and women. It is just as criminal to use violence against [them] as it is against anyone else," wrote a French archbishop.[42]

Exceptionalism

All researchers, then, agree on the importance of a generalized reliance on universal ideals in guiding the altruism of Gentile rescuers. But when we look closely at the minority of rescuers who claim to have been motivated by faith—between 12 and 27 percent of samples in most studies—we encounter a category of motivation Gushee refers to as "a strong sense of religious kinship with Jews as a people."[43] This sense of kinship, which I refer to as "philosemitism," is distinct from the compassion toward other human beings described by many rescuers, religious and nonreligious alike.

Philosemites aided Jews not because they were people in need, but because they were God's people in need. Whether or not they proselytized their guests (and most did not), philosemitic rescuers regarded Jews' presence in their homes, farms, or towns in theological terms that issued in a religious obligation to protect them. Not surprisingly, this philosemitic impulse was often communicated to rescuees. Oliner and Oliner quote one rescued Jew who remembers that "Julian was a very good and decent man. He said that Judaism was the origin of all religions and that the Jews were chosen by God as the first people of the world."[44]

Christian subcultures in which philosemitism has been identified as a factor in encouraging resistance to Nazi anti-Semitism include French Protestant, Ukrainian Baptist, Hungarian Methodist, German Plymouth Brethren, and Seventh-Day Adventist. But the majority of evidence for the phenomenon of philosemitic rescue comes from the Netherlands. Among Dutch Reformed rescuers, Oliner and Oliner note, "all Jews had a special merit regardless of the behaviors or attitudes of individuals, for it was bestowed by God himself." This attitude is evident in some of the interviews they cite:

> When it came to the Jewish people, we were brought up by a tradition in which we had learned that the Jewish people were the people of the Lord.
>
> The main reason [we became involved in rescue] is because we know that they are the chosen people of God. We had to save them. We thought we had to do it—and then you risk everything according to that.
>
> Like I told you, we always liked the Jewish people because the Jewish people are God's people.[45]

The role of philosemitism in Christian rescue can be substantiated statistically as well as anecdotally. Lawrence Baron claims that although the Christian Reformed Church in the Netherlands represented only 8 percent of the country's population, it supplied 25 percent of Dutch rescuers.[46]

However, despite broad recognition of philosemitism's role in motivating rescuers, there is not a clear understanding of the phenomenon. In the popular imagination, it is considered the province of "evangelicals," largely through association with published memoirs such as Corrie ten Boom's *The Hiding Place*, the most popular account of the Holocaust among conservative Christians.[47] Scholars, meanwhile, describe religious "judeophiles" vaguely as "fundamentalist Christians, who grew up with biblical stories" and felt a "religious connection" with Jews.[48]

The Case of Le Chambon-sur-Lignon

Attributing Christian philosemitism to "fundamentalist Christians, who grew up with biblical stories" marginalizes the phenomenon and obscures its importance for understanding Christian rescue. It also ignores one of the most remarkable examples of religiously motivated rescue—Le Chambon-sur-Lignon. This Huguenot community in southwestern France was a mountain hamlet with a population of about five thousand people, who were responsible for saving as many as five thousand Jews during the war years. Research on Le Chambon has revealed that while the Chambonnais were influenced by the conscientious objection, pacifism, and anti-fascism of Reformed pastor André Trocmé, they also shared a sense of special obligation to Jews as God's elect.

Trocmé is quoted as responding to the attempted deportation of Jews with the words, "We do not know what a Jew is. We know only men."[49] These words suggest that Le Chambon was a place where universalism triumphed over any tendency to view Jews as exceptional. But there was also a strong undercurrent of philosemitism in Le Chambon. As Trocmé's assistant, Édouard Theis, explains in the documentary *Weapons of the Spirit,* "The Jews felt close to us because of our ties to the Old Testament, and we felt close to them because they were the people of the Old Testament." Like Trocmé, Theis was a confirmed pacifist, but his words imply that his decision to harbor Jews was as pro-Jewish as it was anti-collaborationist. As a Christian laywoman who was not a member of Theis's church remarks in the film, "For us they remained the people of God; that's what really mattered." Another Chambonnais reflects that "God is sending us these events, so that we can have contact with God's chosen people."[50]

In "Ten Things I Would Like to Know about Le Chambon," filmmaker Pierre Sauvage comments that some of the Jews rescued by righteous Christians in Le Chambon "never got over their astonishment at being not only sheltered but welcomed as the People of God."[51] Likewise, Philip Hallie, author of *Lest Innocent Blood Be Shed: The Story of the Village of Le Chambon and How Goodness Happened There,* tells of a female refugee who was asked by a peasant woman, "Are you Jewish?" Answering in the affirmative, the refugee was terrified of the consequences. But the woman responded by calling for her husband, to whom she exclaimed, "Husband! Look! We have in our home today a representative of the Chosen People." What Hallie calls the "supernatural dimension" of the Chambonnais' rescue activities should not be divorced from their history of being "always ready to help" those in need.[52] Yet it is clear that aid-giving to non-Jews would not have had the same meaning for them.

What are we to make of this complicated tension between a desire to assist fellow human beings in need and a special affinity for the Jewish people? At the very least, it demonstrates the coexistence of motivations for rescue that researchers have tended to categorize separately or even view as mutually exclusive.

Bonhoeffer and the Universalist-Exceptionalist Tension

What we know of Bonhoeffer's reasons for resistance seems to confirm what is suggested by the communal experience of Le Chambon—that despite the tendency to categorize rescuers by motivation, some were driven by a complicated recipe of humanist universalism and Christian philosemitism. Without doubt, Bonhoeffer's decision to resist Hitler was shaped by his involvement in the international peace movement, his commitment to ecumenism, and his opposition to military service. There is evidence, in fact, that humanist thinking was in the foreground of Bonhoeffer's decision to participate in the plot to assassinate Hitler. W. A. Visser 't Hooft recalls:

> In 1939 I was walking with [Bonhoeffer] up and down the platform of Paddington Station in London. Our discussion centered on the likelihood of his conscription when the Hitler regime started a war, and on whether he should not become a conscientious objector. How did it come about then, that he took that great decision to be actively involved in preparing the events which had their explosive effect on 20th July 1944? The answer to this question is that here too he could not stop midway. To reject the political system of that time in theory, to reject it by withdrawing into a spiritual realm, was not enough for him. Such an attitude was schizophrenia, it meant that the challenge was not taken seriously, it meant just talk, not action. That in the first instance the Church fought for its own preservation, filled him with sorrow. In a situation where millions of men were threatened in their

very existence, it was not a question of saving the Church. But it was mankind that had to be saved. The very conviction which had made him a man of peace, led him into active resistance.[53]

The idea that Bonhoeffer was driven by universalist principles seems to find support in the fact that his co-conspirators were inspired by secular morality rather than Christian conviction. Bishop George Bell's eulogy of Bonhoeffer in July 1945 portrayed him in terms of what he shared with these people:

> As one of a noble company of martyrs of differing traditions, he represents the resistance of the believing soul, in the name of God, to the assault of evil, and also the moral and political revolt of the human conscience against injustice and cruelty. . . . And it was this passion for justice that brought him, and so many others . . . into such close partnership with other resisters, who, though outside the Church, shared the same humanitarian and liberal ideals.[54]

Christian humanism alone, however, does not explain Bonhoeffer's decision to join the resistance. For there is evidence that Bonhoeffer's perceived obligation to oppose National Socialism increased in proportion to his awareness of the Jews' vulnerability under Nazism. From "The Church and the Jewish Question" (1933) to the marginal notes in his Bible following *Kristallnacht* (1938) to his statements in *Ethics* connecting Christ with the fate of European Jews, Bonhoeffer's path to resistance was accompanied by a deep-seated conviction that Jewish suffering held unique significance for Christians and called for a singular response. Ann W. Astell refers to this conviction when she claims that Bonhoeffer "was one of the rescuers who discovered the features of the crucified Christ in the persecuted Jews."[55]

Bonhoeffer's complex motivations for resistance should make us wary of interpretive paradigms that encourage thinking about rescue in terms of *either* a humanism so broad that it embraced much-despised Jews, *or* a commitment to protect Jews because of their special relationship with Christians through the Jew Jesus. The centrality and persistence of both impulses in Bonhoeffer—and among the rescuers of Le Chambon-sur-Lignon—imply that this is a false dichotomy.

In fact, testimony cited by Oliner and Oliner suggests that the inextricability of universalism and exceptionalism may be a common characteristic of Christian rescue. According to a Dutch rescuer interviewed for their study: "My background is Christian Reformed; Israel has a special meaning for me. We have warm feelings for Israel—but that means the whole human race. That is the main principal point."[56] Another of their interviewees explains: "My father taught me to love God and my neighbor, regardless of their race or religion. He had always had something special for the Jewish people. To be more precise, my father taught me to love God, to love my neighbor, particularly the Jewish people."[57] The paradoxical nature of these statements, unexamined by the researchers who record them, suggests that Bonhoeffer's amalgamation of humanism and philosemitism was not unusual among Christian rescuers during the Nazi years.[58]

Further, Bonhoeffer demonstrates that philosemitism should not be regarded as the province of "fundamentalists" or hyper-Calvinists. A French Catholic rescuer told researcher Eva Fleischner that "the religious education I had received had instilled in me respect for the Jewish people, and gratitude that they had given us the prophets, the Virgin Mary, Christ and the apostles. Jews were for me people of the Covenant, of God's promises."[59] A bishop of the Lutheran Church of Denmark proclaimed his opposition to persecution of the Jews because

> we shall never be able to forget that the Lord of the Church, Jesus Christ, was born in Bethlehem, of the Virgin Mary into Israel, the people of His possession, according to the promise of God. The history of the Jewish people up to the birth of Christ includes the preparation for the salvation which God has prepared in Christ for all men [and women]. This is also expressed in the fact that the Old Testament is a part of our Bible.[60]

If religious philosemitism can be detected in the testimony of Lutherans and Roman Catholics as well as urban evangelicals like Corrie ten Boom and rural Huguenots like the Chambonnais, it appears to be a more pervasive Christian phenomenon than Holocaust researchers have led us to believe.

Other or Brother?

Bonhoeffer's path to resistance on behalf of Jews can inform not only our understanding of rescue but our quest for a normative post-Holocaust Christian posture toward the Jewish people. Despite almost universal agreement on the need for Christian solidarity with Jews in the wake of the Holocaust, just how this solidarity ought to be conceived remains a perplexing question. Do Christians owe Jews special consideration as sibling children of God, the Father of Jesus Christ, or simply inclusion in the universe of human obligation? Should the church instill in Christian children a sense of religious kinship with Jews, or an attitude of compassion toward anyone in need?

In a world swirling with ethnic stereotypes and religious hatred, universalist perceptions of Jews are considered a welcome defense against the exceptionalist notions that have made Jews so vulnerable to anti-Semitic fantasies in the past. But if normalizing the image of the Jew in the Christian imagination is the church's principal post-Holocaust challenge, we must acknowledge that Bonhoeffer will be of little help in meeting it. For nowhere does he encourage Christians to view Jews *simply* as human beings whose rights must be respected. For Bonhoeffer, the Jew is always the other who is also Christ's brother; the other with whom is tied up the fate of the West; the other whose suffering reflects God's providence and whose treatment discloses the moral condition of church and society. Bonhoeffer's commitment to defend *Jews* may have formed the basis for a theology of solidarity with *others* more generally, but he never conflated the two categories.

In their attempts to fashion his legacy for a religiously plural world, some scholars have ignored the fact that for Bonhoeffer the Jew is always brother before being other. Robert Willis argues that through a growing emphasis on "the concreteness of the requirement of neighbor-love, which permits the Jewish neighbor, especially, to be encountered largely apart from a prior theological scheme that undertakes to 'place' Judaism and the Jewish people in relation to the church," Bonhoeffer successfully overcame the theological apprehension of Jews that clung to Barth's theology.[61] David H. Jensen emphasizes Bonhoeffer's relevance for a dialogical age by exploring the "interfaith promise" of his theology.[62] And Victoria Barnett discovers in *Letters and Papers from Prison* indications of a "real shift" in Bonhoeffer's thinking about Judaism, inasmuch as it contains reflections on the "changed role of Christianity in modern secular society."[63] But these arguments ignore the evidence cited throughout this book that long after 1933 Bonhoeffer continued to view Jews "in a quite special context," as he put it in "The Church and the Jewish Question." The details of this context shifted over time, but the assumption of Israel's unique importance for Christians did not.

If, on the other hand, Christians' post-Holocaust task is the challenge of recalling the unique bond Jews and Christians share in Jesus Christ, Bonhoeffer has much to teach us. At a time when Christians are encouraged to think of Judaism as a "world religion" encountered in the context of "religious pluralism," he reminds us that Christian theology properly reflects on the meaning of Israel when it relies on the language of election, covenant, and redemption. Can our picture of the post-Holocaust Bonhoeffer acknowledge this reality?

THE PARADOX OF BONHOEFFER'S POST-HOLOCAUST LEGACY

Exceptionalism and the Witness-People Tradition

Bonhoeffer's exceptionalism—his habit of viewing Jews as a people uniquely related to God and to Christians—is both the glory and the bane of his post-Holocaust legacy. It led him to claim the Old Testament for Christians when doing so was scandalous. It kept in sight for him the church's obligation to the "weakest and most defenseless brothers and sisters of Jesus Christ" and motivated him to speak out for the despised who were "the apple of God's eye." Ultimately, it led to his involvement in resistance and rescue activities that were nurtured by a philosemitism he shared with many European Christians.

Yet all this grew out of a theological tradition that claimed to understand Jewish identity and Jewish destiny better than did Jews themselves, a tradition that can be used to legitimize Jewish suffering, a tradition that inevitably perceives Jews through the lens of Jesus Christ the crucified Messiah and risen Lord. If these impulses seem hopelessly intertwined in Bonhoeffer's thinking, it is because the reprobationist and preservationist elements of the witness-people myth represent two sides of a potent ambivalence toward Jews that is ingrained in the Christian imagination. Is it possible to retrieve one side of the witness-people tradition in the absence of the other, to maintain a Christian exceptionalism whose implications for Jews are exclusively positive?

Mordechai Paldiel, director of Yad Vashem's Department for the Righteous Among the Nations, expresses his committee's disappointment that this would-be Righteous Gentile publicly condoned certain state measures against unbaptized Jews and upheld "the traditional

Christian delegitimization of Judaism, coupled with a religious justification of the persecution of Jews."[1] Richard L. Rubenstein responds
that in considering Bonhoeffer's words and deeds under Nazism, we
must keep in mind that the resources for his opposition to National
Socialism were located in his faith. As objectionable as we may find
Bonhoeffer's supersessionism, Rubenstein argues, "without it he would
have had no Archimedean point with which to transcend his culture
and oppose Hitler and National Socialism. Regrettably, that faith was
a seamless garment that included a harshly negative evaluation of Jews
and Judaism."[2] I know of no better description of the paradox that is the
post-Holocaust Bonhoeffer.

The depth of this paradox is indicated by Andreas Pangritz, who at the
1996 Bonhoeffer Congress in Cape Town, South Africa, responded to an
earlier version of my analysis of the witness-people myth in Bonhoeffer's
theology of Israel. Pangritz did not dispute Bonhoeffer's debt to this tradition but claimed that a "normalization" of the Christian-Jewish relationship was a liberal illusion. "Unlike Haynes," he wrote, "I would contend
that there is no possibility of 'normal' Jewish-Christian relations after the
Holocaust. What he calls the 'witness-people myth' will remain indispensable as long as the Bible has any relevance to theology, because it
is closely related to the theological concept of Israel as God's Chosen
People."[3]

It is rare that one agrees so wholeheartedly with one's critics. As a
Christian, I share Pangritz's suspicion of the "liberal" notion that the
church ought to respond to the Holocaust by exchanging an emphasis
on its unique organic relationship with Jews for a universal obligation
to protect the vulnerable. As a theologian, I agree with Pangritz that
the obligation to think theologically cannot be forfeited because Christians have failed in the past to discharge it responsibly. As an interpreter
of Bonhoeffer, I share the view that he was correct in maintaining that
the church cannot fathom the Jewish Question entirely in categories
of social morality.[4]

Finally, as a student of the Christian-Jewish encounter, I concur
that after the Holocaust it is misleading for Christians to speak of "normalizing" relations between the two peoples. For as long as Christians
approach the relationship with a biblical-theological mindset, the
witness-people tradition will indeed remain "indispensable" for the
church's reflection on the mystery of Israel. If there is another *Christian*

base from which to approach the Jewish people, I am not aware of it. If there is a way to construct a Christian theology of Israel completely apart from the witness-people tradition, I have not discovered it.[5] If there is an obvious solution to the tension between universalism and exceptionalism in Christian apprehensions of the Jews, it remains obscure.

Beyond Bonhoeffer

I do not think, however, that Christians are destined to recapitulate the perceptions of Judaism that have made Jews so vulnerable in the past—as long, that is, as we become more aware of the ways our theological impulses are implicated in a tradition that is fundamentally ambivalent about Jewish existence and virtually closed to Jewish self-understanding. Inasmuch as Bonhoeffer's legacy represents the pitfalls into which even the most compassionate and insightful Christians have fallen when theologizing about the Jewish people, it should serve to heighten this awareness. It remains an open question, however, whether Christians can learn from Bonhoeffer without reiterating the problems that are part and parcel of the tradition he represents.

Wayne Whitson Floyd Jr. argues that while Christians must learn from Bonhoeffer, we cannot allow ourselves the luxury of merely emulating him.[6] One way post-Holocaust Christians must surpass Bonhoeffer is in their willingness to engage Jews and Judaism on their own terms. Speaking of his realization that Christians had defined Jews "without listening and talking to the Jews themselves," Eberhard Bethge acknowledged that Bonhoeffer was little help in this process.[7] And Pangritz notes how remarkable it is that Bonhoeffer contributed to Christian-Jewish relations "without knowledge of Leo Baeck's theological works, without living Jewish interlocutors, and without an intimate knowledge of the Talmud."[8] What Christian admirers of Bonhoeffer must add to his putative "re-Hebraisation" of church and theology is the experiences that make Jews and Judaism living entities rather than theological or social abstractions.

Since the concepts of election and witness continue to shape Jewish self-understanding, Christians who listen to Jews may hear familiar affirmations that have the ironic effect of investing the Christian witness-people tradition with renewed credibility. This problem is evident among post-Holocaust theologians such as Paul van Buren and Franklin Littell, whose attentiveness to Jewish self-understanding has only strengthened their reliance on witness-people thinking.[9]

A Final Word

Based on the evidence in this study, Bonhoeffer the redeemer of post-Holocaust Christian theology seems to bear a striking resemblance to Bonhoeffer the father of Anglo-American radical theology. The initial enthusiasm generated by the radical portrait of the German theologian ultimately yielded to the realization that the depiction of Bonhoeffer by death-of-God thinkers was a creative misuse that ignored threads of continuity in his writings. This realization was hastened by the publication and assimilation of texts that undermined the edifice of the secular Bonhoeffer, chief among them Bethge's biography and Bonhoeffer's Christology lectures. When Bonhoeffer's prison writings were read in light of his life and his christologically framed theology, they took on an entirely new hue.

Similarly, published writings from across Bonhoeffer's career, when exposed to careful scrutiny, reveal that the Bonhoeffer who is heralded as a guide through the dilemmas of post-Holocaust Christianity may be no more credible than Bonhoeffer the Christian atheist. Both portraits, in fact, can be sustained only by ignoring significant continuities in Bonhoeffer's theology, continuities that are clear enough when we look for them.

NOTES

All URLs—dated and undated—were active at the time this book went to press. All references to the Bonhoeffer Archive are to the archival collection of Bonhoeffer materials at Burke Library, Union Theological Seminary, New York.

Preface

1. See Eberhard Bethge, *Dietrich Bonhoeffer: Theologian, Christian, Man for His Times: A Biography*, rev. ed., ed. Victoria J. Barnett (Minneapolis: Fortress Press, 2000), 267.

2. In a letter dated October 24, 1933, regarding a post at Lazarus Church in Berlin, Bonhoeffer wrote: "I knew I could not accept the pastorate I longed for in this particular neighborhood without giving up my attitude of unconditional opposition to *this* church, without making myself untrustworthy to my people from the start, and without betraying my solidarity with the Jewish Christian pastors" (Bethge, *Dietrich Bonhoeffer*, 232).

3. Bethge, *Dietrich Bonhoeffer*, 314–15.

4. Eberhard Bethge writes that "the verse 'Open thy mouth for the dumb' appears soon after Bonhoeffer's move from Berlin to London (fall 1933), and we find it repeatedly from then on in all sorts of connections." Bethge cites three examples of Bonhoeffer referring to the verse between January 1934 and August 1935. See "Dietrich Bonhoeffer and the Jews," in *Ethical Responsibility: Bonhoeffer's Legacy to the Churches*, Toronto Studies in Theology, vol. 6, ed. John D. Godsey and Geffrey B. Kelly (New York: Edwin Mellen, 1981), 43–96.

5. Victoria Barnett, "Dietrich Bonhoeffer," http://www.ushmm.org/bonhoeffer/b4.htm.

6. Of his time in London, Bonhoeffer wrote: "Besides my parish work, I have countless . . . visitors, most of them Jews, who know me from somewhere and want something of me" (Bethge, *Dietrich Bonhoeffer*, 330).

7. Ibid., 540.

8. Ibid., 631–32.

9. Ibid., 814–17.

10. In Berlin in September 1941 Bonhoeffer witnessed Jews wearing the yellow star and became aware that an elderly friend of the family was being evacuated to Theresienstadt. "The first day Dietrich Bonhoeffer collected all the facts he could confirm, to pass them on to sympathizers in the army command. [Friedrich Justus] Perels helped him get information from elsewhere in the Reich. By 18 October 1941 they had completed a report describing what was happening in Berlin, and mentioning similar proceedings in Cologne, Düsseldorf, and Elberfeld. On 20 October a more detailed report was concluded, and warned that further deportations were expected on the nights of 23 and 28 October. . . . Perels and Bonhoeffer gave the reports to Dohnanyi to pass on to Oster and Beck, in the hope that the military would either agree to intervene or accelerate its preparations for revolt (Bethge, *Dietrich Bonhoeffer*, 745–46).

11. Dietrich Bonhoeffer, *Letters and Papers from Prison*, enlarged ed., ed. Eberhard Bethge (New York: Macmillan, 1972), 194–45. See also Ruth Zerner's "Chronicle of Compassion and Courage," in "Church, State, and the Jewish Question," in John de Gruchy, ed., *A Cambridge Companion to Dietrich Bonhoeffer* (Cambridge: Cambridge University Press, 1999), 190–205; 197.

12. Pinchas E. Lapide, "Bonhoeffer und das Judentum," in *Verspieltes Erbe: Dietrich Bonhoeffer und der deutsche Nachkriegsprotestantismus*, ed. Ernst Feil (Munich: Kaiser, 1979), 116–30; 118. Translations of this work cited in this book are by the author.

13. *The Rule of Saint Benedict*, ed. Timothy Fry, O.S.B., Vintage Spiritual Classics (New York: Vintage, 1998), xxiii. Recent studies continue to demonstrate that continuity between intellectual reflection and personal commitment is central to Bonhoeffer's perennial relevance. See Keith Clements: "He overcame in himself...the dichotomy between intellect and activity—what in Christian contexts has been a faithless divorce between theology and commitment" (Keith W. Clements, *What Freedom? The Persistent Challenge of Dietrich Bonhoeffer* [Bristol: Bristol Baptist College, 1990], 10); Stanley Hauerwas: "Anyone who has read Eberhard Bethge's *Dietrich Bonhoeffer: A Biography* knows it is impossible to distinguish between Bonhoeffer's life and work" (*Performing the Faith: Bonhoeffer and the Practice of Nonviolence* [Grand Rapids, Mich.: Brazos, 2004], 34); Stephen Plant: "Bonhoeffer's writing only makes sense if read against the events which he lived because as much as for any theologian, his life and theology are intertwined" (*Bonhoeffer*, Outstanding Christian Thinkers Series [London: Continuum, 2004], x);

and Craig J. Slane: "In an age of asymmetry in belief and behavior, [martyrs] spawn hope that I might yet weave my own life into a unity of word and deed. . . . I want to illumine the passageway between belief and behavior with the use of martyrdom" (*Bonhoeffer as Martyr: Social Responsibility and Modern Christian Commitment* [Grand Rapids, Mich.: Brazos, 2004], 12, 119).

14. Renate Wind, *Dietrich Bonhoeffer: A Spoke in the Wheel*, trans. John Bowden (Grand Rapids, Mich.: Eerdmans, 1992), 70.

15. The phrase "the Jews" is used in this study because it is the phrase favored by those who have previously written on the topic. I place it in quotation marks here and elsewhere in order to indicate awareness of the essentialism it may imply.

16. While this is not Bonhoeffer's phrase, Eberhard Bethge does use it to describe Bonhoeffer's theological reflection on the meaning of Jews and Judaism. See especially "One of the Silent Bystanders? Bonhoeffer on November 9, 1938," in *Friendship and Resistance: Essays on Dietrich Bonhoeffer* (Grand Rapids, Mich.: Eerdmans, 1995) 58–71; 59, 63, 65.

17. Plant, *Bonhoeffer*, 9.

18. Franklin H. Littell, *The Crucifixion of the Jews: The Failure of Christians to Understand the Jewish Experience* (Macon, Ga.: Mercer University Press, 1986 [1975]), 51. See also Ruth Zerner, "German Protestant Responses to Nazi Persecution of the Jews," in *Perspectives on the Holocaust*, ed. Randolph L. Braham (Boston: Luwer-Nijhoff Publishing, 1983), 64–65.

19. Cited in Andreas Pangritz, "Sharing the Destiny of His People," in *Bonhoeffer for a New Day: Theology in a Time of Transition*, ed. John W. de Gruchy (Grand Rapids, Mich.: Eerdmans, 1997), 258–77; 275. Ruth Zerner makes a similar argument in her seminal article "Dietrich Bonhoeffer and the Jews: Thoughts and Actions, 1933–45," *Jewish Social Studies* 37:3–4 (Summer–Fall, 1975): 235–50.

20. Slane, *Bonhoeffer as Martyr*, 249, 97. In a similar vein, Slane writes: "On a clearly reasoned yet sophisticated theological foundation, Bonhoeffer freely brought his faith into the *polis*—brought his confession to action—entering into solidarity with and sacrificing himself for the Jews of the Holocaust, and thus, like Jesus, he laid down his life for others" (248).

21. Richard Rubenstein, "Was Dietrich Bonhoeffer a 'Righteous Gentile'?" paper presented at the American Academy of Religion and Society of Biblical Literature annual meeting, Nashville, November 20, 2000, 7.

22. Pangritz, "Sharing the Destiny of His People," 271.

23. A. James Rudin, "Dietrich Bonhoeffer: A Jewish Perspective," paper presented at the Evangelische Akademie Nordelbien, Hamburg, Germany, June 17, 1987, 16, in the Bonhoeffer Archive.

Chapter 1: Bonhoeffer and the Jews in Popular Memory

1. A mid-1960s turning point for attention to the Jews in Bonhoeffer studies is supported by a survey of the major critical and biographical studies of the period. John D. Godsey's *The Theology of Dietrich Bonhoeffer* (Philadelphia: Westminster, 1960) contains only a superficial discussion of "The Church and the Jewish Question" (109ff.) and has no index entries for "Jews," "Israel," or "anti-Semitism." However, Mary Bosanquet's *The Life and Death of Dietrich Bonhoeffer* (New York: Harper & Row, 1968) includes no less than twenty references to the "Jewish Problem"; Edwin H. Robertson's *Dietrich Bonhoeffer* (Richmond: John Knox, 1967) includes a brief section devoted to "the Jews" (26–28); and William Kuhns's *In Pursuit of Dietrich Bonhoeffer* (Dayton, Ohio: Pflaum, 1967) notes Bonhoeffer's "mild anti-Semitism" in 1933. The critical silence on "Bonhoeffer and the Jews" has not been entirely overcome, however, as Wayne Whitson Floyd Jr. notes in his discussion of Georg Huntemann's *The Other Bonhoeffer* in "Bonhoeffer's Many Faces," *Christian Century* (April 26, 1995): 444–45.

2. A. James Rudin, "Dietrich Bonhoeffer: A Jewish Perspective," paper presented at the Evangelische Akademie Nordelbien, Hamburg, Germany, June 17, 1987, 3–4.

3. See John S. Conway, "Historiography of the German Church Struggle," *Journal of Bible and Religion* (July 1964): 221–30; "The German Church Struggle and Its Aftermath," in *Jews and Christians after the Holocaust*, ed. Abraham J. Peck (Philadelphia: Fortress Press, 1982), 39–52; and "Coming to Terms with the Past: Interpreting the German Church Struggles 1933–1990," *German History* 16:3 (1998): 377–96.

4. Jürgen Fangmeier and Hinrich Stoevesandt, eds., *Karl Barth, Letters 1961–68*, trans. Geoffrey W. Bromiley (Edinburgh: T & T Clark, 1981), 250.

5. See Franklin H. Littell and Hubert G. Locke, eds., *The German Church Struggle and the Holocaust* (San Francisco: Mellen Research, 1990).

6. William Jay Peck, "From Cain to the Death Camps: An Essay on Bonhoeffer and Judaism," *Union Seminary Quarterly Review* 28:2 (Winter 1973): 158–76; 158. An earlier version of the paper was delivered at the first International Bonhoeffer Congress, Kaiserwerth, Germany, 1971.

7. John S. Conway, "Bonhoeffer, Dietrich," *Encyclopedia of the Holocaust*, ed. Israel Gutman (New York: Macmillan, 1990), 1:230–31.

8. See Renate Bethge, *Dietrich Bonhoeffer: A Brief Life*, trans. K. C. Hanson (Minneapolis: Fortress Press, 2004).

9. John W. de Gruchy, *Daring, Trusting Spirit: Bonhoeffer's Friend Eberhard Bethge* (Minneapolis: Fortress Press, 2005), xiii.

10. Ibid., 142, 210.

11. Eberhard Bethge, "Unfulfilled Tasks," *Dialog* 34:1 (Winter 1995): 30–31; 30. According to Clifford Green, it was the eighth edition of Bethge's biography of Bonhoeffer, published in 1994, that reflected Bethge's ongoing work related to the Jews. See Green's foreword to Eberhard Bethge, *Dietrich Bonhoeffer: A Biography*, rev. and ed. Victoria J. Barnett (Minneapolis: Fortress Press, 2000), x.

12. This evolution is evident in the volume of Bethge's collected papers published in 1979. See *Am gegebene Ort: Aufsätze und Reden, 1970–1979* (Munich: Kaiser, 1979). In this volume, according to de Gruchy, Bethge "seeks to interpret Bonhoeffer's legacy for today, reflecting on the *Kirchenkampf* and the significance of Auschwitz, anti-Judaism and anti-Semitism" (*Daring, Trusting Spirit*, 204).

13. Eberhard Bethge, "The Holocaust and Christian Anti-Semitism: Perspectives of a Christian Survivor," *Union Seminary Quarterly Review* 32:3–4 (1977): 141–55; 141. In this connection, Bethge mentions his friendship with H. G. Adler, an Auschwitz survivor, "from whom I have learned continuously since our first meeting in 1953" (149). Bethge also enjoyed a friendship with British Rabbi Albert H. Friedlander. See Friedlander's "Bonhoeffer and Baeck: Theology after Auschwitz," *European Judaism* 14 (Summer 1980): 26–32; 26.

14. De Gruchy, *Daring, Trusting Spirit*, 159.

15. Ibid., 165.

16. Ibid., 174–75.

17. Ibid., 176.

18. Eberhard Bethge, "The Legacy of the Confessing Church: Transporting Experience across Historical Turning Points," *Church and Society* 85:6 (July–August, 1995): 78–92; 82–83.

19. Ibid., 88.

20. De Gruchy, *Daring, Trusting Spirit*, 182.

21. In Keith W. Clements, *What Freedom? The Persistent Challenge of Dietrich Bonhoeffer* (Bristol, UK: Bristol Baptist College, 1990), 34.

22. Eberhard Bethge, "The Holocaust as Turning-Point," editor's introduction in *Christian Jewish Relations* 22:3–4 (1989): 55–67; 55.

23. In a discussion of Bethge's influence on perceptions of Bonhoeffer at the AAR/SBL Annual Meeting in 2005, Ruth Zerner supplemented de Gruchy's reading of Bethge's turn toward the importance of the "Jewish Question" by recalling some of Bethge's encounters with Jews in New York during the 1950s. These included reading Elie Wiesel's *Night*, meeting Wiesel, working in proximity to Jewish Theological Seminary, and encountering a Jewish banker who reacted emotionally to hearing Bethge and his wife conversing in German (Bonhoeffer: Theology

and Social Analysis Group, AAR/SBL Annual Meeting, Philadelphia, November 20, 2005).

24. Eberhard Bethge, "Research-Mediation-Commemoration: Steps to Combating Forgetting," in *Friendship and Resistance: Essays on Dietrich Bonhoeffer* (Grand Rapids, Mich.: Eerdmans, 1995), 106–7.

25. In Clements, *What Freedom?* 34.

26. Pinchas E. Lapide, "Bonhoeffer und das Judentum," in Ernst Feil, ed., *Verspieltes Erbe: Dietrich Bonhoeffer und der deutsche Nachkriegsprotestantismus* (Munich: Kaiser, 1979), 116–130.

27. Eberhard Bethge, "Dietrich Bonhoeffer and the Jews," in *Ethical Responsibility: Bonhoeffer's Legacy to the Churches*, Toronto Studies in Theology, vol. 6, ed. John D. Godsey and Geffrey B. Kelly (New York: Edwin Mellen, 1981), 43–96; 49.

28. For a recent citation of Lapide's statement, see Robert O. Smith, "Reclaiming Bonhoeffer after Auschwitz," *Dialog* 43:3 (Fall 2004): 205–20; 213.

29. De Gruchy, *Daring, Trusting Spirit*, 185–86.

30. Ibid., 191.

31. See Stephen R. Haynes, *The Bonhoeffer Phenomenon: Portraits of a Protestant Saint* (Minneapolis: Fortress Press, 2004), ch. 5.

32. In *Bonhoeffer*, directed by Martin Doblmeier (New York: First Run Features, 2004).

33. Dietrich Bonhoeffer, *Ethics*, "Editor's Introduction to the English Edition" Dietrich Bonhoeffer Works, vol. 6, ed. Clifford J. Green, trans. Reinhard Krauss, Charles C. West, and Douglas W. Stott (Minneapolis: Fortress Press, 2005), 4.

34. This statement appears in promotional material for the film *Bonhoeffer: Agent of Grace* (directed by Eric Till [Gateway Films, 1999]).

35. Michael Phillips, *The Eleventh Hour* (Wheaton, Ill.: Tyndale, 1993).

36. Ibid., 120.

37. Denise Giardina, *Saints and Villains* (New York: Fawcett, 1998), 12. See also 33, 96, 100, 112, 115, 116, 119, 124, 132, 135, 139, 142f., 157, 170, 173, 177f., 182, 213, 225, 234, 238, 241, 252, 255, 256, 268, 270, 276, 287, 291, 292, 294, 295, 302, 310, 321, 349, 398, 409, 418, 427, 435, 436, 438, 446, 451, 454–56, and 479.

38. Ibid., 216, 225, 270, 301, 272, 297, 298.

39. Ibid., 480.

40. Mary Glazener, *The Cup of Wrath: A Novel Based on Dietrich Bonhoeffer's Resistance to Hitler* (Macon, Ga.: Smith & Helwys, 1992). See, for example, chs. 3, 4, 14, 23, and 31.

41. Ibid., 140. In another episode some Nazi agents in search of a "Herr Libowitz" arrive at Bonhoeffer's door by mistake. After their departure, Bonhoeffer attempts to

contact Mordecai Libowitz and warn him (175–76). For her part, Giardina is careful not to overplay the success of Bonhoeffer's efforts to protect Jews. During his imprisonment, Dietrich's evil *Doppelgänger* Alois Bauer taunts him with the claim, "I've saved more Jews than you have" (*Saints and Villains*, 456).

42. Michael van Dyke, *Dietrich Bonhoeffer: Opponent of the Nazi Regime*, Heroes of the Faith (Ulrichsville, Ohio: Barbour, 2001), 30. According to Bethge, Bonhoeffer did not dissociate himself from the Hedgehogs until its pro-Nazi stance became clear after 1933 (*Dietrich Bonhoeffer: A Biography*, 49).

43. Andrew Chandler, "The Quest for the Historical Bonhoeffer," *Journal of Ecclesiastical History* 54:1 (January 2003): 89–96; 89–90.

44. Franklin H. Littell, *The Crucifixion of the Jews: The Failure of Christians to Understand the Jewish Experience* (Macon, Ga.: Mercer University Press, 1986 [1975]), 44–45. Littell relates this view of the Church Struggle to memories of Bonhoeffer: "And now the purveyors of cheap grace are beginning to use the faithfulness of a few Christians like Dietrich Bonhoeffer to boast of the church's record of courage in the face of the spiritual enemy!" (44).

45. Alice L. Eckardt, "The Holocaust, the Church Struggle, and Some Christian Reflections," in *Faith and Freedom: A Tribute to Franklin H. Littell*, ed. Richard Libowitz (New York: Pergamon, 1987): 31–44; 35.

46. Eberhard Bethge, *Bonhoeffer: Exile and Martyr* (New York: Seabury, 1975), 66.

47. Ibid., 110, 72.

48. Geffrey B. Kelly, "Bonhoeffer and the Jews: Implications for Jewish-Christian Relations," in *Reflections on Bonhoeffer: Essays in Honor of F. Burton Nelson*, ed. Geffrey B. Kelly and C. John Weborg (Chicago: Covenant, 1999), 133–66; 145.

49. For example, *Christianity Today*'s "This Week in Christian History" feature referred to the Confessing Church at least eight times between 2000 and mid-2002.

50. The Confessing Church Movement is "a continually growing, unstructured, grassroots collection of independently gathered churches and individuals within the Presbyterian Church (USA) that have agreed to assert the reaffirmation of three basic confessional statements": (1) that Jesus Christ alone is Lord of all and the way of salvation; (2) that Holy Scripture is the triune God's revealed Word, the Church's only infallible rule of faith and life; and (3) that God's people are called to holiness in all aspects of life, which "includes honoring the sanctity of marriage between a man and a woman, the only relationship within which sexual activity is appropriate." As of July 2005 the movement boasted 1,310 PCUSA congregations with 433,773 members. See "The Confessing Church Movement within the

Presbyterian Church (U.S.A.)," *The Layman Online,* http://www.confessingchurch. homestead.com/. For information on the confessing church movement within the United Methodist Church, see http://www.confessingumc.org/. Conservative forces in the Anglican Communion invoke the Confessing Church in similar ways: "The vast majority of the German Church rolled over to Hitler. It was a small band of confessing Christians under Dietrich Bonhoeffer that opposed Hitler and his co-opting of the church for state purposes." See David W. Virtue, "Opposing Views on Sexuality in North and South," *VirtueOnline: The Voice for Global Orthodox Anglicanism* (July 2005), http://www.virtueonline.org/portal/modules/news/article. php?storyid=2716&com_id=16451&com_rootid=14841&com_mode=thread&# comment16451.

51. See Haynes, *The Bonhoeffer Phenomenon,* 169–75.

52. Evan Silverstein, "Confessing Church Movement Grows Rapidly: Prospect of Per-Capita Withholding Gets PC(USA) Officials' Attention," *PCUSA News* (September 6, 2001), http://www.wfn.org/2001/09/msg00021.html.

53. William Stacy Johnson, "Regaining Perspective," *Presbyterian Outlook* 183:19 (May 21, 2001): 11.

54. Geffrey B. Kelly and F. Burton Nelson, *The Cost of Moral Leadership: The Spirituality of Dietrich Bonhoeffer* (Grand Rapids: Eerdmans, 2003), 118.

55. Stephen A. Wise, "Why Isn't Bonhoeffer Honored at Yad Vashem?" *Christian Century* 115 (February 25, 1998): 202–4.

56. Victoria Barnett, "Dietrich Bonhoeffer," publication of the United States Holocaust Memorial Museum, http://www.ushmm.org/bonhoeffer/b6.htm.

57. Wise, "Why Isn't Bonhoeffer Honored at Yad Vashem?" 203.

58. Ibid., 202.

59. Letter posted at www.cyberword.com/bonhoef (January 1999). Henry R. Huttenbach calls Paldiel's October 28, 1998, letter to Wise "a model of Bureau-speak and self-serving logic." See "Guarding the Gates: On Being a Survivor and Becoming a Righteous Gentile," *The Genocide Forum: A Platform for Post-Holocaust Commentary* 5:3 (January–February 1999), http://www.chgs.umn.edu/ Educational_Resources/Newsletter/The_Genocide_Forum/Yr_5/Year_5__No__3/ year_5__no__3.html#guardinggates. Daniel McGown suggests that perhaps the real reason for Yad Vashem's refusal to honor Bonhoeffer is the day of his execution, "three years to the day before the massacre" of Deir Yassin ("RighteousJews.org," http://www.williambowles.info/mideast/righteous_jews.html).

60. Marilyn Henry, "Who, Exactly, Is a 'Righteous Gentile'?" *Jerusalem Post* (April 22, 1998): 12. Victoria Barnett agrees with Hoffman's assessment of the matter: "I suspect that the real reason for Yad Vashem's decision is based upon

Bonhoeffer's connections to the *Abwehr* resistance circles operating out of Wilhelm Canaris' office. This is also probably why a petition (submitted during the 1980s) to recognize Hans von Dohnanyi was turned down as well. . . . Whatever their innermost thoughts or convictions may have been, these individuals continued to be high-ranking members of the Nazi machine well into the war" ("Response to Richard L. Rubenstein," paper presented at the AAR/SBL Annual Meeting, Nashville, November 20, 2000).

61. Richard L. Rubenstein, "Was Dietrich Bonhoeffer a 'Righteous Gentile'?" paper presented at the AAR/SBL Annual Meeting, Nashville, November 20, 2000. An earlier version of the paper was published in the *International Journal on World Peace* 17:2 (2000). The significant role played by Bonhoeffer's theology of the Jews in Paldiel's view of the case is clear in a document titled "Bonhoeffer Dietrich, Germany–File 890, Analysis of the Case and the Evidential Material," compiled by Mordechai Paldiel, dated April 30, 2001, and shared with the author by Stephen Wise.

62. Richard L. Rubenstein, "Was Dietrich Bonhoeffer a 'Righteous Gentile'?" 7, 10. Responses to Rubenstein's presentation were offered by Robert Ericksen and Victoria Barnet, scholars possessing both interest and expertise in this matter. Ericksen admitted that in the aftermath of the Holocaust "we feel a special need for heroes. But we must balance our desire for heroes with some sense of the magnitude of the disaster." With respect to Bonhoeffer, he concluded that while he may have been good at opposing Hitler and National Socialism, "it is less certain that he was good on the 'Jewish Question'" ("Response to Richard L. Rubenstein," AAR/SBL Annual Meeting, Nashville, November 20, 2000).

63. The heading on the main page of "holocaust-heroes.com" reads simply "Bonhoeffer Deserves to Be Named 'Righteous among the Nations.'" The site features background on the designation "Righteous Gentile" as bestowed by Yad Vashem's Commission for the Designation of the Righteous; summarizes the argument made by Bonhoeffer's petitioners that he "clearly risked his life in numerous ways to save Jews"; and claims that he was never really a member of German counterintelligence. The site also includes excerpts from Eberhard Bethge's affidavit in support of Bonhoeffer's candidacy.

64. While concluding that he "did not save any Jews," the Yad Vashem press release acknowledged that Bonhoeffer referred a convert to the care of his brother-in-law von Dohnanyi for inclusion in "Operation-7" and in 1937 assisted in the emigration of the Leibholzes. In April 1933 he justified the persecution of Jews from a theological perspective, and he was arrested and executed for his opposition to the Nazi regime. Wise is referred to as "a person who did not know" Bonhoeffer,

whose support is based on the fact that "following the war he became a symbol of pure Christian resistance to the Nazis and paid with his life" (October 2, 2003, http://www1.yadvashem.org/about_yad/press_room/press_releases/Court.html).

Chapter 2: Bonhoeffer and the Jews in Scholarship

1. Stephen S. Schwarzschild, "Survey of Current Theological Literature: 'Liberal Religion (Protestant),'" *Judaism* 9 (August 1960): 366–71; 366–67. Schwarzschild notes that Bonhoeffer's "polemic against Karl Barth . . . sounds very familiar to the Jewish ear."

2. Eugene B. Borowitz, "Current Theological Literature: Bonhoeffer's World Comes of Age," *Judaism* 14:1 (Winter 1965): 81–87; 82.

3. Stephen S. Schwarzschild, "Bonhoeffer and the Jews," *Commonweal* 83:3 (November 26, 1965): 227, 253–54.

4. Emil L. Fackenheim, "On the Self-Exposure of Faith to the Modern-Secular World: Philosophical Reflections in the Light of Jewish Experience," in *The Quest for Past and Future: Essays in Jewish Theology* (Bloomington: Indiana University Press, 1968), 278–305; 282–83.

5. Ibid., 284.

6. Ibid. See Fackenheim's comments on the matter in 1977, when he referred to Bonhoeffer as "that great saint" and opined that "if there will still be a world 2000 years from now," those who will be heard will include "those among our Christian friends who represent today the spirit of that great saint, Dietrich Bonhoeffer"; and 1994, when he wrote that "Bonhoeffer, if he had lived, would probably be the greatest theological friend we have today." See Emil L. Fackenheim, "Fackenheim on Bonhoeffer," *Newsletter of the International Bonhoeffer Society for Archive and Research, English Language Section* 11 (November 1977): 2–4; 3, 4; and Joshua O. Haberman, *The God I Believe In: Conversations about Judaism* (New York: Free Press, 1994), 40.

7. Fackenheim, "On the Self-Exposure of Faith to the Modern-Secular World," 318–19n24. In a subsequent publication, Fackenheim mentioned a letter he received from Bethge in 1979 that claimed Bonhoeffer "belongs to those making possible a [Christian] theology [after the Holocaust]," and this despite the fact that "to expect such a theology from him is impossible." "I agree with this assessment" was Fackenheim's response. See *To Mend the World: Foundations of Post-Holocaust Jewish Thought* (New York: Schocken, 1982), 293.

8. Emil L. Fackenheim, "(Kritik) Besprechung," review of *Konsequenzen: Dietrich Bonhoeffers Kirchenverständnis Heute*, ed. Ernst Feil and Ilse Tödt, and *Ethik im Ernstfall: Dietrich Bonhoeffers Stellung zu den Juden und ihre Aktualität*, ed.

Wolfgang Huber and Ilse Tödt, *IBK Bonhoeffer Rundbrief* 20 (November 1985): 16–18; 16.

9. Eva Fleischner, *Judaism in German Christian Theology since 1945: Christianity and Israel Considered in Terms of Mission,* American Theological Library Association Monograph Series 8 (Metuchen, N.J.: Scarecrow, 1975), 24–25.

10. Pinchas E. Lapide, "Bonhoeffer und das Judentum," in *Verspieltes Erbe: Dietrich Bonhoeffer und der deutsche Nachkriegsprotestantismus,* ed. Ernst Feil (Munich: Kaiser, 1979), 116–30.

11. Ibid., 118.

12. Ibid., 126.

13. Ibid., 128.

14. Ibid., 117.

15. Ibid., 122.

16. Ibid., 119, 123, 124, 130.

17. Ibid., 124.

18. Stanley R. Rosenbaum, "Dietrich Bonhoeffer: A Jewish View," *Journal of Ecumenical Studies* 18:2 (Spring 1981): 301–7; 301.

19. Ibid., 303.

20. Ibid., 306. Fackenheim also complains of Bonhoeffer's ignorance of Jewish thought past and present. See "(Kritik) Besprechung," 17.

21. Ibid., 305.

22. Ibid., 307. Several years later, *The Jewish Spectator* took note of Rosenbaum's article, opining that "Jews familiar with the life of Dietrich Bonhoeffer, the Protestant theologian murdered by the Nazis because of his resistance to Hitler and his hordes, will be shocked to learn that Bonhoeffer, who was involved in a plot to assassinate Hitler and who helped his baptized brother-in-law and fourteen prominent Jews to escape from Germany, regarded Judaism as obsolete and Jews as in need of salvation by baptism." See *The Jewish Spectator,* "Bonhoeffer and Judaism" (Winter 1985–Spring 1986): 65.

23. A. James Rudin, "Dietrich Bonhoeffer: A Jewish Perspective," paper presented at the Evangelische Akademie Nordelbien, Hamburg, Germany, June 17, 1987, 1, in the Bonhoeffer Archive.

24. Ibid., 10.

25. Ibid., 13. Rudin's comments concerning the other side of the Bonhoeffer coin are dependent on the work of Walter Harrelson, Ruth Zerner, Emil Fackenheim, and Richard Rubenstein; however, they do reflect the way reservations about Bonhoeffer have reverberated through the Jewish community.

26. Ibid., 14–15.

27. Ibid., 16–17.

28. Albert H. Friedlander, "Israel and Europe: Meditations for the Bonhoeffer Conference, 15.6.88," paper presented at the International Bonhoeffer Congress, Amsterdam, 7, 8, in the Bonhoeffer Archive.

29. Ibid., 4.

30. Albert H. Friedlander, "Bonhoeffer and Baeck: Theology after Auschwitz," *European Judaism* 14 (Summer 1980): 26–32; 30, 31.

31. Richard L. Rubenstein and John K. Roth, *Approaches to Auschwitz: The Holocaust and Its Legacy* (Louisville: Westminster John Knox, 2003). That Rubenstein is primarily responsible for the section of the revised edition on Bonhoeffer (262–65) can be demonstrated by comparing it to his paper "Was Dietrich Bonhoeffer a 'Righteous Gentile'?" presented at the AAR/SBL Annual Meeting, Nashville, November 20, 2000, and published in the *International Journal for World Peace* 17:2 (2000).

32. Rubenstein finds "no evidence that Bonhoeffer manifested any curiosity concerning Jews or Judaism during his 1930–31 stay in America" ("Was Dietrich Bonhoeffer a 'Righteous Gentile'?" 8).

33. Rubenstein and Roth, *Approaches to Auschwitz*, 264.

34. Richard L. Rubenstein, "Dietrich Bonhoeffer and Pope Pius XII," in *The Century of Genocide: Selected Papers from the 30th Anniversary Conference of the Annual Scholars' Conference on the Holocaust and the Churches*, ed. Daniel J. Curran Jr., Richard Libowitz, and Marcia Sachs Littell (Merion Station, Pa.: Merion Westfield, 2002), 193–218; 202.

35. Irving Greenberg, "Partnership in the Covenant: Dietrich Bonhoeffer and the Future of Jewish-Christian Dialogue," 2, paper presented at the Sixth International Bonhoeffer Congress, New York, 1992, in the Bonhoeffer Archive.

36. Ibid., 11, 12.

37. Walter Harrelson, "Bonhoeffer and the Bible," in *The Place of Bonhoeffer: Problems and Possibilities in His Thought*, ed. Martin E. Marty (New York: Association Press, 1962), 115–39.

38. Ibid., 131.

39. Ibid., 129–30 (emphasis in the original). In 1975 Frances I. Andersen reached a similar conclusion relative to a Bonhoeffer sermon outline on Isaiah 53: "Not a single exegetical issue is faced or argued. He does not seem to be interested in the historical meaning of the passage. When he says that the finger of the Prophet points to Christ, this is of course what Christians have believed from the beginning." See "Dietrich Bonhoeffer and the Old Testament," *Reformed Theological Review* 34:2 (May–August 1975): 33–44; 43.

40. Ibid., 132. See Harrelson's discussion of Bonhoeffer's prison letters, 133ff.

41. William Jay Peck, "From Cain to the Death Camps: An Essay on Bonhoeffer and Judaism," *Union Seminary Quarterly Review* 28:2 (Winter 1973): 158–76; 158.

42. Ibid., 169.

43. Ibid., 172.

44. Ibid. Peck dismisses "mythological" aspects of Bonhoeffer's theology (such as his 1933 claim that "the chosen people who nailed the Savior of the world to the cross must bear the curse for their deed during a long history of suffering") yet cites approvingly sections from Bonhoeffer's *Ethics* that reiterate the "witness-people myth" that will be analyzed in chapter 3.

45. Ibid., 162.

46. Zerner's paper was published the following year as "Dietrich Bonhoeffer and the Jews: Thoughts and Actions, 1933–1945," *Jewish Social Studies* 37:3–4 (1975): 235–50.

47. Ibid., 236.

48. Ibid., 241.

49. Ibid., 248.

50. Ibid., 250.

51. Ibid., 249.

52. Bethge, "Dietrich Bonhoeffer and the Jews," in *Ethical Responsibility: Bonhoeffer's Legacy to the Churches*, Toronto Studies in Theology, vol. 6, ed. John D. Godsey and Geffrey B. Kelly (New York: Edwin Mellen, 1981), 43–96. This is the published version of a paper presented at the Third International Bonhoeffer Congress, Oxford, 1980.

53. Ibid., 45–46.

54. "The young Bonhoeffer, as far as I can discern, did not establish links during the twenties with that Jewish revival which is so spectacular in its religious and philosophical meaning for us today, and which at that time was going on, so to speak, just around the corner, centering upon names such as Franz Rosenzweig, Martin Buber, Eugen Rosenstock and Leo Baeck" (Bethge, "Dietrich Bonhoeffer and the Jews," 52).

55. Ibid., 54–55. The quotation is from student notes taken at a "Contemporary Theology" lecture given by Bonhoeffer in 1932–33.

56. Ibid., 56.

57. Ibid., 60. Evidence that Bonhoeffer transcended curse theology in this essay is offered in the claims that his statements regarding divine judgment are not employed to justify Jews' social disenfranchisement, but to fight against it; and that they are not intended as independent statements about the Jews, but as a warning to the church.

58. Ibid., 62.

59. Ibid., 63.

60. Ibid., 65.

61. Ibid., 67.

62. Ibid., 75.

63. Ibid., 76.

64. Ibid., 80.

65. Ibid., 82.

66. Ibid., 83.

67. Ibid., 90.

68. Robert E. Willis, "Bonhoeffer and Barth on Jewish Suffering: Reflections on the Relationship between Theology and Moral Sensibility," *Journal of Ecumenical Studies* 24:4 (Fall 1987): 598–615.

69. Ibid., 601.

70. Ibid., 603.

71. Ibid., 605.

72. Ibid., 608.

73. What emerges in *Church Dogmatics*, according to Willis, "is that curious species, *Judaeos theologicum*, which bears no relationship whatever to real Jews" ("Bonhoeffer and Barth on Jewish Suffering," 612).

74. Ibid., 615.

75. Edwin Robertson, "A Study of Dietrich Bonhoeffer and the Jews, January–April, 1933," 121–29, and James Patrick Kelley, "The Best of the German Gentiles: Dietrich Bonhoeffer and the Rights of Jews in Hitler's Germany," 80–92, in *Remembering for the Future: Working Papers and Addenda*, vol. 1, *Jews and Christians during and after the Holocaust*, ed. Yehuda Bauer et al. (Oxford: Pergamon, 1989). Robertson's essay was later published as "A Study of Dietrich Bonhoeffer and the Jews, January–April, 1933" in *Bonhoeffer's Ethics: Old Europe and New Frontiers*, ed. Guy Carter, René van Eyden, Hans-Dirk van Hoogstraten, and Jurjen Wiersma (Kampen, Netherlands: Kok Pharos, 1991), 121–30.

76. Robertson, "A Study of Dietrich Bonhoeffer and the Jews, January–April, 1933," 126.

77. Ibid., 126.

78. Ibid., 128.

79. Kelley, "The Best of the German Gentiles," 87.

80. Ibid., 89.

81. Christine-Ruth Müller, *Dietrich Bonhoeffers Kampf gegen die nationalsozialistische Verfolgung und Vernichtung der Juden: Bonhoeffers Haltung zur Juden-*

frage im Vergleich mit Stellungnahmen aus der evangelischen Kirche und Kreisen des deutschen Widerstandes, Heidelberger Untersuchungen zu Widerstand, Judenverfolgung und Kirchenkampf im Dritten Reich, Band 5 (München: Kaiser, 1990). Translations of this work cited in this book are by the author.

82. Ibid., 17.

83. Ibid., 49.

84. See, for example, Christian Gremmels's contribution to a volume of essays from the Sixth International Bonhoeffer Congress, New York, 1992, "Bonhoeffer, the Churches, and Jewish-Christian Relations," in *Theology and the Practice of Responsibility: Essays on Dietrich Bonhoeffer*, ed. Wayne Whitson Floyd Jr. and Charles Marsh (Valley Forge, Pa: Trinity Press International, 1994), 295–305; and F. Burton Nelson's article in the proceedings of the 1985 Scholars' Conference, "Dietrich Bonhoeffer and the Jews: An Agenda for Exploration and Contemporary Dialogue," in *The Holocaust Forty Years After*, ed. Marcia Littell, Richard Libowitz, and Evelyn Bodek Rosen (Lewiston, N.Y.: Edwin Mellen, 1989), 87–93.

85. Alejandro Zorzin, "Church versus State: Human Rights, the Church, and the Jewish Question," in *Bonhoeffer for a New Day: Theology in a Time of Transition*, ed. John W. de Gruchy (Grand Rapids, Mich.: Eerdmans, 1997), 236–57.

86. Cited in ibid., 246.

87. Ibid., 248.

88. Ibid., 257.

89. Ibid.

90. Andreas Pangritz, "Sharing the Destiny of His People," in *Bonhoeffer for a New Day: Theology in a Time of Transition*, 258–77.

91. Andreas Pangritz, "'Mystery and Commandment' in Leo Baeck and Dietrich Bonhoeffer," *European Judaism* 30:2 (Autumn 1997): 44–57.

92. Ibid., 45. Pangritz identifies common ground between Baeck and Bonhoeffer in their loyalty to Prussia and the Prussian "idea" that perished in World War I, in "a common ambiguity in their loyalty to Germany as the locus of responsibility still under the conditions of the Nazi State" (46), and in the similar formulations found in Baeck's *The Essence of Judaism* and Bonhoeffer's *Discipleship* and *Letters and Papers from Prison*. The major difference between the two thinkers, according to Pangritz, is that while Baeck's thinking was in continuity with his tradition, Bonhoeffer's later theology was consciously in conflict with his own (53). Pinchas Lapide, too, imagines how enriching an encounter between these two prisoners would have been ("Bonhoeffer und das Judentum," 122).

93. Ibid., 53.

94. Jane Pejsa, ". . . They Burned All the Meeting Places of God in the Land," in *Reflections on Bonhoeffer: Essays in Honor of F. Burton Nelson*, ed. Geffrey B. Kelly and C. John Weborg (Chicago: Covenant, 1999), 129–32; 129.

95. Ibid., 130, 131.

96. Geffrey B. Kelly, "Bonhoeffer and the Jews: Implications for Jewish-Christian Relations," in *Reflections on Bonhoeffer: Essays in Honor of F. Burton Nelson*, 133–66; 135, 137.

97. Ibid., 158.

98. Robert O. Smith, "Reclaiming Bonhoeffer after Auschwitz," *Dialog* 43:3 (Fall 2004): 205–20; 213.

99. Ibid., 218.

100. Ibid., 215.

101. Among the scholars who cite Bethge's conclusion that "Bonhoeffer's primary motivation for entering the active political conspiracy was the treatment of Jews at the hands of the Nazis" are F. Burton Nelson, "Dietrich Bonhoeffer and the Jews: An Agenda for Exploration and Contemporary Dialogue," in *The Holocaust Forty Years After*, 88; Geffrey B. Kelly, "Bonhoeffer and the Jews: Implications for Jewish-Christian Relations," 133–66; 156; Geffrey B. Kelly and F. Burton Nelson, *The Cost of Moral Leadership: The Spirituality of Dietrich Bonhoeffer* (Grand Rapids, Mich.: Eerdmans, 2003), 22; and Clifford Green, "The Holocaust and the First Commandment" (1992), 7, in the Bonhoeffer Archive. The influence of Bethge is less traceable but no less real in the work of scholars like Larry Rasmussen, whose 1972 study on Bonhoeffer's "great decision to be actively involved in preparing the events that had their explosive effect on July 20, 1944," barely mentions Jews, but who in 1995 was claiming that Bonhoeffer "joined the conspiracy against Hitler in large part *because of* German crimes against the Jews." See Larry L. Rasmussen, *Dietrich Bonhoeffer: Reality and Resistance*, Studies in Christian Ethics (Nashville: Abingdon, 1972); and Larry L. Rasmussen, "Dietrich Bonhoeffer and the Holocaust: Lessons for Lutherans," in *Planning for the Future: LECNA at 85, Papers and Proceedings of the 81st Annual Meeting of the Lutheran Education Conference of North America* (Washington, D.C.: LECNA, 1995), 6–17; 7 (emphasis in original).

102. Bethge, "Dietrich Bonhoeffer and the Jews," 45–46.

103. Wolfgang Gerlach, *And the Witnesses Were Silent: The Confessing Church and the Persecution of the Jews*, ed. and trans. Victoria J. Barnett (Lincoln: University of Nebraska Press, 2000), 27.

104. Clifford Green, "The Holocaust and the First Commandment" (1992), 5–6, in the Bonhoeffer Archive.

105. In a letter from Stephen Wise to Yehuda Bauer, David Bankier, and Mordecai Paldiel (March 19, 2001), shared with the author. In his campaign to have Bonhoeffer recognized by Yad Vashem, Wise has solicited testimony affirming Bonhoeffer's concern for unbaptized Jews from Franklin H. Littell, Rabbi Balfour Brickner, and Gerhart M. Riegner, among others.

106. Bethge, *Dietrich Bonhoeffer: A Biography*, 273, 276.

107. Ibid., 486, 488, 489.

108. For instance, Elizabeth Raum writes that the *Bethel Confession* "issued a strong call for the church to remain true to the Bible. It presented a theological argument that recognized Israel as the Holy Land and the Jews as God's people." See *Dietrich Bonhoeffer: Called by God* (New York: Continuum, 2002), 75.

109. Geffrey B. Kelly, *Liberating Faith: Bonhoeffer's Message for Today* (Minneapolis: Augsburg Publishing House, 1984), 99.

110. Smith, "Reclaiming Bonhoeffer after Auschwitz," 212, 215.

111. In a remarkable document submitted as part of Stephen Wise's petition to have Bonhoeffer honored as a Righteous Gentile by Yad Vashem, Anneliese Schnurmann, aware that Bonhoeffer's 1933 essay on the Jewish Question represents a barrier to his case, writes: "I distinctly recall [Bonhoeffer] saying to me at various times during 1933 that his remarks about the 'curse' and 'deicide' were wrong . . . , that he had refused to sign the Bethel Confession because it was not clear enough in condemning the Nazis' terror against the Jews in August of 1933, and that he had had to battle hard to obtain the passage at the conference in Sofia of the resolution which did 'deplore . . . the State measures against the Jews in Germany in September of 1933.' In my conversations with him, I could tell how deeply he felt these statements and that they were genuinely stated, not just for my benefit as a Jew. And he made other such statements as occasions of Nazi terror occurred over the years" (affidavit dated March 19, 2001, and shared with the author by Stephen Wise).

112. Charlotte Klein, *Anti-Judaism in Christian Theology*, trans. Edward Quinn (Minneapolis: Fortress Press, 1978), 118.

113. Geoffrey Wigoder, *Jewish-Christian Relations since the Second World War*, Sherman Studies of Judaism in Modern Times (New York: Manchester University Press, 1988), 3.

114. Franklin H. Littell, *The Crucifixion of the Jews: The Failure of Christians to Understand the Jewish Experience* (Macon: Mercer University Press/Rose Reprints, 1986 [1975]), 51. Significantly, Littell has been part of the campaign to have Bonhoeffer recognized as a Righteous Gentile. In a document of testimony compiled by Stephen Wise, Littell writes that "he is *not* . . . one of those who opposed

the Nazi church politics only because of the churches' machinery or because of danger to baptized Jews, *although this is frequently charged by those who have read only his early writings and assume that he neither changed nor grew during the decade before his martyrdom*" ("Answers to the Commission's Questions, by the Individual Supporters of Recognition," October 17, 2000, document shared with the author).

115. Sidney G. Hall III, *Christian Anti-Semitism and Paul's Theology* (Minneapolis: Fortress Press, 1993), 48.

116. Nicholls says of Barth and Bonhoeffer that they "did stand up to the Nazi onslaught on the Church with great courage, and Bonhoeffer defended Jews within the Church, but even they failed to grasp the theological significance of the fact that Hitler's real conflict was not with the German church but with the Jewish people. The theologians did not know how to teach Christians to stand up for the Jews when they were in mortal peril." See *Christian Anti-Semitism: A History of Hate* (Northvale, N.J.: Jason Aronson, 1993), 352, 426.

117. Clarke Williamson, *Has God Rejected His People? Anti-Judaism in the Christian Church* (Nashville: Abingdon, 1982), 103.

118. Stephen G. Ray Jr., *Do No Harm: Social Sin and Christian Responsibility* (Minneapolis: Fortress Press, 2003).

119. Discursive economies, according to Ray, are "the complex of ideas and customs of knowing that underlie particular forms of our cultural and social 'common sense'" (*Do No Harm*, 22).

120. Ray, *Do No Harm*, 91, 93.

121. Ibid., 77.

122. Ibid., 94. Ray also accuses Bonhoeffer of a "functionalist view of Israel," of ascribing to the church a knowledge of Israel and its destiny that Jews did not possess (87), and of using curse-language that constitutes a "rationalization" of Israel's history of oppression (88).

Chapter 3: The German Church Struggle in Post-Holocaust Perspective

1. Charlotte Klein, *Anti-Judaism in Christian Theology*, trans. Edward Quinn (Minneapolis: Fortress Press, 1978), 118, 119.

2. Christine-Ruth Müller, *Dietrich Bonhoeffers Kampf gegen die nationalsozialistische Verfolgung und Vernichtung der Juden: Bonhoeffers Haltung zur Judenfrage im Vergleich mit Stellungnahmen aus der evangelischen Kirche und Kreisen des deutschen Widerstandes*, Heidelberger Untersuchungen zu Widerstand, Judenverfolgung und Kirchenkampf im Dritten Reich, Band 5 (München: Kaiser, 1990), 71.

3. Richard L. Rubenstein, "Dietrich Bonhoeffer and Pope Pius XII," in *The Century of Genocide: Selected Papers from the 30th Anniversary Conference of the Annual Scholars' Conference on the Holocaust and the Churches*, ed. Daniel J. Curran Jr., Richard Libowitz, and Marcia Sachs Littell (Merion Station, Pa.: Merion Westfield, 2002), 193–218; 198.

4. Geffrey B. Kelly, "Bonhoeffer and the Jews: Implications for Jewish-Christian Relations, in *Reflections on Bonhoeffer: Essays in Honor of F. Burton Nelson*, ed. Geffrey B. Kelly and C. John Weborg (Chicago: Covenant, 1999), 133–66; 136–37.

5. Cited in Andreas Pangritz, "Sharing the Destiny of His People," in *Bonhoeffer for a New Day: Theology in a Time of Transition*, ed. John W. de Gruchy (Grand Rapids, Mich.: Eerdmans, 1997), 258–77; 259. Tödt's analysis is confirmed in the work of Christine-Ruth Müller.

6. Ruth Zerner, "Dietrich Bonhoeffer and the Jews: Thoughts and Actions, 1933–1945," *Jewish Social Studies* 37:3–4 (1975): 235–50; 245.

7. Pangritz, "Sharing the Destiny of His People," 259.

8. Robert O. Smith, "Reclaiming Bonhoeffer after Auschwitz," *Dialog* 43:3 (Fall 2004): 205–20; 207.

9. See Stephen R. Haynes, *Reluctant Witnesses: Jews and the Christian Imagination* (Louisville: Westminster John Knox, 1995), 8–9.

10. Adolf Köberle, "Die Judenfrage im Lichte der Christusfrage" (1933), in Wolfgang Gerlach, *And the Witnesses Were Silent: The Confessing Church and the Persecution of the Jews*, ed. and trans. Victoria J. Barnett (Lincoln: University of Nebraska Press, 2000), 7. In the wake of the Nazi boycott of Jewish businesses in 1933, Christian novelist Jochen Klepper affirmed "God's mystery, which he established in Judaism" (13).

11. Lecture delivered before the Conference of Brethren in Lippe, Germany, April 30, 1933, cited in Gerlach, *And the Witnesses Were Silent*, 22–23.

12. Ibid., 83.

13. From an April 1937 *Gutachten* (professional opinion) requested by the Old Prussian Union Council of Brethren (ibid., 106).

14. Eric Gross, "The Jewish Question in Light of the Bible," cited in Gerlach, *And the Witnesses Were Silent*, 106.

15. Cited in Gerlach, *And the Witnesses Were Silent*, 112.

16. Wilhelm Halfmann, cited in ibid., 106.

17. Cited in ibid., 151 (emphasis in original).

18. Ibid., 216 (emphasis in original). The memorandum went on to claim that because the church is bound in guilt and promise to Judaism, it is obligated to

interpret "the phenomenon of the Jews, in whom the prophetic predication that 'I will make them . . . to be a curse, a terror, a hissing, and a reproach among all the nations where I have driven them' (Jer. 29:18) is fulfilled."

19. The Freiburg Circle Memorandum titled "Church and World," cited in Gerlach, *And the Witnesses Were Silent*, 211.

20. Ibid., 228–29.

21. The Kittel quote is in Klein, *Anti-Judaism in Christian Theology*, 13. The Niemöller sermon is from 1937 and may be found in Richard Gutteridge, *The German Evangelical Church and the Jews, 1879–1950* (New York: Barnes & Noble, 1976), 103–4. See also the statement of Wilhelm Bousset and Hugo Gressman: "In bitter resentment Judaism withdrew from the world, a nation which could neither live nor die, a Church which did not break away from national life and therefore remained a sect" (in Klein, *Anti-Judaism in Christian Theology*, 33).

22. Daniel Jonah Goldhagen, *Hitler's Willing Executioners: Ordinary Germans and the Holocaust* (New York: Knopf, 1996), 73.

23. Doris L. Bergen, "Catholics, Protestants, and Antisemitism in Nazi Germany," *Central European History* 27:3 (1994): 329–48; 333.

24. Ibid., 336.

25. Ibid., 333.

26. Ibid.

27. Doris L. Bergen, *Twisted Cross: The German Christian Movement in the Third Reich* (Chapel Hill: University of North Carolina Press, 1996), 31–32. German Christians associated "Jewishness" with secularism, atheism, Marxism, and an international conspiracy against Germany; they also employed the adjective "Jewish" to refer to "legalistic or dogmatic tendencies."

28. Uriel Tal, "Aspects of Consecration of Politics in the Nazi Era," in *Papers Presented to the International Symposium on Judaism and Christianity under the Impact of National-Socialism (1919–1945)* (Jerusalem: Historical Society of Israel, 1982), 62–63.

29. Ibid., 64. Tal exposes a similar rhetoric in the comments of Adolf Schlatter, who wrote of Aryan enthusiasts, "Their thinking is completely Jewish."

30. Uriel Tal, "On Modern Lutheranism and the Jews," in *Year Book of the Leo Baeck Institute* (London: Secker & Warburg, 1985): 203–13; 203.

31. Ibid., 204.

32. Ibid., 207.

33. Ibid., 209.

34. Ibid., 204.

35. Ibid., 211.

36. Kenneth C. Barnes, *Nazism, Liberalism, and Christianity: Protestant Social Thought in Germany and Great Britain 1925–1937* (Lexington: University Press of Kentucky, 1991), 140–41.

37. Gerlach, *And the Witnesses Were Silent*, 236.

38. Ronald J. Berger, *Fathoming the Holocaust: A Social Problems Approach* (New York: Aldine de Gruyter, 2002), xi.

39. Ibid., 24.

40. Ibid., 28.

41. Paul Lawrence Rose, *German Question/Jewish Question: Revolutionary Antisemitism from Kant to Wagner* (Princeton: Princeton University Press, 1990).

42. Ibid., 5.

43. Victor von Istoczy, *Manifesto to the Governments and Peoples of the Christian Countries Endangered by Judaism* (1882), cited in Uriel Tal, *Christians and Jews in Germany: Religion, Politics and Ideology in the Second Reich*, trans. Noah Jonathan Jacobs (Ithaca: Cornell University Press, 1975), 248.

44. Cited in Tal, *Christians and Jews in Germany*, 137.

45. Klaus P. Fischer, *The History of an Obsession: German Judeophobia and the Holocaust* (New York: Continuum, 1998), 127.

46. Goldhagen, *Hitler's Willing Executioners*, 432.

47. Fischer, *The History of an Obsession*, 54.

48. Shelley Baranowski, "The Confessing Church and Antisemitism," in *Betrayal: German Churches and the Holocaust*, ed. Robert P. Ericksen and Susannah Heschel (Minneapolis: Fortress Press, 1999), 99.

49. Ibid., 42.

50. Gerlach, *And the Witnesses Were Silent*, 4, 5. A series of study guides on the issue published in Germany during the 1920s indicates that pastors had become quite susceptible to racial understandings of *die Judenfrage*.

51. This discussion is based on Robert P. Ericksen, *Theologians under Hitler: Gerhard Kittel, Paul Althaus, Emanuel Hirsch* (New Haven: Yale University Press, 1985), 54ff.

52. Ibid., 58. For Kittel, the Jewish Question developed with the transition from Old Testament Israelites to "Jewry" in the postexilic period.

53. Lecture delivered before the Conference of Brethren in Lippe, Germany, April 30, 1933, cited in Gerlach, *And the Witnesses Were Silent*, 23.

54. "The Evangelical Church and Its Jewish Christians," published by the regional church of Baden, cited in Gerlach, *And the Witnesses Were Silent*, 54.

55. Walter Michaelis, writing in *Licht und Leben*, cited in Gerlach, *And the Witnesses Were Silent*, 68. Anti-Semitism is justified, the same journal proclaimed in another issue, as long as it remains "within the limits shown in the Bible."

56. An official church memorandum from mid-1933, cited in Gerlach, *And the Witnesses Were Silent*, 56.

57. Barnes, *Nazism, Liberalism, and Christianity*, 141.

58. Director of the Protestant Charitable Service in Zehlendorf, cited in Gerlach, *And the Witnesses Were Silent*, 83. Martin Rade, editor of *Christlicher Welt*, wrote of the Nazi Nuremberg Laws that they formed the basis "for a positive solution to the Jewish question" (cited in Gerlach, *And the Witnesses Were Silent*, 101).

59. "Principles Regarding the Aryan Question in the Church" (November 1933), cited in Gerlach, *And the Witnesses Were Silent*, 48.

60. Cited in Gerlach, *And the Witnesses Were Silent*, 149.

61. Ibid., 195.

62. Ibid., 213.

63. Ibid., 223. In May 1942 the Spiritual Confidential Council of the Evangelical Church Chancellery noted that "without question, Jewry is an enemy people for us Germans" (197).

64. Cited in Gerlach, *And the Witnesses Were Silent*, 112.

65. Wilhelm Rehm, cited in ibid., 113.

66. Ibid., 85.

67. Ibid., 68. Similarly, Michael Cardinal Falhauber declared in his Advent sermons of 1933 that while the church "has stretched forth her protecting hand over the Scriptures of the Old Testament," Christianity does not thereby "become a Jewish religion. These books were not composed by Jews; they are inspired by the Holy Ghost." See George Mosse, *Nazi Culture: A Documentary History* (New York: Random House, 1966), 258. While Falhauber's sermons espoused a "rejection of the Nazi anti-Semitic propaganda" at a crucial juncture in the National Socialist revolution, they also trafficked in religious propaganda that played into Nazi hands by highlighting Jewish perfidy and normalizing Jewish suffering and dispersion.

68. "Luther und das Alte Testament," *Junge Kirche* (1937), cited in Gerlach, *And the Witnesses Were Silent*, 112.

69. Dietrich Bonhoeffer, *No Rusty Swords: Letters, Lectures, and Notes, 1928–1936, from the Collected Works of Dietrich Bonhoeffer*, vol. 1, ed. Edwin H. Robertson, trans. Edwin H. Robertson and John Bowden (New York: Harper & Row, 1965), 211.

70. Cited in Gerlach, *And the Witnesses Were Silent*, 104. The Vienna paper *Gerechtigkeit* responded to Schlatter's text by asking: "Does he really believe that he

can struggle successfully [against the Nazi state] if he mocks, ridicules, and slanders other victims of National Socialism who are persecuted, tormented, and oppressed even more than the Protestants loyal to the confession?" (105).

71. Martin Niemöller, *Here Stand I!* trans. Jane Lymburn (Chicago: Willett, Clark & Co., 1937), 196.

72. Gerlach, *And the Witness Were Silent*, 196. Similarly, in 1927 Paul Althaus warned against the "Jewish threat" while at the same time condemning "anti-Semitic Pharisaism" (ibid., 40).

73. Ibid., 144, 147, 148–49.

74. Ibid., 165.

75. Katharina Staritz, a Confessing Church vicar, writing in 1941, cited in ibid., 170.

76. Cited in ibid., 105.

77. Ibid., 201. The phrase is from a letter by Confessing Church bishop Theophil Wurm, written March 14, 1943.

78. The Godesberg Declaration of 1939, cited in Gerlach, *And the Witnesses Were Silent*, 179.

79. Cited in Gerlach, *And the Witnesses Were Silent*, 201, 204.

Chapter 4: Bonhoeffer's Early Anti-Nazi Writings in Post-Holocaust Perspective

1. Konrad Raiser, "Bonhoeffer and the Ecumenical Movement," in *Bonhoeffer for a New Day: Theology in a Time of Transition*, ed. John W. de Gruchy (Grand Rapids, Mich.: Eerdmans, 1997), 319–39; 335.

2. For example, in the glossary of *The Cambridge Companion to Dietrich Bonhoeffer*, we read that "*Judenfrage*" refers to "the Nazi policy toward people of Jewish descent," as if the Nazis had invented the term. See John W. de Gruchy, *The Cambridge Companion to Dietrich Bonhoeffer* (Cambridge: Cambridge University Press, 1999), xxii. In an equally misleading passage, Susan Martins Miller defines the Jewish Question as "the debate in German churches about how to respond to Hitler's policies of discrimination and persecution of Jews. Churches debated whether they should be concerned only with Christian Jews or with helping all people of Jewish descent." See Susan Martins Miller, *Dietrich Bonhoeffer*, Men of Faith (Minneapolis: Bethany House, 2002), 136–37. Even Eberhard Bethge is guilty in this regard, as he claims that the title "The Church and the Jewish Question" is of little importance since Bonhoeffer was actually already concerned with the "Christian Question." See Eberhard Bethge, "Dietrich Bonhoeffer and the Jews," in *Ethical Responsibility: Bonhoeffer's Legacy to the Churches*, ed. John D.

Godsey and Geffrey B. Kelly, Toronto Studies in Theology, vol. 6 (New York: Edwin Mellen, 1981), 43–96; 58.

3. Stephen G. Ray Jr., *Do No Harm: Social Sin and Christian Responsibility* (Minneapolis: Fortress Press, 2003), 77–78, 81, 86. Ray observes that "the term *Jewish Question* functioned in the German cultural context in much the same way that Negro Problem functioned in the American context. The phrase encapsulated a cultural common sense that the place of Jewish persons and their communities was continually an open question, and one that presented somewhat of a conundrum for German society" (150n8).

4. Dietrich Bonhoeffer, *No Rusty Swords: Letters, Lectures, and Notes, 1928–1936, from the Collected Works of Dietrich Bonhoeffer*, vol. 1, ed. Edwin H. Robertson, trans. Edwin H. Robertson and John Bowden (New York: Harper & Row, 1965), 223.

5. Cited in Wolfgang Gerlach, *And the Witnesses Were Silent: The Confessing Church and the Persecution of the Jews*, ed. and trans. Victoria J. Barnett (Lincoln: University of Nebraska Press, 2000), 40–41.

6. Bonhoeffer, *No Rusty Swords*, 226–27. In a message received when this book was already in proofs, Geffrey Kelly pointed out that the translation of this passage in *No Rusty Swords* is misleading, since Bonhoeffer does not write that "the state is justified" (*gerechtfertigt*) but that "the state has the right" (*ohne Zweifel ist der Staat berechtigt, hier neue Wege zu gehen*). E-mail message to the author, January 31, 2006. Bonhoeffer invoked the term "*Judenfrage*" again in 1935 in a lecture to members of the Confessing Church. According to surviving notes, Bonhoeffer's address "The Interpretation of the New Testament" included these comments: "The service of the church has to be given to those who suffer violence and injustice. The Old Testament still demands right-dealing of the state, the New Testament no longer does so. Without asking about justice or injustice, the church takes to itself all the sufferers, all the forsaken of every party and of every status. 'Open your mouth for the dumb' (Prov. 31:8). Here the decision will really be made whether we are still the church of the present Christ. The Jewish question." See Bonhoeffer, *No Rusty Swords*, 325. Geffrey Kelly and F. Burton Nelson opine that a message of solidarity with Jews emerges here when we "put aside [Bonhoeffer's] spurious differentiation between the Old and New Testaments. . . ." See Geffrey B. Kelly and F. Burton Nelson, *The Cost of Moral Leadership: The Spirituality of Dietrich Bonhoeffer* (Grand Rapids, Mich.: Eerdmans, 2003), 46.

7. Bonhoeffer, *No Rusty Swords*, 229.

8. Doris L. Bergen, *Twisted Cross: The German Christian Movement in the Third Reich* (Chapel Hill: University of North Carolina Press, 1996), 32.

9. Bonhoeffer, "The Church and the Jewish Question," in *No Rusty Swords*, 227–28.

10. At first glance it appears that this "divine law" refers to Jewish legal stipulations. But as Bonhoeffer's argument develops, it seems that the "divine law" he is thinking of is racial identity. If this is the case, then Bonhoeffer would seem to be implying what many Protestant theologians on the German Christian side were arguing at the time: that race must be regarded as an ordinance of creation.

11. Stephen S. Schwarzschild, "Bonhoeffer and the Jews," *Commonweal* 83:3 (November 26, 1965): 227, 253–54; 254.

12. Ray, *Do No Harm*, 89, 90.

13. Eberhard Bethge, *Dietrich Bonhoeffer: A Biography*, rev. and ed. Victoria J. Barnett (Minneapolis: Fortress Press, 2000), 288. Bonhoeffer returns to this argument in *Life Together* (1938). See Dietrich Bonhoeffer, *Life Together and Prayerbook of the Bible*, ed. Geffrey B. Kelly, trans. Daniel W. Bloesch and James H. Burtness, Dietrich Bonhoeffer Works, vol. 5 (Minneapolis: Fortress Press, 1996), 71.

14. "Principles of the Rhineland Brotherhood of Pastors against the Twenty-eight Theses," *Junge Kirche* (June 1934). The principles were written in response to "Twenty-Eight Theses of the Saxon People's Church on the Internal Organization of the German Evangelical Church," adopted the previous December. Cited in Gerlach, *And the Witnesses Were Silent*, 70.

15. Wilhelm Rehm, cited in Gerlach, *And the Witnesses Were Silent*, 113.

16. Schwarzschild, "Bonhoeffer and the Jews," 254.

17. Cited in Eberhard Bethge, *Bonhoeffer: Exile and Martyr* (New York: Seabury, 1975), 66.

18. Bonhoeffer, *No Rusty Swords*, 226.

19. Robert E. Willis, "Bonhoeffer and Barth on Jewish Suffering: Reflections on the Relationship between Theology and Moral Sensibility," *Journal of Ecumenical Studies* 24:4 (Fall 1987): 598–615; 605.

20. See Ruth Zerner, "Dietrich Bonhoeffer and the Jews: Thoughts and Actions, 1933–1945," *Jewish Social Studies* 37:3–4 (1975): 235–50; 240.

21. Kenneth C. Barnes, "Dietrich Bonhoeffer and Hitler's Persecution of the Jews," in *Betrayal: German Churches and the Holocaust*, ed. Robert P. Ericksen and Susannah Heschel (Minneapolis: Fortress Press, 1999), 114.

22. Bethge, "Dietrich Bonhoeffer and the Jews," 63.

23. See Bethge, "Dietrich Bonhoeffer and the Jews," 74–75; and Zerner, "Dietrich Bonhoeffer and the Jews," 245.

24. Bonhoeffer, *No Rusty Swords*, 226.

25. Ibid., 221–22. For a discussion of these Luther quotes and their importance, see Edwin H. Robertson, "A Study of Dietrich Bonhoeffer and the Jews, January–April, 1933," in *Bonhoeffer's Ethics: Old Europe and New Frontiers*, ed. Guy Carter, René van Eyden, Hans-Dirk van Hoogstraten, and Jurjen Wiersma (Kampen, Netherlands: Kok Pharos, 1991), 121–30; 127.

26. Paul Lawrence Rose, *German Question/Jewish Question: Revolutionary Antisemitism from Kant to Wagner* (Princeton: Princeton University Press, 1990), 5.

27. Ibid.

28. Ray, *Do No Harm*, 88.

29. The term *"Heimkehr Israels"* goes back at least to the seventeenth-century German theologian Philip Jacob Spener. I am indebted to Professor Erich Geldbach of Ruhr-Universität Bochum for this observation.

30. Geffrey B. Kelly, "Bonhoeffer and the Jews: Implications for Jewish-Christian Relations," in *Reflections on Bonhoeffer: Essays in Honor of F. Burton Nelson*, ed. Geffrey B. Kelly and C. John Weborg (Chicago: Covenant, 1999), 133–66; 142.

31. Ibid., 143–44.

32. Craig J. Slane, *Bonhoeffer as Martyr: Social Responsibility and Modern Christian Commitment* (Grand Rapids, Mich.: Brazos, 2004), 103. Slane focuses on Bonhoeffer's contributions to the confession's article on Christology.

33. Edwin Robertson, "A Study of Dietrich Bonhoeffer and the Jews, January–April, 1933," in *Remembering for the Future: Working Papers and Addenda*, vol. 1, *Jews and Christians during and after the Holocaust*, ed. Yehuda Bauer et al. (Oxford: Pergamon, 1989), 121–29; 128.

34. Guy Christopher Carter, "Confession at Bethel, August 1933 — Enduring Witness: The Formation, Revision and Significance of the First Full Theological Confession of the Evangelical Church Struggle in Nazi Germany" (Ph.D. dissertation, Marquette University, 1987).

35. *No Rusty Swords*, 240–42.

36. Ibid., 242.

37. Ibid., 229, 241.

38. Ibid., 226.

39. Ibid., 241.

40. Carter, "Confession at Bethel, August 1933 — Enduring Witness," 313. It is interesting to compare this paragraph with two documents from July 1933. One is Bonhoeffer's "Church Election Sermon" of July 23 in which he mentions "the crowds who on Palm Sunday would cry out 'Hosanna' and on Good Friday, 'Crucify

him.'" Another is an election pamphlet drafted by Bonhoeffer's friend Franz Hildebrandt, which reads in part: "The German Christians say: The voice of the people is the voice of God (Declaration by Müller). The Bible says: Everyone who is of the truth hears my voice.—They cried out again, 'Not this man, but Barabbas!' Now Barabbas was a robber (John 18:37, 40)." See Bonhoeffer, *No Rusty Swords,* 209.

41. Carter, "Confession at Bethel, August 1933—Enduring Witness," 316.

42. Ibid., 317.

43. Ibid.

44. Ibid., 319.

45. Ibid. This statement was retained in later versions.

46. The only section of the August chapter on "The Church and the Jews" that was completely removed in November deals with the witness-people theme of God's preserving a holy remnant that bears the indelible character of the chosen people; the necessity of maintaining a mission to the Jews was softened but maintained. See ibid., 334–36.

47. Ibid., 336b. Also appearing for the first time in the November version of the *Bethel Confession* is the statement that "God rules His kingdom according to His plan, which is hidden from human comprehension. All human attempts to bring about such reign of God are therefore laughable presumption. With the Reformers we reject such *iudaicae opiniones* [Jewish notions] in every form whether they appear in the form of apocalyptic phantasies or secular utopias such as faith in progress or pacifism" (338b).

48. Edwin H. Robertson, "A Study of Dietrich Bonhoeffer and the Jews, January–April, 1933," 128; Walter Harrelson, "Bonhoeffer and the Bible," 115–39, in *The Place of Bonhoeffer: Problems and Possibilities in His Thought,* ed. Martin E. Marty (New York: Association Press, 1962), 141n27; Bethge, "Dietrich Bonhoeffer and the Jews," 60; Kelly, "Bonhoeffer and the Jews: Implications for Jewish-Christian Relations," 135; Willis, "Bonhoeffer and Barth on Jewish Suffering," 607; Kelly and Nelson, *The Cost of Moral Leadership,* 21; Robert O. Smith, "Reclaiming Bonhoeffer after Auschwitz," *Dialog* 43:3 (Fall 2004): 205–20; 209.

49. Josiah Ulysses Young III, *No Difference in the Fare: Dietrich Bonhoeffer and the Problem of Racism* (Grand Rapids, Mich.: Eerdmans, 1998), 137. Robert F. Koch, "The Theological Responses of Karl Barth and Deitrich Bonhoeffer to Church-State Relations in Germany, 1933–1945" (Ph.D. dissertation, Northwestern University, 1988), 239. Ann W. Astell, "Reading the Bible with Holocaust Survivors and Rescuers: A New Biblical Spirituality," *Interpretation* 56:2 (April 2002): 181–92; 184.

50. Robertson, "A Study of Dietrich Bonhoeffer and the Jews, January–April, 1933," 128.

51. David H. Jensen, "Religionless Christianity and Vulnerable Discipleship: The Interfaith Promise of Bonhoeffer's Theology," *Journal of Ecumenical Studies* 38:3 (Spring–Summer 2001), 151–67.

52. Victoria Barnett, "Response to Richard Rubenstein," paper presented at the AAR/SBL Annual Meeting, Nashville, November 20, 2000.

53. Geffrey B. Kelly, "Bonhoeffer and the Jews: Implications for Jewish-Christian Relations," 135; Ruth Zerner, "Church, State and the 'Jewish Question,'" 200.

54. Barnes, "Dietrich Bonhoeffer and Hitler's Persecution of the Jews," 116.

Chapter 5: Bonhoeffer and Post-Holocaust Theology

1. Writing on "Bonhoeffer's Legacy" for the Public Broadcasting Service website, Clifford Green claims that Bonhoeffer "outgrew traditional Christian anti-Jewish attitudes. He became an advocate for and rescuer of Jews in Nazi Germany, and ended his life sharing the same fate as the victims of the Holocaust. His witness was a direct inspiration to the Lutheran church in America (ELCA) to publicly repudiate in 1994 Luther's anti-Jewish writings" (2000, www.pbs.org/opb/bonhoeffer/legacy).

2. Cited in Eberhard Bethge, "Dietrich Bonhoeffer and the Jews," in *Ethical Responsibility: Bonhoeffer's Legacy to the Churches*, ed. John D. Godsey and Geffrey B. Kelly, Toronto Studies in Theology, vol. 6 (New York: Edwin Mellen, 1981), 43–96; 45.

3. Eberhard Bethge, "Christians and Jews in Germany Today, and Bonhoeffer's Sustaining Legacy," in *Burning Memory: Times of Testing and Reckoning*, ed. Alice L. Eckardt (Oxford: Pergamon, 1993), 297–311; 308.

4. Eberhard Bethge, "The Legacy of the Confessing Church: Transporting Experience across Historical Turning Points," *Church and Society* 85:6 (July–August 1995): 78–92; 82–83.

5. Douglas K. Huneke, *The Stones Will Cry Out: Pastoral Reflections on the Shoah (with Liturgical Resources)*, Contributions to the Study of Religion 39 (Westport, Conn: Greenwood, 1995), 61.

6. Ernst Feil, *Bonhoeffer Studies in Germany: A Survey of Recent Literature*, ed. James H. Burtness, trans. Jonathan Sorum (Philadelphia: Bonhoeffer Center, 1997), 29–33.

7. Douglas C. Bowman, "Bonhoeffer and the Possibility of Judaizing Christianity," in *A Bonhoeffer Legacy: Essays in Understanding*, ed. A. J. Klassen

(Grand Rapids, Mich.: Eerdmans, 1981), 76–86; 77. Such a re-imagining of the faith, Bowman opines, would involve revising notions of humanity's nature and capacities, diminishing theology's importance, and appropriating "the whole ethical tenor—the *pan-halakic* character—of the Jewish tradition" (78). Bowman observes these very processes under way in the "emergence of Judaizing tendencies" in Bonhoeffer's late writings—particularly his reading of the Old Testament, his comments on Christian versus Jewish anthropology, and his concept of Jesus as "the man for others," which for Bowman "amounts to nothing short of the typical rabbinic displacement of theology by ethics" (81). Bowman believes that Bonhoeffer would have found "congenial" recent Judaizing developments in Christian thought, particularly the picture of a "'non-religious' Jesus . . . who is thoroughly one with Old Testament roots and first-century culture" (83–84).

8. Cited in Geffrey B. Kelly, "Bonhoeffer and the Jews: Implications for Jewish-Christian Relations," in *Reflections on Bonhoeffer: Essays in Honor of F. Burton Nelson*, ed. Geffrey B. Kelly and C. John Weborg (Chicago: Covenant, 1999), 133–66; 160.

9. Wayne Whitson Floyd Jr., "Bonhoeffer's Many Faces," *Christian Century* 112 (April 26, 1995): 444–45.

10. Kelly, "Bonhoeffer and the Jews: Implications for Jewish-Christian Relations," 162.

11. For both men, "ours is a new era that carries with it an altered relationship to the Ancient of Days. We stand, both men say, awkwardly astride a break in time. Bonhoeffer calls it 'the world coming of age,' Greenberg describes it in conjunction with 'the third great cycle of Jewish history.'" In other words, both men share a "strikingly similar judgment" about the relationship of divine presence and human power. Bonhoeffer began to search for the meaning of a new age of power, Rasmussen claims, after discerning in his fellow resisters "the incarnation of responsibility and the morally sensitive use of power." Like Greenberg, Bonhoeffer saw "religious and moral reconstruction in the form of concrete, secular acts of responsibility toward history." See Larry Rasmussen with Renate Bethge, *Dietrich Bonhoeffer: His Significance for North Americans* (Minneapolis: Fortress Press, 1990), 113, 119, 121, 133.

12. Robert O. Smith, "Reclaiming Bonhoeffer after Auschwitz," *Dialog* 43:3 (Fall 2004): 205–20. See also Richard Harries, *After the Evil: Christianity and Judaism in the Shadow of the Holocaust* (Oxford: Oxford University Press, 2003), where the author cites Bonhoeffer's *Letters and Papers from Prison* and *The Cost of Discipleship*.

13. Craig J. Slane, *Bonhoeffer as Martyr: Social Responsibility and Modern Christian Commitment* (Grand Rapids, Mich.: Brazos, 2004), 96.

14. Kelly, "Bonhoeffer and the Jews: Implications for Jewish-Christian Relations," 146–49.

15. Cited in Keith W. Clements, *What Freedom? The Persistent Challenge of Dietrich Bonhoeffer* (Bristol, UK: Bristol Baptist College, 1990), 27.

16. Slane, *Bonhoeffer as Martyr*, 246.

17. John W. de Gruchy, "Editor's Introduction to the English Edition," in Dietrich Bonhoeffer, *Creation and Fall: A Theological Exposition of Genesis 1–3*, ed. John W. DeGruchy, trans. Douglas Stephen Bax, Dietrich Bonhoeffer Works, vol. 3 (Minneapolis: Fortress Press, 1997), 9.

18. Martin Rüter and Ilse Tödt, "Editors' Afterword to the German Edition," in Bonhoeffer, *Creation and Fall*, 172.

19. De Gruchy, "Editor's Introduction to the English Edition," in Bonhoeffer, *Creation and Fall*, 11.

20. Eberhard Bethge, *Dietrich Bonhoeffer: A Biography*, rev. and ed. Victoria J. Barnett (Minneapolis: Fortress Press, 2000), 188–89.

21. Letter dated April 8, 1936, cited in Slane, *Bonhoeffer as Martyr*, 163.

22. A. James Rudin, "Dietrich Bonhoeffer: A Jewish Perspective," paper presented at the Evangelische Akademie Nordelbien, Hamburg, Germany, June 17, 1987, 13, in the Bonhoeffer Archive.

23. Irving Greenberg, "Partnership in the Covenant; Dietrich Bonhoeffer and the Future of Jewish-Christian Dialogue," 11, 12, paper presented at the Sixth International Bonhoeffer Congress, New York, 1992, in the Bonhoeffer Archive.

24. Martin Kuske, *The Old Testament as the Book of Christ: An Appraisal of Bonhoeffer's Interpretation*, trans. S. T. Kimbrough Jr. (Philadelphia: Westminster, 1976), 1, 18. Helmut Gollwitzer recalls that he and Bonhoeffer "made a fresh discovery of the Old Testament as a book of the Christian Church" as the necessity of warding off attacks against the Old Testament led them more deeply into a knowledge of this portion of the Bible. See "The Way of Obedience," in *I Knew Dietrich Bonhoeffer*, ed. Wolf-Dieter Zimmerman and Ronald Gregor Smith, trans. Käthe Gregor Smith (New York: Harper & Row, 1966), 138–44; 140.

25. Kuske, *The Old Testament as the Book of Christ*, 9.

26. Ibid., 24. In a 1935 lecture titled "Christ in the Psalms," Bonhoeffer wrote that David could pray Psalm 58 only because Jesus Christ, the guiltless one, was in him (85).

27. Ibid., 44.

28. Clements, *What Freedom?* 141, 146, 152.

29. Dietrich Bonhoeffer, *Life Together and Prayerbook of the Bible*, ed. Geffrey B. Kelly, trans. Daniel W. Bloesch and James H. Burtness, Dietrich Bonhoeffer Works, vol. 5 (Minneapolis: Fortress Press, 1996), 53–19.

30. Ibid., 143.

31. Kuske, *The Old Testament as the Book of Christ*, 50, 58. Kuske argues that "typological exegesis proceeds from the essential correlation of the Old and New Testaments in the mutual possession of the revelation of God. It seeks to grasp the text as clearly as possible according to its inner Old Testamental meaning" (79–80).

32. See, for example, Bonhoeffer, *Life Together*, 48: "The Old Testament day begins on one evening and ends with the sundown of the next evening. That is the time of expectation. The day of the New Testament church begins at sunrise in the early morning and ends with the dawning light of the next morning. That is the time of fulfillment, the resurrection of the Lord."

33. Kuske, *The Old Testament as the Book of Christ*, 45.

34. Bethge, *Dietrich Bonhoeffer: A Biography*, 565.

35. Bethge, "Dietrich Bonhoeffer and the Jews," 85, 87. Bethge claims that "this shows a relation to the Torah like that brought to our attention by the Jewish New Testament scholar David Flusser in his work on the antitheses of Jesus in the Sermon on the Mount." Bethge also quotes two passages from *Ethics* dealing with the commandment of God that he believes present the author "like an interpreter of the Torah" who refused to write Christology without its ethical implications. "Maybe he was nearer to Jewish tradition than he knew himself," Bethge muses.

36. Kelly, "Bonhoeffer and the Jews: Implications for Jewish-Christian Relations," 147. See Dietrich Bonhoeffer, *Discipleship*, ed. and trans. Geffrey B. Kelly and John D. Godsey, Dietrich Bonhoeffer Works, vol. 4 (Minneapolis: Fortress Press, 2003), 285.

37. Smith, "Reclaiming Bonhoeffer after Auschwitz," 211. The passage is from Bonhoeffer, *Discipleship*, 123.

38. Bonhoeffer, *Discipleship*, 117.

39. Ibid., 118.

40. Ibid., 121.

41. Ibid., 123. Oddly, the editors attach a note to this sentence reminding us of Bonhoeffer's oral remark that "only those who cry out for the Jews may sing Gregorian chants" (123).

42. Both Walter Harrelson and Stanley Rosenbaum quote *The Cost of Discipleship*, rev. ed. (New York: Macmillan, 1959), 224. The new edition of *Discipleship* softens the passage by omitting the sentence "Such was the condition of the

people when Jesus came" (184). See Walter Harrelson, "Bonhoeffer and the Bible," 115–39, in *The Place of Bonhoeffer: Problems and Possibilities in His Thought*, ed. Martin E. Marty (New York: Association Press, 1962), and Stanley R. Rosenbaum, "Dietrich Bonhoeffer: A Jewish View," *Journal of Ecumenical Studies* 18:2 (Spring 1981): 301–7; 305.

43. Charlotte Klein summarizes the view this way: "The centuries between the Babylonian exile and the emergence of Christianity was a time of decadence, of internal and external decline for Judaism. It had no longer any history properly speaking, its faith was externalized and rigid, God had become a distant God and the prophetic message was forgotten" (*Anti-Judaism in Christian Theology*, trans. Edward Quinn [Philadelphia: Fortress Press, 1978], 38).

44. This ambiguity is reflected in Bonhoeffer's depiction of the Pharisees. Although their devotion to the law is characterized quite positively, Bonhoeffer uses the phrase "'Pharisaic' visibility" as a foil to Christian discipleship (*Discipleship*, 113).

45. Eberhard Bethge, "One of the Silent Bystanders? Bonhoeffer on November 9, 1938," in *Friendship and Resistance: Essays on Dietrich Bonhoeffer* (Grand Rapids, Mich.: Eerdmans, 1995), 58–71; 71, 59. It is interesting that Bonhoeffer's response to *Kristallnacht* receives less than a page of attention in Bethge's biography. See *Dietrich Bonhoeffer: A Biography*, 607. Jane Pejsa concurs that *Kristallnacht* was "the critical turn in Bonhoeffer's life journey," after which "circumstances were leading him rather to view his own fate as intertwined with that of the Jews in his land." See ". . . They Burned All the Meeting Places of God in the Land," in *Reflections on Bonhoeffer: Essays in Honor of F. Burton Nelson*, ed. Geffrey B. Kelly and C. John Weborg (Chicago: Covenant, 1999), 129–132; 129, 130. A similar view is articulated by Otto Dudzus, "Discipleship and Worldliness in the Thinking of Dietrich Bonhoeffer," *Religion in Life* 35 (Spring 1966): 230–40; 233.

46. Bethge, "One of the Silent Bystanders?" 64.

47. Wolfgang Gerlach, *And the Witnesses Were Silent: The Confessing Church and the Persecution of the Jews*, ed. and trans. Victoria J. Barnett (Lincoln: University of Nebraska Press, 2000), 147.

48. Bethge, "Dietrich Bonhoeffer and the Jews," 75; and "One of the Silent Bystanders?" 65–67. Bethge emphasizes that Bonhoeffer's pencil marks at Psalm 74 were not "added as a result of later reflection." See also Hans-Werner Jensen: "There are still some marginal comments to the psalms in my Bible which date from the Gross-Schlönwitz time, for instance the date 10th November 1938, the 'Crystal Night', beside Psalm lxxiv, 8: 'They burned all the meeting places of God in the land'" (in *I Knew Dietrich Bonhoeffer*, 153).

49. Bethge, "One of the Silent Bystanders?" 66.

50. Clements, *What Freedom?* 137.

51. See Augustine, *City of God*, 18:46, in A Select Library of the Nicene and Post-Nicene Fathers of the Christian Church Series, 8 vols., ed. Philip Schaff (Grand Rapids, Mich.: Eerdmans, 1955).

52. Cited in Marc Saperstein, *Moments of Crisis in Jewish-Christian Relations* (Philadelphia: Trinity Press International, 1989), 19. See also David Berger, "The Attitude of St. Bernard of Clairvaux to the Jews," *PAAJR* 40 (1972): 89–108.

53. Bethge, "One of the Silent Bystanders?" 64.

54. Ibid. (emphasis added).

55. Hans-Werner Jensen, "Life Together," in *I Knew Dietrich Bonhoeffer*, 152–55.

56. Gottfried Maltusch, "When the Synagogues Burnt," in *I Knew Dietrich Bonhoeffer*, 150. Bethge says of the "great discussion" described by Maltusch that it "certainly represented fairly accurately what was then thought or not thought about Jews in the Confessing Church. . . . Today it is difficult to imagine how the centuries-old notions of divine curse, punishment and replacement were taken for granted even by us in the Confessing Church" ("One of the Silent Bystanders?" 62).

57. Christine-Ruth Müller, *Dietrich Bonhoeffers Kampf gegen die nationalsozialistische Verfolgung und Vernichtung der Juden: Bonhoeffers Haltung zur Judenfrage im Vergleich mit Stellungnahmen aus der evangelischen Kirche und Kreisen des deutschen Widerstandes*, Heidelberger Untersuchungen zu Widerstand, Judenverfolgung und Kirchenkampf im Dritten Reich, Band 5 (Munich: Kaiser, 1990), 159.

58. Bethge, "Dietrich Bonhoeffer and the Jews," 81.

59. Kenneth C. Barnes, "Dietrich Bonhoeffer and Hitler's Persecution of the Jews," in *Betrayal: German Churches and the Holocaust*, ed. Robert P. Ericksen and Susannah Heschel (Minneapolis: Fortress Press, 1999), 126.

60. Kelly, "Bonhoeffer and the Jews: Implications for Jewish Christian Reconciliation," 151.

61. Andreas Pangritz, "Sharing the Destiny of His People," in *Bonhoeffer for a New Day: Theology in a Time of Transition*, ed. John W. de Gruchy (Grand Rapids, Mich.: Eerdmans, 1997), 258–77; 271.

62. Pinchas E. Lapide, "Bonhoeffer und das Judentum," in *Verspieltes Erbe: Dietrich Bonhoeffer und der deutsche Nachkriegsprotestantismus*, ed. Ernst Feil (Munich: Kaiser, 1979), 116–30.

63. Dietrich Bonhoeffer, *Ethics*, ed. Clifford J. Green, trans. Reinhard Krauss, Charles C. West, and Douglas W. Stott, Dietrich Bonhoeffer Works, vol. 6 (Minneapolis: Fortress, 2005), 105.

64. William Jay Peck, "From Cain to the Death Camps: An Essay on Bonhoeffer and Judaism," *Union Seminary Quarterly Review* 28:2 (Winter 1973): 158–76; 158.

65. Kelly, "Bonhoeffer and the Jews: Implications for Jewish-Christian Relations," 152, and "Bonhoeffer's Theology of Liberation," *Dialog* 34:1 (Winter 1995), 22–29; 24.

66. James Patrick Kelley, "The Best of the German Gentiles: Dietrich Bonhoeffer and the Rights of Jews in Hitler's Germany," 80–92, in *Remembering for the Future: Working Papers and Addenda*, vol. 1, *Jews and Christians during and after the Holocaust*, ed. Yehuda Bauer et al. (Oxford: Pergamon, 1989), 87.

67. Bonhoeffer, *Ethics*, 139.

68. Bethge, "Dietrich Bonhoeffer and the Jews," 81.

69. Clifford Green, "The Holocaust and the First Commandment" (1992), 8, paper in the Bonhoeffer Archive.

70. Smith, "Reclaiming Bonhoeffer after Auschwitz," 212, 215.

71. Bonhoeffer, *Ethics*, 61.

72. Ibid., 54 (emphasis in original).

73. Ibid., 356, 75.

74. Clifford J. Green, "Editor's Introduction to the English Edition," in Bonhoeffer, *Ethics*, 6.

75. Amos Yong, "Globalizing Christology: Jesus Christ in World Religious Context," *Religious Studies Review* 30:4 (October 2004): 259–66; 263.

76. See, for example, "the most hypocritical of all Pharisees" (80); "Pharisaism"(86), "pharisaical criticism" (90); "pharisaical refusal of love for the wicked" (156); "unbearable Pharisaism" (195); "from Pharisaism to complete rejection of God" (210); "a pharisaical kind of self-examination" (325); "Pharisees and hypocrites" (348); and "pharisaical arrogance" (399).

77. Bonhoeffer, *Ethics*, 195n85.

78. Ibid., 80n13.

79. Ibid., 311.

80. Ibid., 317.

81. Ibid., 314.

82. Ibid., 327, 329.

83. Klein, *Anti-Judaism in Christian Theology*, chs. 3 and 4.

84. Bonhoeffer, *Ethics*, 310n40.

85. It should be noted, though, that in its universal aspect Bonhoeffer's portrait of the Pharisee contains a certain sympathetic dimension. Pharisees, he writes, are "those human beings, admirable to the highest degree, who subject their entire lives to the knowledge of good and evil and who judge themselves as sternly as their

neighbors—and all to the glory of God, whom they humbly thank for this knowledge." Ibid., 309–10.

86. Ibid., 310. References to "pharisaism" may also be found in Bonhoeffer's letters and papers. In "After Ten Years" (Christmas 1942), Bonhoeffer writes that he who seeks the sanctuary of private virtuousness runs the risk of becoming "the most hypocritical of Pharisees" (Dietrich Bonhoeffer, *Letters and Papers from Prison*, enlarged ed., ed. Eberhard Bethge [New York: Macmillan, 1972], 5). On June 22, 1939, Bonhoeffer wrote his parents from New York about the situation there being "terribly sensational and full of hatred and horribly pharisaic." On July 25, 1942, he wrote to Winfried Krause complaining of Christians' "dogmatic pharisaism" in response to Bultmann's demythologizing project (Bethge, *Dietrich Bonhoeffer: A Biography*, 645, 712).

87. Bonhoeffer, *Ethics*, 311.

88. Rosenbaum writes of this passage, "If this is a euphemism for Jews, one wonders why it is necessary." Rosenbaum discounts the possibility of censorship, noting that Bonhoeffer was still free when he wrote these words, but fails to realize that Bonhoeffer had much to fear from the Gestapo, who were keeping close tabs on his travel and writing at this time. See Rosenbaum, "Dietrich Bonhoeffer: A Jewish View," 305.

89. Slane, *Bonhoeffer as Martyr*, 108. See also Bonhoeffer, *Ethics*, 253, where he writes that "in Christ we see God in the form of the poorest of our brothers and sisters."

90. Kelley, "The Best of the German Gentiles," 89. Kelley's reading of this passage is so dubious that it deserves to be cited:

> Bonhoeffer appears here to suggest that Christian faith cannot be reduced to a position which is held with pure, unquestioning commitment and without any doubt. For such reasons, the Jewish faith, by rejecting Jesus' messiahship in the sense held by Christians, is essential to preserve Christian faith as a real faith rather than some kind of human certainty. According to this view, the Jews' questioning what Christians believe is the essential other side of their faith. The impossible expulsion of the Jews would destroy Christianity itself, since Christ himself was a Jew. It would also remove "the sign" of the necessary dialogue of commitment and doubt which is essential to faith, falsely resolve in a final way "the question of Christ," and make authentic faith in Christ impossible even for Christians. Here is a dialectic, both a difference and an indissoluble linkage between its two forms. For Bonhoeffer at this time, such a relation characterizes the two covenants and the "two peoples of God."

91. Bonhoeffer's claim that "the Jews . . . are the sign of God's free, gracious election and of God's rejecting wrath" resonates unmistakably with Barth's discussion titled "Israel and the Church" in *Church Dogmatics* 2:2. Given that Bonhoeffer apparently read this text in proofs in May 1942, and that its influence is apparent in "The 'Ethical' and the 'Christian' as a Topic," one is tempted to conclude that "Heritage and Decay" was influenced by Barth's discussion titled "The Election of the Community" in *CD* 2:2. Yet according to the critical edition of *Ethics*, "Heritage and Decay" was completed by the end of 1941. If there is no direct influence here, we have an even stronger basis for assuming that both men drew on a common theological tradition in reflecting on the mystery of Israel.

Also intriguing is the similarity between Bonhoeffer's contention that "an expulsion of the Jews from the west must necessarily bring with it the expulsion of Christ. For Jesus Christ was a Jew" and Barth's 1938 statement that "whoever rejects and persecutes the Jew, rejects and persecutes the one who died for the sins of the Jews and only thereby for our sins." On Barth, see Stephen R. Haynes, *Prospects for Post-Holocaust Theology: "Israel" in the Theologies of Karl Barth, Jürgen Moltmann, and Paul van Buren*, American Academy of Religion Academy Series 77 (Atlanta: Scholars, 1991).

92. Slane, *Bonhoeffer as Martyr*, 107.

93. This problem was recognized by Theodore A. Gill in the 1970s: "I simply cannot get gooseflesh," Gill wrote, "over . . . the declaration that the attacks on the Jews must be resisted because they are really attacks on Jesus Christ. . . .We have little to learn from a church or a prophet who cannot recognize murder until it is murder in the cathedral. . . ." Cited in Emil L. Fackenheim, "Fackenheim on Bonhoeffer," *Newsletter of the International Bonhoeffer Society for Archive and Research, English Language Section* 11 (November 1977): 2–4; 3.

94. Clifford Green detects expressions of compassion for Jews before Bonhoeffer's arrest in April 1943. Referring to the famous statement in "After Ten Years" that "we [in the Resistance] have for once learnt to see the great events of world history from below, . . . from the perspective of those who suffer," Green writes that "there can be no doubt that this passage reflects Bonhoeffer's response to the genocide Jews were suffering under Hitler." See Clifford Green, "Sharing the Sufferings of God: The Challenge of the Holocaust to Religious Faith" (1985), 12, paper in the Bonhoeffer Archive.

95. See, for example, Bonhoeffer, *Letters and Papers from Prison*, letters of May 15, 1943 (40); November 18, 1943 (129); November 20, 1943 (134); November 21, 1943 (135); December 5, 1943 (156–57); December 15, 1943 (163); January 29–30, 1944 (199); March 19, 1944 (234); April 30, 1944 (282); May 5, 1944 (286);

May 20, 1944 (303); June 2, 1944 (315); June 27, 1944 (336–37); July 16, 1944 (359); and July 28, 1944 (374). See also "Thoughts on the Day of the Baptism of Dietrich Wilhelm Rüdiger Bethge," May 1944 (294–300).

96. David E. Timmer makes Bonhoeffer's "striking evaluation of the Old Testament" in the letter dated December 5, 1943, a jumping-off point for his discussion of Christian apprehensions of the Old Testament in "The Bible between Church and Synagogue: Thoughts on the Interpretation of the Hebrew Scriptures," *Reformed Review* 39:2 (Winter 1986): 94–103. Alan Ecclestone is another scholar who notes Bonhoeffer's ruminations on the Old Testament in his letter of December 5, 1943, and perceives in them a path out of the dilemma of Christian theology after the Holocaust. See Alan Ecclestone, *The Night Sky of the Lord* (London: Darton Longman & Todd, 1980), 218–20.

97. Bonhoeffer, *Letters and Papers from Prison*, 156–57.

98. Ibid., 369.

99. Ibid., 145.

100. Francis I. Andersen, "Dietrich Bonhoeffer and the Old Testament," *The Reformed Theological Review* 34:2 (May–August 1975): 33–44; 33.

101. David F. Ford, *Self and Salvation: Being Transformed* (Cambridge: Cambridge University Press, 1999), 262.

102. Bonhoeffer, *Letters and Papers from Prison*, 282.

103. R. Kendall Soulen, *The God of Israel and Christian Theology* (Minneapolis: Fortress Press, 1996), 21. It must be said that if Soulen had offered a full analysis of Bonhoeffer's writings on the Old Testament, he would have had to explain how the prison writings eclipse the "economic supersessionism" that characterizes Bonhoeffer's other published writings—an approach to the Hebrew Scriptures that, according to Soulen, "logically entails the ontological, historical, and moral obsolescence of Israel's existence after Christ." In fact, what Soulen calls the "standard model" for unifying the Christian canon "completely neglects the Hebrew Scriptures, with the exception of Genesis 1–3," the subject of Bonhoeffer's only self-published study of the Old Testament (30).

104. Bonhoeffer, *Letters and Papers from Prison*, 336.

105. Ibid., 282, 312, 391 (emphasis added).

106. Kuske summarizes the agreement this way: "There is One God throughout the entire Bible whose action in Christ and upon Israel is related, the destiny of Jesus Christ is a repetition of the destiny of Israel, the Old Testament is the witness of God's accepting, judging, and renewing love" (*The Old Testament as the Book of Christ*, 59). Speaking for the many scholars who regard Christology as the primary source of continuity in Bonhoeffer's thought, Stephen Plant writes that "the

christology Bonhoeffer formed in his 1933 lectures constitutes the central light that illuminates many of the political, theological and ethical subjects he attends to. Christ is at the centre of the *Sanctorum Communio*; christology is *the* academic discipline because with christology alone is the one central question of human life asked 'Who is Jesus Christ for you today?' *Discipleship* is following Christ's call; in the *Ethics* believers are described as conformed to Christ; and in prison Jesus is the man for others and the presence of God is made visible in the weakness and suffering of the cross. Christ is the *cantus firmus* in the polyphony of Bonhoeffer's theology." See Stephen Plant, *Bonhoeffer*, Outstanding Christian Thinkers (London: Continuum, 2004), 146.

107. Bonhoeffer, *Creation and Fall*, 9.

108. Harrelson, "Bonhoeffer and the Bible," 133. Harrelson regards Bonhoeffer's celebrated comment that "it is only when one knows the ineffability of the Name of God that one can utter the name of Jesus Christ" as "quite ambiguous," noting that it could be interpreted to mean that the Old Testament witnesses to humanity's need of redemption rather than to God the Redeemer (131, 132, 134).

109. Rosenbaum, "Dietrich Bonhoeffer: A Jewish View," 304.

110. This paradox is expressed by Stephen Plant, who writes that "the uncompromising Christocentrism of Bonhoeffer's reading of the Hebrew Bible, in the wake of the Holocaust, creates obvious theological problems; but this should not obfuscate the originality of Bonhoeffer's commitment to recovering the Old Testament for Christian theology in a climate in which it was widely dismissed as irrelevant" (*Bonhoeffer*, 87). This comment, specifically addressed to *Creation and Fall* (1933), may be applied to Bonhoeffer's entire corpus.

111. Stephen S. Schwarzschild, "Survey of Current Theological Literature: 'Liberal Religion (Protestant),'" *Judaism* 9 (August 1960): 366–71; 366–67.

112. In his introduction to *Prayerbook of the Bible* (1940), Geffrey B. Kelly remarks that in Bonhoeffer's discussion of the psalms of lament, it is "obvious that Bonhoeffer felt that there could be no specific mention of the Jews, given the rigorous censorship to which his book was submitted." This is a reasonable explanation; less convincing is Kelly's claim that it is "equally clear that even when he speaks openly only of the suffering of Christians, he is likewise describing the crucifixion of the Jews of Europe to whom he was viscerally bound during the church struggle." See Bonhoeffer, *Life Together and Prayerbook of the Bible*, 151–52.

113. Vivienne Blackburn surmises that in a section of *Ethics* dealing with "Christian solutions for world problems" (*Gibt es überhaupt christliche Lösungen für weltliche Probleme?*), there may be "a veiled reference to the tragic *Lösung* [solution]

developed by the regime to the 'Jewish question' (the reference would necessarily be veiled in case Bonhoeffer's papers fell into the hands of the Gestapo) . . . that behind the question as to whether there are Christian solutions to worldly problems, there is a reference to the Nazi 'solution' of genocide." Though probably unfalsifiable, the claim is a dubious attempt to connect Bonhoeffer with the Holocaust. See Vivienne Blackburn, *Dietrich Bonhoeffer and Simone Weil: A Study in Christian Responsiveness*, Religions and Discourse (New York: Peter Lang, 2004), 184.

114. Ruth Zerner, "Dietrich Bonhoeffer and the Jews: Thoughts and Actions, 1933–1945," *Jewish Social Studies* 37:3–4 (1975): 235–50; 248.

115. Bonhoeffer, "King David," cited in Bethge, "Dietrich Bonhoeffer and the Jews," 56; and Bonhoeffer, *Life Together*, 62.

116. Bethge, "Dietrich Bonhoeffer and the Jews," 67–68. "The significant point," according to Bethge,

is that such formulae are hardly ever repeated in later manuscripts, articles, sermons and letters. Instead, certain key words and phrases reveal a new degree of solidarity with the persecuted Jews, and this makes it difficult to think any longer in the old simplistic terms. In this sense a noticeable hermeneutical change occurs as discrimination and persecution of the Jews continues to escalate. The changing situation simply forbids certain concepts to pass his lips, silences certain old formulas both inside the church and in communications for Jewish addresses. Key words alone do not represent any further development toward a "theology after the Holocaust," but in hindsight they prove themselves to have been signs of an incubation period. (68–69)

117. Dietrich Bonhoeffer, *No Rusty Swords: Letters, Lectures, and Notes, 1928–1936, from the Collected Works of Dietrich Bonhoeffer*, vol. 1, ed. Edwin H. Robertson, trans. Edwin H. Robertson and John Bowden (New York: Harper & Row, 1965), 226.

118. Bonhoeffer, *Ethics*, 105.

119. This appears to be what has happened in Yad Vashem's analysis of Bonhoeffer's candidacy for the designation "righteous among the nations."

120. Huneke, *The Stones Will Cry Out*, 61.

Chapter 6: Bonhoeffer and the Holocaust

1. F. Burton Nelson, "Dietrich Bonhoeffer and the Jews: An Agenda for Exploration and Contemporary Dialogue," in *The Holocaust Forty Years After*, ed. Marcia

Littell, Richard Libowitz, and Evelyn Bodek Rosen (Lewiston, N.Y.: Edwin Mellen, 1989), 87–93; 89.

2. Sidney G. Hall III, *Christian Anti-Semitism and Paul's Theology* (Minneapolis: Fortress Press, 1993), 48.

3. R. Kendall Soulen, *The God of Israel and Christian Theology* (Minneapolis: Fortress Press, 1996), 17, 18. Eva Fogelman writes that Bonhoeffer was deported to a concentration camp for "anti-Nazi sermons." See *Conscience and Courage: Rescuers of Jews during the Holocaust* (New York: Anchor, 1994), 170.

4. Craig J. Slane, *Bonhoeffer as Martyr: Social Responsibility and Modern Christian Commitment* (Grand Rapids, Mich.: Brazos, 2004), 95, 115.

5. Ann W. Astell, "Reading the Bible with Holocaust Survivors and Rescuers: A New Biblical Spirituality," *Interpretation* 56:2 (April 2002): 181–92; 187.

6. Rasmussen writes as though Bonhoeffer and the Holocaust can only be understood together, referring to what can be learned "from Bonhoeffer and the Holocaust," what "the Holocaust reveals and Bonhoeffer tried to address," "the point made by both Bonhoeffer and the Holocaust," and "the rupture Bonhoeffer and Holocaust reflection are trying to name." See "Dietrich Bonhoeffer and the Holocaust: Lessons for Lutherans," in *Planning for the Future: LECNA at 85, Papers and Proceedings of the 81st Annual Meeting of the Lutheran Education Conference of North America* (Washington, D.C.: LECNA, 1995): 6–17; 9–12.

7. Geffrey B. Kelly, "Bonhoeffer and the Jews: Implications for Jewish-Christian Relations," in *Reflections on Bonhoeffer: Essays in Honor of F. Burton Nelson*, ed. Geffrey B. Kelly and C. John Weborg (Chicago: Covenant Publications, 1999), 133–66; 162.

8. Eberhard Bethge, "Dietrich Bonhoeffer and the Jews," in *Ethical Responsibility: Bonhoeffer's Legacy to the Churches*, ed. John D. Godsey and Geffrey B. Kelly, Toronto Studies in Theology, vol. 6 (New York: Edwin Mellen, 1981), 43–96; 80.

9. Ibid., 46. Ruth Zerner has been particularly sensitive to the temptation of making Bonhoeffer a post-Holocaust critic of the Christian tradition. In 1973 William Jay Peck claimed that Bonhoeffer had developed a "deep revulsion . . . toward the whole religious tradition that has contributed so much to anti-Semitism and the coming of the 'final solution.'" But Zerner pointed out shortly thereafter the problems with such an assumption: "Implicit in Peck's comments is the suggestion that Bonhoeffer finally recognized how insidiously his own religious tradition had encouraged anti-Semitic persecution. Bonhoeffer's scant comments on the Jews during his last years hardly provide sufficient proof for such an assumption. Unlike his heroic acts, Bonhoeffer's ideas (even in his later writings) on Jews and their Bible continue to contain elements of ambivalence and ambiguity; the traditional

Christian image of the 'cursed Jews' lingers on. This does not make Bonhoeffer less heroic, only more human." See Ruth Zerner, "Dietrich Bonhoeffer and the Jews: Thoughts and Actions, 1933–1945," *Jewish Social Studies* 37:3–4 (1975): 235–50; 250–80.

10. Probably nothing written subsequently is as blunt and condemnatory as Karl Barth's response to Bonhoeffer's decision to take a pastorate in London in October 1933. See Barth's letter of November 20, 1933, in Dietrich Bonhoeffer, *No Rusty Swords: Letters, Lectures, and Notes, 1928–1936, from the Collected Works of Dietrich Bonhoeffer*, vol. 1, ed. Edwin H. Robertson, trans. Edwin H. Robertson and John Bowden (New York: Harper & Row, 1965), 237–40.

11. Kenneth C. Barnes, "Dietrich Bonhoeffer and Hitler's Persecution of the Jews," in *Betrayal: German Churches and the Holocaust*, ed. Robert Ericksen and Susannah Heschel (Minneapolis: Fortress Press, 1999), 112.

12. Eberhard Bethge, "One of the Silent Bystanders? Bonhoeffer on November 9, 1938," in *Friendship and Resistance: Essays on Dietrich Bonhoeffer* (Grand Rapids, Mich.: Eerdmans, 1995), 58–71. See also Ruth Zerner, "Martin Niemöller: Activist as Bystander: The Oft-Quoted Reflection," in *Jewish-Christian Encounters over the Centuries*, ed. Marvin Perry and Frederick M. Schweitzer (New York: Peter Lang, 1994), 327–38.

13. Bethge, "One of the Silent Bystanders?" 58–59.

14. See Robert E. Willis, "Bonhoeffer and Barth on Jewish Suffering: Reflections on the Relationship between Theology and Moral Sensibility," *Journal of Ecumenical Studies* 24:4 (Fall 1987): 598–615; 599–600; and Ruth Zerner, "German Protestant Responses to Nazi Persecution of the Jews," in *Perspectives on the Holocaust*, ed. Randolph L. Braham (Boston: Luwer-Nijhoff, 1983), 61–64, where the attitudes of Walter Künneth, Martin Niemöller, and Karl Barth are compared with Bonhoeffer's.

15. Zerner, "Dietrich Bonhoeffer and the Jews," 238.

16. Eberhard Bethge, *Dietrich Bonhoeffer: A Biography*, rev. and ed. Victoria J. Barnett (Minneapolis: Fortress Press, 2000), 275–76.

17. Cited in ibid., 505–6.

18. "The Church and the Jewish Question," in Bonhoeffer, *No Rusty Swords*, 221–29; 225.

19. "The Church and the Jews," in Bonhoeffer, *No Rusty Swords*, 241.

20. In October 1943 the last Confessional Synod of the Old Prussian Union asserted that although Israel had rejected the Christ of God, "it is not we human beings or even we Christians who are called upon to punish Israel's disbelief." Cited in Wolfgang Gerlach, *And the Witnesses Were Silent: The Confessing Church and*

the Persecution of the Jews, ed. and trans. Victoria J. Barnett (Lincoln: University of Nebraska Press, 2000), 207.

21. Ervin Staub, *The Roots of Evil: The Origins of Genocide and Other Group Violence* (Cambridge: Cambridge University Press, 1989), 18.

22. Robert Jay Lifton, *The Nazi Doctors: Medical Killing and the Psychology of Genocide* (New York: Basic, 1986), 431.

23. Karl Barth, *Church Dogmatics*, vol. III/3, 2nd ed., ed. G. W. Bromiley and T. F. Torrance, trans. G. W. Bromiley (Edinburgh: T & T Clark, 1975), 222.

24. Claudia Koonz, "Ethical Dilemmas and Nazi Eugenics: Single Issue Dissent in Religious Contexts," in *Resistance against the Third Reich, 1933–1990*, ed. Michael Geyer and John W. Boyer (Chicago: University of Chicago Press, 1992), 15–38; 15.

25. Eberhard Bethge, "Between Confession and Resistance," in *Friendship and Resistance*, 15–29; 24.

26. "Sharing the Destiny of His People," in *Bonhoeffer for a New Day: Theology in a Time of Transition*, ed. John W. de Gruchy (Grand Rapids, Mich.: Eerdmans, 1997), 258–77; 271.

27. See Bethge, "Dietrich Bonhoeffer and the Jews," 76–77; and Barnes, "Dietrich Bonhoeffer and Hitler's Persecution of the Jews," 124–25. William Jay Peck argued in 1973 that Bonhoeffer's reference in "The Church and the Jewish Question" to jamming a spoke in the wheel of the state "provides important evidence linking the plight of the Jews with Bonhoeffer's eventual decision to join the resistance movement after the other less potent options had failed." See "From Cain to the Death Camps: An Essay on Bonhoeffer and Judaism," *Union Seminary Quarterly Review* 28:2 (Winter 1973): 158–76; 168.

28. John W. de Gruchy, *Daring, Trusting Spirit: Bonhoeffer's Friend Eberhard Bethge* (Minneapolis: Fortress Press, 2005), 184.

29. Inge Scholl, *The White Rose: Munich 1942–1943*, trans. Arthur R. Schultz (Middletown, Conn.: Wesleyan University Press, 1983), 78.

30. Ibid.

31. See Bethge, *Dietrich Bonhoeffer: A Biography*, 515.

32. From Lawrence L. Langer, *Versions of Survival: The Holocaust and the Human Spirit* (Albany: State University of New York Press, 1982), 72–73, excerpted at www.facing.org/facing/fhao2.nsf/scholars.

33. Bethge, *Dietrich Bonhoeffer: A Biography*, 655.

34. Steven S. Schwarzschild, "Survey of Current Theological Literature: 'Liberal Religion (Protestant),'" *Judaism* 9 (Autumn 1960): 366–71; 366. See also Slane, *Bonhoeffer as Martyr*, 114.

35. A. James Rudin, "Dietrich Bonhoeffer: A Jewish Perspective," paper presented at the Evangelische Akademie Nordelbien, Hamburg, Germany, June 17, 1987, 17, paper in the Bonhoeffer Archive.

36. Eberhard Bethge, "Christians and Jews in Germany Today, and Bonhoeffer's Sustaining Legacy," in *Burning Memory: Times of Testing and Reckoning*, ed. Alice L. Eckardt (Oxford: Pergamon, 1993), 297–311; 310.

37. Bethge, *Bonhoeffer: Exile and Martyr* (New York: Seabury, 1975), 160–61. Slane obscures this issue by arguing that "in the Holocaust context, the totalitarian encroachment of the state upon nearly all social institutions and relationships took from Bonhoeffer the decision *whether* to become political. Only the *form* of his political involvement was in question" (*Bonhoeffer as Martyr*, 111).

38. Geffrey B. Kelly, *Liberating Faith: Bonhoeffer's Message for Today* (Minneapolis: Augsburg Publishing House, 1984), 160.

39. Clifford Green, "The Holocaust and the First Commandment" (1992), 5, 8, paper in the Bonhoeffer Archive.

40. Alf Lüdtke, "The Appeal of Exterminating 'Others': German Workers and the Limits of Resistance," in *Resistance against the Third Reich, 1933–1990*, ed. Michael Geyer and John W. Boyer (Chicago: University of Chicago Press, 1992), 53–74; 53. Traces of the victimization myth can still be detected in German political rhetoric, which by necessity must refer to the end of the Nazi era as a liberation from tyranny.

41. For examples of such images, see Scholl, *The White Rose*, 11, 16–19, 36, 44.

Chapter 7: Bonhoeffer and Christian Rescue

1. Andreas Pangritz, "Sharing the Destiny of His People," in *Bonhoeffer for a New Day: Theology in a Time of Transition*, ed. John W. de Gruchy (Grand Rapids, Mich.: Eerdmans, 1997), 275.

2. Yad Vashem press release, October 2, 2003, http://www1.yadvashem.org/about_yad/press_room/press_releases/Court.html.

3. David Gushee, *The Righteous Gentiles of the Holocaust: A Christian Interpretation* (Minneapolis: Fortress Press, 1994), 99. According to Gushee, religion does not appear to be a significant predictor of rescue behavior, since no measure of religious affiliation or commitment differentiates rescuers from nonrescuers. More rescuers than nonrescuers describe themselves as "very" religious at each stage of life. However, the fact that rescuers are more likely than nonrescuers to describe themselves as "not at all" religious suggests that rescuers may have stronger convictions about religion, whether positive or negative.

4. See Gushee, *Righteous Gentiles of the Holocaust*, ch. 5.

5. Samuel P. Oliner and Pearl M. Oliner, *The Altruistic Personality: Rescuers of Jews in Nazi Europe* (New York: Free Press, 1988), 249–51.

6. See Ruth Zerner, "Dietrich Bonhoeffer and the Jews: Thoughts and Actions, 1933–1945," *Jewish Social Studies* 37:3–4 (1975): 235–50; 239.

7. Eberhard Bethge, "Dietrich Bonhoeffer and the Jews," in *Ethical Responsibility: Bonhoeffer's Legacy to the Churches*, ed. John D. Godsey and Geffrey B. Kelly, Toronto Studies in Theology, vol. 6 (New York: Edwin Mellen, 1981), 43–96; 50. Kenneth C. Barnes notes that Bonhoeffer's neighborhood of Grünewald had a higher percentage of Jewish residents than any district in Berlin, a city in which the proportion of Jews was nearly five times greater than in Germany as a whole. See "Dietrich Bonhoeffer and Hitler's Persecution of the Jews," in *Betrayal: German Churches and the Holocaust*, ed. Robert Ericksen and Susannah Heschel (Minneapolis: Fortress Press, 1999), 110. For a different perspective, see Stanley R. Rosenbaum, "Dietrich Bonhoeffer: A Jewish View," *Journal of Ecumenical Studies* 18:2 (Spring 1981): 301–7; 307: "[Bonhoeffer's] first close friendship with anyone of even minimally Jewish background did not occur until 1927."

8. On Hildebrandt, see Eberhard Bethge, *Dietrich Bonhoeffer: A Biography*, rev. and ed. Victoria J. Barnett (Minneapolis: Fortress Press, 2000), 138: "His friendship with Franz Hildebrandt would have numerous consequences for Bonhoeffer, and would last for the rest of his life."

9. Edwin H. Robertson, *The Shame and the Sacrifice: The Life and Teaching of Dietrich Bonhoeffer* (London: Hodder & Stoughton, 1987), 162–63.

10. Cited in Ruth Zerner, "Dietrich Bonhoeffer and the Jews: Thoughts and Actions, 1933–1945," 244. James McClendon observes that when Bonhoeffer "no longer had any resource for Christian resistance . . . he turned to the time-honored practices and skills of his family." See Michael Goldberg, "Bonhoeffer and the Limits of Jewish-Christian Dialogue," *Books and Religion* 14:3 (March 1986): 3–4; 4.

11. See Bethge, *Dietrich Bonhoeffer: A Biography*, 273, 436, 598.

12. On the influences of Leibholz and von Dohnanyi on Bonhoeffer's initial response to Nazism in 1933, see James Patrick Kelley, "'The Best of the German Gentiles': Dietrich Bonhoeffer and the Rights of Jews in Hitler's Germany," in *Remembering for the Future: Working Papers and Addenda*, vol.1, *Jews and Christians during and after the Holocaust*, edited by Yehuda Bauer et al. (Oxford: Pergamon, 1989), 80–92; 81.

13. Raymond Mengus, "Dietrich Bonhoeffer and the Decision to Resist," in *Resistance against the Third Reich, 1933–1990*, ed. Michael Geyer and John W. Boyer (Chicago: University of Chicago Press, 1992), 200–213; 204.

14. Oliner and Oliner, *The Altruistic Personality*, 249.

15. Ibid., 252.

16. Eberhard Bethge inadvertently endorses this view in his description of the decision to return to Germany from New York in 1939: "Bonhoeffer had made the great decision of his life entirely alone" (*Dietrich Bonhoeffer*, 653). Bethge also speaks of Bonhoeffer's "complete moral loneliness" in the conspiracy. See "Turning Points in Bonhoeffer's Life and Thought," in *Bonhoeffer in a World Come of Age*, ed. Peter Vorkink II (Philadelphia: Fortress Press, 1968), 26.

17. George W. Bush, Commencement Address at Concordia University, Mequon, Wisconsin, May 14, 2004, http://www.whitehouse.gov/news/releases/2004/05/20040414-4.html.

18. Nechama Tec, *When Light Pierced the Darkness: Christian Rescuers of Jews in Nazi-Occupied Poland* (New York: Oxford University Press, 1986), 188.

19. Ibid., 190–91.

20. Ibid., 189.

21. Oliner and Oliner, *The Altruistic Personality*, 257.

22. Ibid., 199.

23. Michael F. Moeller, "The Lonely Resister: Dietrich Bonhoeffer, Protestant Martyr," August 2002, http://www.beliefnet.com/story/6/story_687_1.html.

24. Bethge, *Dietrich Bonhoeffer: A Biography*, 595.

25. On Dietrich's relationships with family members, see Ronald Gregor Smith and Wolf-Dieter Zimmerman, eds., *I Knew Dietrich Bonhoeffer* (New York: Harper & Row, 1966), especially Sabine Leibholz, "Childhood and Home," 19–33; Hans-Werner Jensen, "Life Together," where the author notes Dietrich's "close attachment to his mother" during the late 1930s (154); and Eberhard Bethge, "Friends," where we learn that Erwin Sutz, the Swiss friend Dietrich met in New York, "was amazed that anybody was prepared to waste so much money on the post office and the Western Union to keep in touch with his family by telegram or telephone; there was a continuous dispatching of congratulations, an endless discussion of the problems of innumerable and distant relatives" (46). Keith W. Clements writes that "one of the most striking things about Bonhoeffer—and never more so than in the prison writings—is his intense devotion to his family and above all to his parents." See Keith W. Clements, *A Patriotism for Today: Love of Country in Dialogue with the Witness of Dietrich Bonhoeffer* (London: Collins Liturgical, 1984), 21. See also Larry Rasmussen with Renate Bethge, "Bonhoeffer's Family and Its Significance for His Theology," in *Bonhoeffer's Significance for North Americans* (Minneapolis: Fortress Press, 1990).

26. Victoria Barnett emphasizes that the influence of Bonhoeffer's ecumenical friends cannot be overestimated in the final period of his life ("Dietrich Bonhoeffer,

the Ecumenical Movement, and the Holocaust," paper presented at Zion Lutheran Church, Baltimore, March 1995). See also "Dietrich Bonhoeffer's Ecumenical Vision," *Christian Century* 112 (April 26, 1995): 454–57, where Barnett laments the lack of attention to "the influence of [Bonhoeffer's] ecumenical contacts and world-view on his theology and praxis" (454).

27. Bethge, *Dietrich Bonhoeffer: A Biography*, 581.

28. Ibid., 677.

29. Oliner and Oliner, *The Altruistic Personality*, 258.

30. Ibid., 260.

31. After reviewing several studies of rescue, Craig Slane writes that they "reinforce the basic notion of universality or omnipartiality so crucial to risk-laden intervention for others" (*Bonhoeffer as Martyr*, 245).

32. Oliner and Oliner, *The Altruistic Personality*, 254.

33. Tec, *When Light Pierced the Darkness*, 188.

34. Ibid., 148–49. Even the small minority of Polish rescuers Tec defines as "deeply religious" were not influenced by a sense of spiritual connection with Jews. Rather, their brand of religiosity demanded "high humanitarian standards" that trumped the church's pronouncements when the two were in conflict.

35. Ibid., 189.

36. Ibid.

37. Oliner and Oliner, *The Altruistic Personality*, 156.

38. Ibid., 166–67, 169

39. Ibid., 166, 170.

40. Eva Fogelman, *Conscience and Courage: Rescuers of Jews during the Holocaust* (New York: Anchor, 1995), 165, 169, 173. The book grew out of more than three hundred in-depth interviews conducted for the Rescuer Project at the City University of New York.

41. Gushee, *Righteous Gentiles of the Holocaust*, 113.

42. Ibid., 134–35.

43. Ibid., 119.

44. Oliner and Oliner, *The Altruistic Personality*, 155.

45. Ibid., 154–55.

46. Cited in Gushee, *Righteous Gentiles of the Holocaust*, 130. Eva Fogelman explains that many Dutch rescuers belonged to the Anti-Revolutionary Church Party, whose members "felt a spiritual connection with Jews through stories from the Hebrew Bible and through stories about Jesus. Jews were brothers and sisters to them, not alien beings" (*Conscience and Courage*, 164).

47. Ten Boom's love for Jews has attracted the attention of millions of readers, as well as rescue researchers. Her love for the Hebrew Scriptures contributed to an affinity for the Jewish people as divinely elected. Because the Jews are God's chosen people—"the apple of God's eye" according to Corrie's father—Christians are obligated to protect them. See Corrie ten Boom with John and Elizabeth Sherrill, *The Hiding Place* (Washington Depot, Conn.: Chosen Books, 1971).

48. Fogelman, *Conscience and Courage*, 191. "Judeophiles" are one of five distinct groups in Fogelman's taxonomy of rescue. In this category, the second largest, Fogelman places persons with a variety of experiences and motivations. Some, like Oskar Schindler, were driven by commitment to a close Jewish friend or a Jewish spouse. Other judeophiles were motivated by economic factors (the rescued Jews possessed resources that aided the survival of the host family); some had or suspected they had Jewish blood; others had been in romantic relationships with Jews that were forbidden by their families; others thought they might be the illegitimate offspring of a secret Jewish liaison. Fogelman's other four categories of rescuers are "moral," "network," "concerned professionalism" and "children."

49. Cited in Slane, *Bonhoeffer as Martyr*, 243.

50. *Weapons of the Spirit*, directed, written, and produced by Pierre Sauvage (The Chambon Foundation, 1989).

51. Pierre Sauvage, "Ten Things I Would Like to Know about Righteous Conduct in Le Chambon and Elsewhere during the Holocaust," address at "Faith in Humankind: Rescuers of Jews during the Holocaust" conference, United States Holocaust Memorial Museum, Washington, D.C., September 19, 1984, http://www.chambon.org/chambon_ten_things.htm.

52. Philip Hallie, "Rescue and Goodness: Reflections on the Holocaust" (Washington, D.C.: United States Holocaust Memorial Museum, 1993), 6.

53. W. A. Visser 't Hooft, "An Act of Penitence," in *I Knew Dietrich Bonhoeffer*, 193 (emphasis added).

54. Cited in Bethge, *Dietrich Bonhoeffer: A Biography*, 931.

55. Ann W. Astell, "Reading the Bible with Holocaust Survivors and Rescuers: A New Biblical Spirituality," *Interpretation* 56:2 (April 2002): 181–93; 185. Andreas Pangritz points out that Karl Barth may be an even more provocative example of this combination of motivations for solidarity with Jews (e-mail message to the author, September 7, 2004).

56. Oliner and Oliner, *The Altruistic Personality*, 157.

57. Ibid., 166.

58. The same melding of universal and exclusive ideas is evident in an official statement of the Confessing Church from 1943. "The Christian's neighbor," the statement declares, "is always the one who is helpless and who especially needs him, and this irrespective of race, *Volk*, and religion. For the life of all human beings belongs to God alone. The life of the people of Israel is holy to Him. Israel, certainly, has rejected the Christ of God, but it is not we human beings or even we Christians who are called upon to punish Israel's disbelief" (statement of the Confessional Synod of the Old Prussian Union, October 1943). Cited in Wolfgang Gerlach, *And the Witnesses Were Silent: The Confessing Church and the Persecution of the Jews*, ed. and trans. Victoria J. Barnett (Lincoln: University of Nebraska Press, 2000), 207.

59. Gushee, *Righteous Gentiles of the Holocaust*, 120–21.

60. Ibid., 121.

61. Robert E. Willis, "Bonhoeffer and Barth on Jewish Suffering: Reflections on the Relationship between Theology and Moral Sensibility," *Journal of Ecumenical Studies* 24:4 (Fall 1987): 598–615; 612, 615.

62. While acknowledging the "troubling implications" of Bonhoeffer's early thought, David Jensen identifies his "vision of 'religionless Christianity' and vulnerable discipleship" as a distinctive contribution to the current dialogical scene. See David H. Jensen, "Religionless Christianity and Vulnerable Discipleship: The Interfaith Promise of Bonhoeffer's Theology," *Journal of Ecumenical Studies* 38:3 (Spring–Summer 2001): 151–67.

63. Barnett, "Dietrich Bonhoeffer, the Ecumenical Movement, and the Holocaust."

Chapter 8: The Paradox of Bonhoeffer's Post-Holocaust Legacy

1. Cited in Richard L. Rubenstein, "Was Dietrich Bonhoeffer a 'Righteous Gentile'?" 2, paper presented at the AAR/SBL Annual Meeting, Nashville, November 20, 2000, and graciously shared with the author. An earlier version of the paper was published in the *International Journal on World Peace* 17:2 (2000).

2. Richard L. Rubenstein and John K. Roth, *Approaches to Auschwitz: The Holocaust and Its Legacy*, rev. ed. (Louisville, Ky.: Westminster John Knox, 2003), 264. Similarly, Andreas Pangritz argues that without a theological conception of the relationship between the church and Israel, Bonhoeffer would not have been able to develop the sort of paradoxical patriotism that brought him back to Germany in 1939 with the aim of joining the resistance. See Andreas Pangritz,

"Sharing the Destiny of His People," in *Bonhoeffer for a New Day: Theology in a Time of Transition,* ed. John W. de Gruchy (Grand Rapids, Mich.: Eerdmans, 1997), 258–77; 271.

3. Ibid., 260.

4. Ibid.

5. See Stephen R. Haynes, *Reluctant Witnesses: Jews and the Christian Imagination* (Louisville, Ky.: Westminster John Knox, 1995).

6. Wayne Whitson Floyd Jr., "'These People I Have Loved Now Live': Commemorating Dietrich Bonhoeffer after Auschwitz," unpublished manuscript, Lutheran Theological Seminary at Philadelphia, 1995.

7. Eberhard Bethge, "The Chronicler of an Era," in *Friendship and Resistance: Essays on Dietrich Bonhoeffer* (Grand Rapids, Mich.: Eerdmans, 1995), 11–12.

8. Andreas Pangritz, "'Mystery and Commandment' in Leo Baeck and Dietrich Bonhoeffer," *European Judaism* 30:2 (Autumn 1997): 44–57; 54.

9. I am thankful to Andreas Pangritz for reminding me of this fact (e-mail message to the author, September 7, 2004). See Haynes, *Reluctant Witnesses,* ch. 8.

BIBLIOGRAPHY

All URLs—dated and undated—were active at the time this book went to press.
All references to the Bonhoeffer Archive are to the archival collection of Bonhoeffer materials at Burke Library, Union Theological Seminary, New York.

Andersen, Francis I. "Dietrich Bonhoeffer and the Old Testament." *Reformed Theological Review* 34:2 (May–August 1975): 33–44.

Arnold, E. R. "Who's Afraid of Dietrich Bonhoeffer?" *Journal of Reformed Theology* 29:1 (1972): 57–75.

Astell, Ann W. "Reading the Bible with Holocaust Survivors and Rescuers: A New Biblical Spirituality." *Interpretation* 56:2 (April 2002): 181–93.

Augustine, *City of God.* In A Select Library of the Nicene and Post-Nicene Fathers of the Christian Church Series, 8 volumes. Edited by Philip Schaff. Grand Rapids: Eerdmans, 1955.

Axelrod, Nancy. "Knight: A Play in Two Acts." 1995. Bonhoeffer Archive, Bonhoeffer Secondary Papers, series 3 box 1.

Barnes, Kenneth C. "Dietrich Bonhoeffer and Hitler's Persecution of the Jews." In *Betrayal: German Churches and the Holocaust.* Edited by Robert Ericksen and Susannah Heschel. Minneapolis: Fortress Press, 1999.

———. *Nazism, Liberalism, and Christianity: Protestant Social Thought in Germany and Great Britain 1925–1937.* Lexington: University Press of Kentucky, 1991.

Barnett, Victoria. "Dietrich Bonhoeffer." Publication of the United States Holocaust Memorial Museum. http://www.ushmm.org/bonhoeffer/b6.htm.

———. "Dietrich Bonhoeffer, the Ecumenical Movement, and the Holocaust." Unpublished manuscript.

———. "Dietrich Bonhoeffer's Ecumenical Vision." *Christian Century* 112:14 (April 26, 1995): 454–57.

———. "Response to Richard L. Rubenstein." Paper presented at the AAR/ SBL Annual Meeting, Nashville, November 20, 2000. Bonhoeffer Archive, Bonhoeffer Secondary Papers, series 1A box 3.

Barth, Karl. *Church Dogmatics*. Edited by G. W. Bromiley and T. F. Torrance. Translated by G. W. Bromiley. 2nd ed. Edinburgh: T & T Clark, 1975–.

Bergen, Doris L. "Catholics, Protestants, and Antisemitism in Nazi Germany." *Central European History* 27:3 (1994): 329–48.

———. *Twisted Cross: The German Christian Movement in the Third Reich*. Chapel Hill: University of North Carolina Press, 1996.

Benedict. *The Rule of Saint Benedict in English*. Edited by Timothy Fry, O.S.B. Vintage Spiritual Classics. New York: Vintage, 1998.

Berger, David. "The Attitude of St. Bernard of Clairvaux to the Jews." *Proceedings of the American Academy of Jewish Research* 40 (1972): 89–108.

Berger, Ronald J. *Fathoming the Holocaust: A Social Problems Approach*. New York: Aldine de Gruyter, 2002.

Bethge, Eberhard. "Aftermath of Flossenbürg: Bonhoeffer, 1945–1970." *Christian Century* 87 (May 27, 1970): 656–59.

———. *Bonhoeffer: Exile and Martyr*. New York: Seabury, 1975.

———. "Christians and Jews in Germany Today, and Bonhoeffer's Sustaining Legacy," 297–311. In *Burning Memory: Times of Testing and Reckoning*, edited by Alice L. Eckardt. Oxford: Pergamon Press, 1993.

———. *Dietrich Bonhoeffer: Man of Vision, Man of Courage*. New York: Harper & Row, 1977.

———. *Dietrich Bonhoeffer: A Biography*. Revised and edited by Victoria J. Barnett. Minneapolis: Fortress Press, 2000.

———. "Dietrich Bonhoeffer 1906–1945." *Christianity and Crisis* 25 (April 19, 1965): 75.

———. "Dietrich Bonhoeffer and the Jews," 43–101. In *Ethical Responsibility: Bonhoeffer's Legacy to the Churches*, edited by John D. Godsey and Geffrey B. Kelly. Toronto Studies in Theology 6. New York: Edwin Mellen, 1981.

———. *Friendship and Resistance: Essays on Dietrich Bonhoeffer*. Grand Rapids, Mich.: Eerdmans, 1995.

———. *Am gegebene Ort: Aufsätze und Reden, 1970–1979*. Munich: Kaiser, 1979.

———. "The Holocaust and Christian Anti-Semitism: Perspectives of a Christian Survivor." *Union Seminary Quarterly Review* 32:3–4 (1977): 141–55.

———. "The Holocaust as Turning-Point." *Christian Jewish Relations* 22:3–4 (1989): 55–67.

———. "My Friend Dietrich." *Christian History* 10:4 (issue 32, 1991): 41.

———. "One of the Silent Bystanders? Bonhoeffer on November 9, 1938," 58–71. In *Friendship and Resistance: Essays on Dietrich Bonhoeffer*. Grand Rapids, Mich.: Eerdmans, 1995.

———. "Unfulfilled Tasks." *Dialog* 34:1 (Winter 1995): 30–31.

Bethge, Renate. *Dietrich Bonhoeffer: A Brief Life*. Translated by K. C. Hanson. Minneapolis: Fortress Press, 2004.

Blackburn, Vivienne. *Dietrich Bonhoeffer and Simone Weil: A Study in Christian Responsiveness*. Religions and Discourse. New York: Peter Lang, 2004.

Bonhoeffer. Directed by Bill Alden, Bekah Dannelley, and Andrzej Krakowski. West Tisbury, Mass.: Pilgrim Productions, 2000.

Bonhoeffer. Directed by Martin Doblmeier. New York: First Run Features, 2004.

Bonhoeffer, Dietrich. *The Cost of Discipleship*. Revised edition. New York: Macmillan, 1959.

———. *Creation and Fall: A Theological Exposition of Genesis 1–3*. Edited by John W. DeGruchy. Translated by Douglas Stephen Bax. Dietrich Bonhoeffer Works, vol. 3. Minneapolis: Fortress Press, 1997.

———. *Discipleship*. Edited by Geffrey B. Kelly and John D. Godsey. Dietrich Bonhoeffer Works, vol. 4. Minneapolis: Fortress Press, 2003.

———. *Ethics*. Edited by Clifford J. Green. Translated by Reinhard Krauss, Charles C. West, and Douglas W. Stott. Dietrich Bonhoeffer Works, vol. 6. Minneapolis: Fortress Press, 2005.

———. *Letters and Papers from Prison*. Edited by Eberhard Bethge. New York: Macmillan, 1972.

———. *Life Together and Prayerbook of the Bible*. Edited by Geffrey B. Kelly. Translated by Daniel W. Bloesch and James H. Burtness. Dietrich Bonhoeffer Works, vol. 5. Minneapolis: Fortress Press, 1996.

———. *No Rusty Swords: Letters, Lectures, and Notes, 1928–1936, from the Collected Works of Dietrich Bonhoeffer*. Vol. 1. Edited by Edwin H. Robertson. Translated by Edwin H. Robertson and John Bowden. New York: Harper & Row, 1965.

Borowitz, Eugene B. "Current Theological Literature: Bonhoeffer's World Come of Age." *Judaism* 14:1 (Winter 1965): 81–87.

Bosanquet, Mary. *The Life and Death of Dietrich Bonhoeffer*. New York: Harper & Row, 1968.

Bowman, Douglas C. "Bonhoeffer and the Possibility of Judaizing Christianity," 76–86. In *A Bonhoeffer Legacy: Essays in Understanding*, edited by A. J. Klassen. Grand Rapids, Mich.: Eerdmans, 1981.

Carter, Guy Christopher. "Confession at Bethel, August 1933—Enduring Witness: The Formation, Revision, and Significance of the First Full Theological Confession of the Evangelical Church Struggle in Nazi Germany." Ph.D. diss., Marquette University, 1987.

Carter, Guy, et al., eds. *Bonhoeffer's Ethics: Old Europe and New Frontiers.* Kampen, Netherlands: Kok Pharos, 1991.

Chandler, Andrew. "The Quest for the Historical Bonhoeffer." *Journal of Ecclesiastical History* 54:1 (January 2003): 89–96.

Clements, Keith W. *A Patriotism for Today: Love of Country in Dialogue with the Witness of Dietrich Bonhoeffer.* London: Collins Liturgical, 1984.

———. *What Freedom? The Persistent Challenge of Dietrich Bonhoeffer.* Bristol, UK: Bristol Baptist College, 1990.

Conway, John S. "Coming to Terms with the Past: Interpreting the German Church Struggles 1933–1990." *German History* 16:3 (1998): 377–96.

———. "Historiography of the German Church Struggle." *Journal of Bible and Religion* 32 (July 1964): 221–30.

———. "The German Church Struggle and Its Aftermath," 39–52. In *Jews and Christians after the Holocaust,* edited by Abraham J. Peck. Philadelphia: Fortress Press, 1982.

DC Talk and The Voice of the Martyrs, *Jesus Freaks: Stories of Those Who Stood for Jesus: The Ultimate Jesus Freaks.* Bloomington, Minn.: Bethany House, 1999.

de Gruchy, John W. *Daring, Trusting Spirit: Bonhoeffer's Friend Eberhard Bethge.* Minneapolis: Fortress Press, 2005.

———, ed. *Bonhoeffer for a New Day: Theology in a Time of Transition.* Grand Rapids, Mich.: Eerdmans, 1997.

———, ed. *The Cambridge Companion to Dietrich Bonhoeffer.* Cambridge: Cambridge University Press, 1999.

———, ed. *Dietrich Bonhoeffer: Witness to Jesus Christ.* The Making of Modern Theology: Nineteenth- and Twentieth-Century Texts. Minneapolis: Fortress Press, 1991.

Dudzus, Otto. "Discipleship and Worldliness in the Thinking of Dietrich Bonhoeffer." *Religion in Life* 35 (Spring 1966): 230–40.

Ecclestone, Alan. *The Night Sky of the Lord.* London: Darton Longman & Todd, 1980.

Eckardt, Alice L. "The Holocaust, The Church Struggle, and Some Christian Reflections," 31–44. In *Faith and Freedom: A Tribute to Franklin H. Littell,* edited by Richard Libowitz. New York: Pergamon, 1987.

Ericksen, Robert. "Response to Richard Rubenstein: Bonhoeffer, the Jews, and Judaism." Paper presented at the AAR/SBL Annual Meeting, Nashville, November 20, 2000.

———. *Theologians under Hitler: Gerhard Kittel, Paul Althaus, Emanuel Hirsch*. New Haven: Yale University Press, 1985.

Ericksen, Robert, and Susannah Heschel, eds. *Betrayal: German Churches and the Holocaust*. Minneapolis: Fortress Press, 1999.

Fackenheim, Emil L. "(Kritik) Besprechung." Review of *Konsequenzen: Dietrich Bonhoeffers Kirchenverständnis Heute*, edited by Ernst Feil and Ilse Tödt, and *Ethik im Ernstfall: Dietrich Bonhoeffers Stellung zu den Juden und ihre Aktualität*, edited by Wolfgang Huber and Ilse Tödt. *IBK Bonhoeffer Rundbrief* 20 (November 1985): 16–18.

———. "Fackenheim on Bonhoeffer." *Newsletter of the International Bonhoeffer Society for Archive and Research, English Language Section* 11 (November 1977): 2–4.

———. *To Mend the World: Foundations of Post-Holocaust Jewish Thought*. New York: Schocken Books, 1982.

———. "On the Self-Exposure of Faith to the Modern-Secular World: Philosophical Reflections in the Light of Jewish Experience," 278–305. In *The Quest for Past and Future: Essays in Jewish Theology*. Bloomington: Indiana University Press, 1968.

Fangmeier, Jürgen, and Hinrich Stoevesandt, eds. *Karl Barth, Letters 1961–68*. Translated by Geoffrey W. Bromiley. Edinburgh: T & T Clark, 1981.

Feil, Ernst. *Bonhoeffer Studies in Germany: A Survey of Recent Literature*. Edited by James H. Burtness. Translated by Jonathan Sorum. Philadelphia: Bonhoeffer Center, 1997.

Fischer, Klaus. *The History of an Obsession: German Judeophobia and the Holocaust*. New York: Continuum, 1998.

Fleischner, Eva. *Judaism in German Christian Theology Since 1945: Christianity and Israel Considered in Terms of Mission*. American Theological Library Association Monograph Series 8. Metuchen, N.J.: Scarecrow, 1975.

Floyd, Wayne Whitson Jr. "Bonhoeffer's Many Faces." *Christian Century* (April 26, 1995): 444–45.

———. "'These People I Have Loved Now Live': Commemorating Bonhoeffer after Fifty Years." Unpublished manuscript, Lutheran Theological Seminary at Philadelphia, 1995.

Floyd, Wayne Whitson, Jr., and Charles Marsh, eds. *Theology and the Practice of Responsibility: Essays on Dietrich Bonhoeffer*. Philadelphia: Trinity Press International, 1994.

Fogelman, Eva. *Conscience and Courage: Rescuers of Jews during the Holocaust.* New York: Anchor, 1995.

Ford, David F. *Self and Salvation: Being Transformed.* Cambridge: Cambridge University Press, 1999.

Friedlander, Albert H. "Bonhoeffer and Baeck: Theology after Auschwitz," *European Judaism* 14 (Summer 1980): 26–32.

————. "Israel and Europe: Meditations for the Bonhoeffer Conference, 15.6.88." In *Bonhoeffer's Ethics: Old Europe and New Frontiers,* edited by Guy Carter et al. Kampen, Netherlands: Kok Pharos, 1991.

Gerlach, Wolfgang. *And the Witnesses Were Silent: The Confessing Church and the Persecution of the Jews.* Edited and translated by Victoria J. Barnett. Lincoln: University of Nebraska Press, 2000.

Giardina, Denise. *Saints and Villains.* New York: Fawcett, 1998.

Glazener, Mary. *The Cup of Wrath: A Novel Based on Dietrich Bonhoeffer's Resistance to Hitler.* Macon, Ga.: Smith & Helwys, 1992.

Godsey, John D. *The Theology of Dietrich Bonhoeffer.* Philadelphia: Westminster, 1960.

Godsey, John D., and Geffrey B. Kelly, eds. *Ethical Responsibility: Bonhoeffer's Legacy to the Churches.* New York: Edwin Mellen, 1981.

Goldberg, Michael. "Bonhoeffer and the Limits of Jewish-Christian Dialogue." *Books and Religion* 14:3 (March 1986): 3–4.

Goldhagen, Daniel Jonah. *Hitler's Willing Executioners: Ordinary Germans and the Holocaust.* New York: Knopf, 1996.

Green, Clifford. "Bonhoeffer's Legacy." Published by Oregon Public Broadcasting and the Public Broadcasting Service online, 2000. http://www.pbs.org/opb/bonhoeffer/legacy.

————. "The Holocaust and the First Commandment." Bonhoeffer Archive, Bonhoeffer Secondary Papers, series 1C box 1.

————. "Sharing the Sufferings of God: The Challenge of the Holocaust to Religious Faith." Bonhoeffer Archive, Bonhoeffer Secondary Papers, series 1C box 1.

Greenberg, Irving. "Partnership in the Covenant: Dietrich Bonhoeffer and the Future of Jewish-Christian Dialogue." Paper presented at the Sixth International Bonhoeffer Congress, New York, 1992. Bonhoeffer Archive, Bonhoeffer Secondary Papers, series 1B box 4.

Gremmels, Christian. "Bonhoeffer, the Churches, and Jewish-Christian Relations," 295–305. In *Theology and the Practice of Responsibility: Essays on Dietrich Bonhoeffer,* edited by Wayne Whitson Floyd Jr. and Charles Marsh. Valley Forge, Pa.: Trinity Press International, 1994.

Gushee, David. *The Righteous Gentiles of the Holocaust: A Christian Interpretation*. Minneapolis: Fortress Press, 1994.

Gutman, Israel, ed. *Encyclopedia of the Holocaust*. New York: Macmillan, 1990.

Gutteridge, Richard. *The German Evangelical Church and the Jews, 1879–1950*. New York: Barnes & Noble, 1976.

Haberman, Joshua O. *The God I Believe In: Conversations about Judaism*. New York: Free Press, 1994.

Hall, Sidney G., III. *Christian Anti-Semitism and Paul's Theology*. Minneapolis: Fortress Press, 1993.

Hallie, Philip. *Rescue and Goodness: Reflections on the Holocaust*. Washington, D.C.: United States Holocaust Memorial Museum, 1993.

Harrelson, Walter. "Bonhoeffer and the Bible," 115–39. In *The Place of Bonhoeffer: Problems and Possibilities in His Thought*, edited by Martin E. Marty. New York: Association Press, 1962.

Harries, Richard. *After the Evil: Christianity and Judaism in the Shadow of the Holocaust*. Oxford: Oxford University Press, 2003.

Hauerwas, Stanley. *Performing the Faith: Bonhoeffer and the Practice of Nonviolence*. Grand Rapids, Mich.: Brazos, 2004.

Haynes, Stephen R. *The Bonhoeffer Phenomenon: Portraits of a Protestant Saint*. Minneapolis: Fortress Press, 2004.

———. *Prospects for Post-Holocaust Theology: "Israel" in the Theologies of Karl Barth, Jürgen Moltmann, and Paul van Buren*. American Academy of Religion Academy Series 77. Atlanta: Scholars, 1991.

———. *Reluctant Witnesses: Jews and the Christian Imagination*. Louisville: Westminster John Knox, 1995.

Haynes, Stephen R., and John K. Roth, eds. *The Death of God and the Holocaust: Radical Theology Encounters the Shoah*. New York: Greenwood, 1997.

Henry, Marilyn. "Who, Exactly, Is a 'Righteous Gentile'?" *Jerusalem Post* (April 22, 1998): 12.

Holland, Scott. "First We Take Manhattan, Then We Take Berlin: Bonhoeffer's New York." *Cross Currents* 50:3 (Fall 2000). http://www.crosscurrents.org/hollandf20.htm.

Huber, Wolfgang. "Answering for the Past, Shaping the Future: In Memory of Dietrich Bonhoeffer." *Ecumenical Review* 47:3 (July 1995): 252–62.

Huneke, Douglas K. *The Stones Will Cry Out: Pastoral Reflections on the Shoah (with Liturgical Resources)*. Contributions to the Study of Religion 39. Westport, Conn.: Greenwood, 1995.

Huttenbach, Henry R. "Guarding the Gates: On Being a Survivor and Becoming a Righteous Gentile." *The Genocide Forum: A Platform for Post-Holocaust Commentary* 5:3 (January–February 1999), http://www.chgs.umn.edu/Educational_Resources/Newsletter/The_Genocide_Forum/Yr_5/Year__5No__3/year_5__no__3.html#guardinggates.

Jensen, David H. "Religionless Christianity and Vulnerable Discipleship: The Interfaith Promise of Bonhoeffer's Theology." *Journal of Ecumenical Studies* 38:3 (Spring–Summer 2001): 151–67.

The Jewish Spectator. "Bonhoeffer and Judaism" (Winter 1985–Spring 1986): 65.

Johnson, William Stacy. "Regaining Perspective." *Presbyterian Outlook* 183:19 (May 21, 2001): 11.

Kelley, James Patrick. "The Best of the German Gentiles: Dietrich Bonhoeffer and the Rights of Jews in Hitler's Germany," 80–92. In *Remembering for the Future: Working Papers and Addenda.* Vol. 1, *Jews and Christians during and after the Holocaust,* edited by Yehuda Bauer et al. Oxford: Pergamon, 1989.

Kelly, Geffrey B. "Bonhoeffer and the Jews: Implications for Jewish-Christian Relations," 133–66. In *Reflections on Bonhoeffer: Essays in Honor of F. Burton Nelson,* edited by Geffrey B. Kelly and C. John Weborg. Chicago: Covenant, 1999.

————. *Liberating Faith: Bonhoeffer's Message for Today.* Minneapolis: Augsburg Publishing House, 1984.

Kelly, Geffrey B., and C. John Weborg, eds. *Reflections on Bonhoeffer: Essays in Honor of F. Burton Nelson.* Chicago: Covenant, 1999.

Kelly, Geffrey B., and F. Burton Nelson. *The Cost of Moral Leadership: The Spirituality of Dietrich Bonhoeffer.* Grand Rapids, Mich.: Eerdmans, 2003.

Klein, Charlotte. *Anti-Judaism in Christian Theology.* Translated by Edward Quinn. Minneapolis: Fortress Press, 1978.

Koch, Robert F. "The Theological Responses of Karl Barth and Deitrich Bonhoeffer to Church-State Relations in Germany, 1933–1945." Ph.D. diss., Northwestern University, 1988.

Koonz, Claudia. "Ethical Dilemmas and Nazi Eugenics: Single Issue Dissent in Religious Contexts," 15–38. In *Resistance against the Third Reich, 1933–1990,* edited by Michael Geyer and John W. Boyer. Chicago: University of Chicago Press, 1992.

Kreilkamp, Hermes Donald. "Dietrich Bonhoeffer: Prophet of Human Solidarity." *Spirituality Today* 36:2 (1984): 151–61.

Kuhns, William. *In Pursuit of Dietrich Bonhoeffer.* Dayton, Ohio: Pflaum, 1967.

Kuske, Martin. *The Old Testament as the Book of Christ: An Appraisal of Bonhoeffer's Interpretation.* Translated by S. T. Kimbrough Jr. Philadelphia: Westminster, 1976.

Langer, Lawrence L. *Versions of Survival: The Holocaust and the Human Spirit.* Albany: State University of New York Press, 1982.

Lapide, Pinchas. "Bonhoeffer und das Judentum," 116–130. In *Verspieltes Erbe: Dietrich Bonhoeffer und der deutsche Nachkriegsprotestantismus,* edited by Ernst Feil. Munich: Kaiser, 1979.

The Layman Online. http://www.confessingchurch.homestead.com/.

Lifton, Robert Jay. *The Nazi Doctors: Medical Killing and the Psychology of Genocide.* New York: Basic, 1986.

Littell, Franklin H. *The Crucifixion of the Jews: The Failure of Christians to Understand the Jewish Experience.* Macon, Ga.: Mercer University Press, 1986 [1975].

Littell, Franklin H., and Hubert G. Locke, eds. *The German Church Struggle and the Holocaust.* San Francisco: Mellen Research Press, 1990.

Lüdtke, Alf. "The Appeal of Exterminating 'Others': German Workers and the Limits of Resistance," 53–74. In *Resistance against the Third Reich, 1933–1990,* edited by Michael Geyer and John W. Boyer. Chicago: University of Chicago Press, 1992.

Marty, Martin E., ed. *The Place of Bonhoeffer: Problems and Possibilities in His Thought.* New York: Association Press, 1962.

Mengus, Raymond. "Dietrich Bonhoeffer and the Decision to Resist," 200–213. In *Resistance against the Third Reich, 1933–1990,* edited by Michael Geyer and John W. Boyer. Chicago: University of Chicago Press, 1992.

Miller, Susan Martins. *Dietrich Bonhoeffer.* Men of Faith. Minneapolis: Bethany House, 2002.

Moeller, Michael F. "The Lonely Resister: Dietrich Bonhoeffer, Protestant Martyr." http://www.beliefnet.com/story/6/story_687_1.html.

Morris, Kenneth Earl. *Bonhoeffer's Ethic of Discipleship: A Study in Social Psychology, Political Thought, and Religion.* University Park: Pennsylvania State University Press, 1986.

Mosse, George. *Nazi Culture: A Documentary History.* New York: Random House, 1966.

Muggeridge, Malcolm. *A Third Testament.* Boston: Little, Brown, 1976.

Müller, Christine-Ruth. *Dietrich Bonhoeffers Kampf gegen die nationalsozialistische Verfolgung und Vernichtung der Juden: Bonhoeffers Haltung zur Judenfrage im Vergleich mit Stellungnahmen aus der evangelischen Kirche und Kreisen des deutschen Widerstandes*. Heidelberger Untersuchungen zu Widerstand, Judenverfolgung und Kirchenkampf im Dritten Reich, Band 5. Munich: Kaiser, 1990.

Nelson, F. Burton. "Dietrich Bonhoeffer and the Jews: An Agenda for Exploration and Contemporary Dialogue," 87–93. In *The Holocaust Forty Years After*, edited by Marcia Littell, Richard Libowitz, and Evelyn Bodek Rosen. Lewiston, N.Y.: Edwin Mellen, 1989.

Nicholls, William. *Christian Anti-Semitism: A History of Hate*. Northvale, N.J.: Jason Aronson, 1993.

Niemöller, Martin. *Here Stand I!* Translated by Jane Lymburn. Chicago: Willett, Clark & Co., 1937.

No Rusty Swords: Letters, Lectures, and Notes, 1928–1936, from the Collected Works of Dietrich Bonhoeffer. See Bonhoeffer, Dietrich. *No Rusty Swords*.

Novak, Michael. "Bonhoeffer's Way." *Book Week* 4 (February 19, 1967): 5–6.

Oliner, Samuel, and Pearl M. Oliner. *The Altruistic Personality: Rescuers of Jews in Nazi Europe*. New York: Free Press, 1988.

Pangritz, Andreas. "'Mystery and Commandment' in Leo Baeck and Dietrich Bonhoeffer." *European Judaism* 30:2 (Autumn 1997): 44–57.

———. "Sharing the Destiny of His People," 258–77. In *Bonhoeffer for a New Day: Theology in a Time of Transition*, edited by John W. de Gruchy. Grand Rapids, Mich.: Eerdmans, 1997.

Peck, Abraham J., ed. *Jews and Christians after the Holocaust*. Philadelphia: Fortress Press, 1982.

Peck, William Jay. "From Cain to the Death Camps: An Essay on Bonhoeffer and Judaism." *Union Seminary Quarterly Review* 28:2 (Winter 1973): 158–76.

Pesja, Jane. ". . . They Burned All the Meeting Places of God in the Land," 129–32. In *Reflections on Bonhoeffer: Essays in Honor of F. Burton Nelson*, edited by Geffrey B. Kelly and C. John Weborg. Chicago: Covenant, 1999.

Phillips, Michael. *The Eleventh Hour*. Wheaton, Ill.: Tyndale, 1993.

Plant, Stephen. *Bonhoeffer*. Outstanding Christian Thinkers. London: Continuum, 2004.

Rasmussen, Larry L. *Dietrich Bonhoeffer: Reality and Resistance*. Studies in Christian Ethics. Nashville: Abingdon, 1972.

———. "Dietrich Bonhoeffer and the Holocaust: Lessons for Lutherans," 6–17. In *Planning for the Future: LECNA at 85, Papers and Proceedings of the 81st Annual Meeting of the Lutheran Education Conference of North America*. Washington, D.C.: LECNA, 1995.

Rasmussen, Larry L., with Renate Bethge. *Dietrich Bonhoeffer: His Significance for North Americans*. Minneapolis: Fortress Press, 1990.

Raum, Elizabeth. *Dietrich Bonhoeffer: Called by God*. New York: Continuum, 2002.

Ray, Stephen G., Jr. *Do No Harm: Social Sin and Christian Responsibility*. Minneapolis: Fortress Press, 2003.

Riccardi, Constantino V. "Egmont and the Theologian." In *The Agony of Shopping and Other Plays*. Redlands, Calif.: Contra Mundum, 1986.

Rice, Chris. "Bonhoeffer after Sixty Years: Dietrich Bonhoeffer as We Understand Him at Jesus People USA Evangelical Covenant Church." http://www.cornerstonemag.com/pages/show_page.asp?694.

Rittner, Carol, and John K. Roth, eds. *Pope Pius XII and the Holocaust*. New York: Leicester University Press, 2002.

Robertson, Edwin H. *Dietrich Bonhoeffer*. Makers of Contemporary Theology. Philadelphia: John Knox, 1966.

———. *The Shame and the Sacrifice: The Life and Teaching of Dietrich Bonhoeffer*. London: Hodder & Stoughton, 1987.

———. "A Study of Dietrich Bonhoeffer and the Jews, January–April, 1933," 121–29. In *Remembering for the Future: Working Papers and Addenda*. Vol. 1, *Jews and Christians during and after the Holocaust*, edited by Yehuda Bauer et al. Oxford: Pergamon, 1989.

Rose, Paul Lawrence. *German Question/Jewish Question: Revolutionary Antisemitism from Kant to Wagner*. Princeton: Princeton University Press, 1990.

Rosenbaum, Stanley R. "Dietrich Bonhoeffer: A Jewish View." *Journal of Ecumenical Studies* 18:2 (Spring 1981): 301–7.

Rubenstein, Richard L. "Dietrich Bonhoeffer and Pope Pius XII," 193–218. In *The Century of Genocide: Selected Papers from the 30th Anniversary Conference of the Annual Scholars' Conference on the Holocaust and the Churches*, edited by Daniel J. Curran Jr., Richard Libowitz, and Marcia Sachs Littell. Merion Station, Pa.: Merion Westfield, 2002.

———. "Was Dietrich Bonhoeffer a 'Righteous Gentile'?" Paper presented at the AAR/SBL Annual Meeting, Nashville, November 20, 2000.

Rubenstein, Richard L., and John K. Roth. *Approaches to Auschwitz: The Holocaust and Its Legacy*. Atlanta: Westminster, 1987. Revised edition. Louisville: Westminster John Knox, 2003.

Rudin, A. James. "Dietrich Bonhoeffer: A Jewish Perspective." Paper presented at the Evangelische Akademie Nordelbien, Hamburg, Germany, June 17, 1987. Bonhoeffer Archive.

Saperstein, Marc. *Moments of Crisis in Jewish-Christian Relations*. Philadelphia: Trinity Press International, 1989.

Sauvage, Pierre. "Ten Things I Would Like to Know about Righteous Conduct in Le Chambon and Elsewhere during the Holocaust." Address at "Faith in Humankind: Rescuers of Jews during the Holocaust" conference, United States Holocaust Memorial Museum, Washington, D.C., September 19, 1984. http://www.chambon.org/sauvage_chambon_ten_things_en.htm.

Scholl, Inge. *The White Rose: Munich, 1942–1943*. Translated by Arthur R. Schultz. Middletown, Conn.: Wesleyan University Press, 1983.

Schulz, Wilfried. "Filme über Dietrich Bonhoeffer." Paper presented at the Eighth International Bonhoeffer Congress, Berlin, August 25, 2000. Bonhoeffer Archive, Bonhoeffer Secondary Papers, series 1B box 7.

Schwarzschild, Stephen S. "Bonhoeffer and the Jews." *Commonweal* 83:3 (November 26, 1965): 227, 253–54.

———. "Survey of Current Theological Literature: 'Liberal' Religion (Protestant)." *Judaism* 9 (Autumn 1960): 366–71.

Selby, Peter. *Grace and Mortgage: The Language of Faith and the Debt of the World*. London: Darton Longman & Todd, 1997.

Silverstein, Evan. "Confessing Church Movement Grows Rapidly: Prospect of Per-Capita Withholding Gets PC(USA) Officials' Attention." *PCUSA News* (September 6, 2001). http://www.wfn.org/2001/09/msg00021.html.

Slane, Craig J. *Bonhoeffer as Martyr: Social Responsibility and Modern Christian Commitment*. Grand Rapids, Mich.: Brazos, 2004.

Smith, Robert O. "Reclaiming Bonhoeffer after Auschwitz." *Dialog* 43:3 (Fall 2004): 205–20.

Snydal, James. *Do Not Surrender: The Faith and Life of Pastor Dietrich Bonhoeffer*. Roseville, Calif.: Dry Bones Press, 2001.

Soulen, R. Kendall. *The God of Israel and Christian Theology*. Minneapolis: Fortress Press, 1996.

Spong, John Shelby. *A New Christianity for a New World: Why Traditional Faith Is Dying and How a New Faith Is Being Born*. San Francisco: HarperSanFrancisco, 2002.

Staub, Ervin. *The Roots of Evil: The Origins of Genocide and Other Group Violence*. Cambridge: Cambridge University Press, 1989.

Staver, Matthew D. "Shedding Our Moral Laryngitis: Silence Is Not an Option for Christians." *National Liberty Journal* (October 2004). http://www.lc.org/radiotv/nlj/nlj2004/nj1004.htm.

Tal, Uriel. "Aspects of Consecration of Politics in the Nazi Era," 49–102. In *Papers Presented to the International Symposium on Judaism and Christianity under the Impact of National-Socialism (1919–1945)*. Jerusalem: Historical Society of Israel, 1982.

———. *Christians and Jews in Germany: Religion, Politics, and Ideology in the Second Reich*. Translated by Noah Jonathan Jacobs. Ithaca: Cornell University Press, 1975.

———. "On Modern Lutheranism and the Jews," 203–13. In *Year Book of the Leo Baeck Institute*. London: Secker & Warburg, 1985.

Tec, Nechama. *When Light Pierced the Darkness: Christian Rescuers of Jews in Nazi-Occupied Poland*. New York: Oxford University Press, 1986.

ten Boom, Corrie, with John and Elizabeth Sherrill. *The Hiding Place*. Washington Depot, Conn.: Chosen Books, 1971.

Timmer, David E. "The Bible between Church and Synagogue: Thoughts on the Interpretation of the Hebrew Scriptures." *Reformed Review* 39:2 (Winter 1986): 94–103.

van Buren, Paul Matthews. *A Theology of the Jewish-Christian Reality*. 3 vols. Vol. 1, *Discerning the Way*. New York: Seabury, 1980. Vol. 2, *A Christian Theology of the People Israel*. San Francisco: Harper & Row, 1987. Vol. 3, *Christ in Context*. San Francisco: Harper & Row, 1988.

van Dyke, Michael. *Dietrich Bonhoeffer: Opponent of the Nazi Regime*. Heroes of the Faith. Ulrichsville, Ohio: Barbour, 2001.

Virtue, David W. "Opposing Views on Sexuality in North and South." *VirtueOnline: The Voice for Global Orthodox Anglicanism* (July 7, 2005). http://www.virtueonline.org/portal/modules/news/article.php?storyid=2716&com_id=16451&com_rootid=14841&com_mode=thread&#comment16451.

Visser 't Hooft, W. A. "Dietrich Bonhoeffer and the Self-Understanding of the Ecumenical Movement." *Ecumenical Review* 27:2 (April 1976): 198–203.

———. "Dietrich Bonhoeffer, 1945–1965." *Ecumenical Review* 17 (July 1965): 224–31.

Vorkink, Peter, II, ed. *Bonhoeffer in a World Come of Age*. Philadelphia: Fortress Press, 1968.

Wallis, Jim, and Joyce Hollyday, eds. *Cloud of Witnesses*. Revised edition. Maryknoll, N.Y.: Orbis, 1991.

Weapons of the Spirit. Directed, written, and produced by Pierre Sauvage. The Chambon Foundation, 1989.

Wigoder, Geoffrey. *Jewish-Christian Relations Since the Second World War.* Sherman Studies of Judaism in Modern Times. New York: Manchester University Press, 1988.

Williamson, Clarke. *Has God Rejected His People? Anti-Judaism in the Christian Church.* Nashville: Abingdon, 1982.

Willis, Robert E. "Bonhoeffer and Barth on Jewish Suffering: Reflections on the Relationship between Theology and Moral Sensibility." *Journal of Ecumenical Studies* 24:4 (Fall 1987): 598–615.

Wise, Stephen A. "Why Isn't Bonhoeffer Honored at Yad Vashem?" *Christian Century* 115 (February 25, 1998): 202–4.

Yong, Amos. "Globalizing Christology: Jesus Christ in World Religious Context." *Religious Studies Review* 30:4 (October 2004): 259–66.

Young, Josiah Ulysses, III. *No Difference in the Fare: Dietrich Bonhoeffer and the Problem of Racism.* Grand Rapids, Mich.: Eerdmans, 1998.

Zerner, Ruth. "Church, State, and the Jewish Question," 190–205. In *A Cambridge Companion to Dietrich Bonhoeffer,* edited by John de Gruchy. Cambridge: Cambridge University Press, 1999.

————. "Dietrich Bonhoeffer and the Jews: Thoughts and Actions, 1933–1945." *Jewish Social Studies* 37:3–4 (1975): 235–50.

————. "German Protestant Responses to Nazi Persecution of the Jews," 57–68. In *Perspectives on the Holocaust,* edited by Randolph L. Braham. Boston: Luwer-Nijhoff, 1983.

————. "Martin Niemöller: Activist as Bystander: The Oft-Quoted Reflection," 327–338. In *Jewish-Christian Encounters over the Centuries,* edited by Marvin Perry and Frederick M. Schweitzer. New York: Peter Lang, 1994.

Zimmerman, Wolf-Dieter, and Ronald Gregor Smith, eds. *I Knew Dietrich Bonhoeffer.* Translated by Käthe Gregor Smith. New York: Harper & Row, 1966.

Zorzin, Alejandro. "Church versus State: Human Rights, the Church, and the Jewish Question," 236–57. In *Bonhoeffer for a New Day: Theology in a Time of Transition,* edited by John W. de Gruchy. Grand Rapids, Mich.: Eerdmans, 1997.

INDEX

213